The
CMO'S
PERIODIC TABLE
A Renegade's Guide to Marketing

Drew Neisser
Founder and CEO, Renegade LLC

THE CMO'S PERIODIC TABLE
A Renegade's Guide to Marketing
Drew Neisser

New Riders
Find us on the Web at www.newriders.com
New Riders is an imprint of Peachpit, a division of Pearson Education.
To report errors, please send a note to errata@peachpit.com

Acquisitions Editor: Nikki Echler McDonald
Production Editor: Danielle Foster
Development Editor: James Houston
Proofreader: Jan Seymour
Compositor: Alan Irikura
Indexer: James Minkin
Cover Design: Alan Irikura
Interior Design: Alan Irikura

ISBN 13: 9780134293783
ISBN 10: 0134293789

9 8 7 6 5 4 3 2

Printed and bound in the United States of America

Praise for
The CMO's Periodic Table

"*The CMO's Periodic Table* is a remarkable collection of advice and ideas from dozens of senior executives. It's a Ph.D. in marketing science, all in one book."

Jay Baer, President of *Convince & Convert* and
New York Times* best-selling author of *Youtility

"Drew is a marketing guru. His interview questions leave no ground uncovered, making you feel as if you're getting crucial insider knowledge from these CMOs. You'll want to keep this book on your desk so you can refer to its content time and again, applying it to your own marketing goals and challenges."

Robin Landa, Distinguished Professor of Design,
Kean University, author of *Graphic Design Solutions, 5th edition*

"Whether you're an entrepreneur or an executive at a Fortune 500 company, Neisser's book is an invaluable guide to the essential elements of marketing with riveting insights from sixty-four of the best and brightest."

Bryan Eisenberg, entrepreneur and
New York Times* best-selling co-author of *Call to Action

"I have been reading Drew's blog for years and found *The CMO's Periodic Table* to be a really useful progression, rich with insights for marketing students and professionals alike. Although all of the interviews are thought provoking, I particularly recommend the element called Marketing as Service, which aligns perfectly with my Marketing with Meaning philosophy!"

Bob Gilbreath, best-selling author of
The Next Evolution of Marketing

"Drew provides invaluable lessons from the CMOs and marketers on the front lines to help you create a disruptive company…or prevent your company from being one that perishes."

Ted Rubin, co-author of *Return on Relationship*

"Along with being written by an exceptional marketing thinker and practitioner, *The CMO's Periodic Table* is an artfully conceived goldmine of marketing wisdom. Drew distills practical guidance from his illustrious interviewees on the very topics—strategy, metrics, data, customer-centricity, innovation, and more—that are essential to every modern marketer."

David Rogers, faculty at Columbia Business School and author of *The Digital Transformation Playbook*

"*The CMO's Periodic Table* opens with a bang and remains a riveting read throughout, thanks to its clever organizational structure and deeply insightful interviews. Drew has gathered an amazing collection of professionals, many of whom share the passion and perseverance that it takes be successful in any field, especially marketing."

Linda Kaplan Thaler, Chairman of Publicis New York, best-selling author, with Robin Koval, of *The Power of Nice* and *Grit to Great*

"This book, with its selection of interviews from marketing, advertising, and media communication experts, is an excellent complement to any undergraduate or graduate marketing course. Students are always eager for advice from practitioners. The interviews cover a wide range of topics that anyone interested in the discipline of marketing needs to understand to excel in the marketplace."

Martha Reeves, Professor of Marketing, Duke University

"Students and marketing executives won't find a better way to learn about cutting-edge marketing than from those who have cracked the code. Drew Neisser has skillfully assembled the combined wisdom of sixty-four CMOs. Insights gained from the book will help executives up their game and students think like a seasoned exec."

C. Samuel Craig, Professor of Marketing, Stern School of Business, co-author of *Global Marketing Strategy*

"Having been a CMO and now an advisor to many, I believe *The CMO's Periodic Table* is a must-have resource for anyone interested in decoding the complexities of marketing. The thought leaders gathered in this book are rich with insights that can save you innumerable missteps whether you're just starting your career or are a veteran looking to sharpen your chops."

Paul Dunay, Financial Services Marketing Leader at PwC, best-selling author of *Facebook Marketing for Dummies*

"Every C-Suite executive has to deliver success—and this book gives CMOs the formula."

Jeffrey Hayzlett, primetime TV & radio host, keynote speaker, best-selling author and Global Business Celebrity

"*The CMO's Periodic Table* is like going to the best marketing buffet you could imagine. Each chapter is a delectable morsel of insightful commentary from some of the tastiest 'chefs' in the biz. Read it from cover to cover and you'll be stuffed with insights you'll be able to apply to just about any marketing challenge on your plate."

Joel Comm, *New York Times* best-selling author of *Twitter Power*

"*The CMO's Periodic Table* is a masterful collection of insights thoughtfully arranged for marketers of all vintages. As a fellow writer, I really appreciate Drew's deft writing style and how he draws out the wisdom of his sixty-four marketing connoisseurs. It is definitely worth reading AND sharing."

Bryan Kramer, CEO of PureMatter, best-selling author of *Shareology*

Periodic Table of Marketing Elements

BASIC ELEMENTS	INTERNAL ELEMENTS	TRANSITIONAL TRENDS	VOLATILE FACTORS	SILICON RALLY		NOBLE PURSUITS	INERT FUNDAMENTALS
Se Setting Expectations	**Bt** Building Trust					**Sr** Marketing as Service	**Sc** Showing Courage
P Planning	**O** Organizing					**Ss** Social Customer Service	**Pb** Personal Branding
R Research	**Ro** Reorganizing	**Ma** Marketing Automation	**Ap** Agency as Partner	**Cr** CRM	**Pc** Pure Creativity		**Li** Listening
S Strategy	**Ga** Global Agendas	**Bb** B2B Content Marketing	**Ca** Changing Agencies	**Md** Mobilizing Digital	**Cc** Customer Centricity		**L** Learning
B Branding	**Re** Retooling	**Bc** B2C Content Marketing	**Rp** Retail Partners	**Im** Integrating Mobile	**Bu** Building Community		**Ev** Evolving
Rb Rebranding	**Lc** Leading Change	**Ug** User-Generated Content	**Rt** Risk-Taking	**Ee** Email Efficacy	**Gg** Going Green		**Em** Empathizing
M Measure	**C** Cohesion	**In** Influencer Marketing	**Bd** Befriending Data	**Rm** Real-Time Marketing	**F** Foundations		**N** Networking
Me Metrics	**Cs** Consultative Selling	**Gm** Grassroots Marketing	**Mm** Media Mixing	**Oo** Online Optimization	**Sd** Sustainable Design		**Pn** Power Networking
Cy Consistency	**Cu** Culture	**St** Storytelling	**Tb** Tiny Budgets	**We** Web Experience	**Lb** Living the Brand		**Sp** Sharing Passion
Np New Products	**E** Empowerment	**Sm** Social Media Success	**Cm** Crisis Management	**Gv** Going Viral	**So** Social Purpose		**Ai** Always Innovating

*To Carl Neisser, my father, best man
and unicameral Board of Directors.*

*To my friend Pete Krainik,
founder of The CMO Club,
home of the best CMO conversations.*

Contents

Foreword

Better Interviews, Better Learning

The CMO's Periodic Table serves up the best, most comprehensive, and most up-to-date lessons the new or seasoned marketing professional can find in one place. Drew Neisser has pulled off this admirable feat by tapping the minds of the most accomplished marketing executives working today. In the pages ahead, Drew asks his most distinguished peers pointed questions informed by his own exemplary career, and persists until reaching one or more invaluable conclusions. He also adds his own breakthrough insights—the same ones that have fueled two decades of success at his NYC-based agency, Renegade LLC.

Reading and pondering these sixty-four one-to-one interviews is to absorb the hard-won wisdom of a select group of very smart marketing practitioners—men and women with genuinely real, market-tested ideas, all of whom have their own reputational skin in the game.

Full disclosure: Drew and I have a history. More than twenty years ago we worked together at the astonishingly creative ad agency Chiat/Day. It was there that I first came in contact with Drew's astronomically high standards when it comes to marketing and advertising, which you'll get to see on display in every chapter of *The CMO'S Periodic Table*.

The subjects of these interviews manage the marketing processes at companies selling products and services ranging from airlines to credit lines, and from the groceries to the Grammys. With each one of these very different perspectives you'll be able to derive an interesting or useful lesson to apply to your own business, whatever that may be.

How does Allstate maintain its "You're in good hands" slogan for more than fifty years? What did Dunkin' Donuts achieve by teaming with Zynga? Why does American Express offer some of the most helpful small-business content marketing anywhere, and make it available even to non-AmEx customers? All is revealed inside. You'll hear the former CMO of AXA Equitable and Vonage, Barbara Goodstein, talk frankly about the whys and hows of changing agencies, freely admitting, "The advertising agency is always at the short end of the straw." Sprint's Doug Duvall will recall his stint as communications director at Freddie Mac, when he had to manage through the crisis created by the suicide of the company's CFO.

These are just a few of the truly fascinating glimpses of life in the CMO lane. Reading *The CMO's Periodic Table,* in fact, feels a bit like browsing through the transcript of a reality TV show starring top CMOs from around the world.

Perhaps, however, because of my own history with Drew at Chiat/Day, some of my favorite stories within these pages come from the CMOs who are prone to push the envelope a little further, taking extraordinary risks in order to make extraordinary gains—as Drew does today at Renegade. At Chiat/Day we used to chuckle to ourselves that you knew it was a good meeting if your presentation made the blood drain from the client's face. Well, there are more than a few blood-draining moments in this book that are a thrill to read as well as very instructive.

For example, when Jack in the Box's CMO Terri Funk Graham launched a breakthrough campaign based on having the brand's smiley-faced Jack character run down by a bus. And at SAP, the mission of the innovation team managed by CMO Jonathan Becher was "to try new things, break rules, make people uncomfortable."

Or consider the implication when Tesco's CEO Sir Terry Leahy tells us about launching his company's groundbreaking Club Card loyalty program more than twenty years ago, long before he became either a CEO or a "Sir." Virtually all grocery chains have loyalty programs now, of course, but Tesco's was really the pioneer in basing such a program entirely on customer data. Launching it meant wagering some 25 percent of the firm's profits on its success. It's not hard to picture the blood draining from the boss's face as Sir Terry pitched the great idea.

If the Papa John's promise is "Better ingredients. Better pizza" (see Element P, for Planning, within), then Drew Neisser's promise with *The CMO's Periodic Table* is "Better interviews. Better learning."

And it's a promise he delivers on.

—Don Peppers, Founding Partner of Peppers & Rogers Group

Introduction

WHAT IS A RENEGADE MARKETER?

I'm not going to presume to give a "sound byte" answer to that question in this short introduction. It's taken me three and a half decades in the trenches of advertising and marketing to form the understanding of Renegade-hood that today guides the work my team and I do at Renegade, LLC.

The fact is that it just can't be boiled down to a sentence, or a paragraph, or even a few pages. It's bigger than that. It would take a whole separate book of its own. (Stay tuned, I'm working on that one right now.)

As far as this book goes, I can promise that after you've read and absorbed these sixty-four targeted interviews with the brightest brains in marketing today, from "living legend" Fortune 100 CMOs to rule-book-torching whiz kids at nimble, disruptive startups, you'll have a strong foundation for understanding how Renegade marketers think—and more importantly, how they act. (And, of course, you'll have a plethora of brilliant new ideas you can apply right away to supercharge your own career.)

This isn't to say that everyone I had the privilege of interviewing for this book would necessarily self-identify as a Renegade. But the work they do and the energy they exude caught my eye so powerfully that I knew I had to sit down with them, hit the "record" button, and get them to talk about what drives their day-in-day-out excellence.

And if there's one thing in the marketing world I've always been inexorably drawn to, it's Renegade thinking. In light of that, I daresay it's not a coincidence that I was hell-bent on interviewing these specific sixty-four luminaries. The work these marketers do resonates—big time—with what matters most to me and to my company. Whatever your core marketing values are, I'm confident these interviews will resonate similarly with you.

It's taken me over five years to track down the folks you'll meet shortly and get them to pry open their vaults of priceless marketing know-how. I shudder just a little to think of all the trial-and-error I could have bypassed with a resource like this at the beginning of my career...heck, at every stage of my career. The ability to instantly reference the pithy-yet-substantive advice of the world's best marketers on today's and tomorrow's most critical marketing competencies is practically an unfair advantage.

If only marketing were a science. We could memorize a bunch of formulas, gather some data, apply category variables, get a few grad students to help with the mixing and measuring, and presto—we'd have a failure-proof, go-to-market plan that builds the brand, generates serious sales, and skyrockets our reputation. Next stop: Nobel Prize. (Or at least a CLIO or a CMO Club Award.)

Alas, reality begs to differ. For one, there's that whole pesky (by which I mean, awesome) element of successful marketing that is at best a distant cousin of science: Art. With all due respect to the great physicists, chemists, and biologists who have made our modern lives possible, if marketing were as objective and predictable as those fields we would lose the creativity that defines the best campaigns.

And now we find ourselves in the era of big data, programmatic media buying, search engine optimization, social platforms, CRM, marketing automation, and (this space reserved for the next hot buzzword). The rate at which our available tools and metrics are changing defies belief, and today's game-changing, must-use software or widget is tomorrow's "remember when?" punchline.

So, a detailed formula for success that will be repeatable for decades to come? Forget about it. Just staying current with the changes and the snowballing complexity of it all is practically a full-time job.

Here's the good news: Marketing does share some important traits with the sciences. And they're traits we marketers can leverage to create better work, faster. There's one such trait I'm excited to focus on in this book.

It emerged, as I conducted more interviews, that effective marketing is like a complex molecule, composed of common "elements" that bond together in a logical, inevitable way. Some elements are universal and timeless—things like leadership, customer-centricity, courage, and innovation. Others are not exactly household names, though they're no less important to the "molecule" performing its unique and vital function.

With each interview it grew clearer that the elements were interrelated and begging to be categorized. It was a short hop from there to start thinking in terms of this Periodic Table. And so with a nod to Russian chemist Dmitri Mendeleev, who in 1869 created the earliest version of the table we all studied in high school chemistry, I set out to do the same with the elements of marketing.

The table I offer you now may or may not do justice to Mendeleev's astonishingly logical arrangement, but I do promise you this: When you have a firm grasp of these sixty-four elements, it's as certain as the attraction between a proton and an electron that you will generate state-of-the-art value for your company and your customers.

You can read this book front-to-back, consuming the interviews in order. Believe it or not, there is a method to the madness herein. But you can also jump straight to the elements that interest you most, whether they're urgent issues you need help with right away or just something you've always wanted to know more about. I don't know any great marketers who approach learning (or anything else) in a totally linear fashion, and accordingly this book is designed to be conducive to jumping around.

As you'll see when you immerse yourself in these conversations, the interviewees and I were ourselves prone to a little jumping around—but only when we stumbled upon a truly exciting and valuable sidetrack from the primary topic. There are so many overlaps in this business, and no element of marketing can be tied up with a neat ribbon—especially as the purview of marketers continues to expand into areas like customer experience and product development.

However you choose to process this material, I urge you to pause after each interview and carefully consider how its content might be applied to your marketing goals and challenges. Perhaps imagine the subject of the interview you're reading will be calling you in twenty-four hours expecting an outline of your action plan based on their advice.

The most essential characteristic of a marketing Renegade is a voracious hunger for new perspectives and ideas. Without this, there's no escaping business as usual. *The CMO's Periodic Table* is a record of my ongoing (and never-ending) attempt to satiate that hunger within myself. If I've done my job, it will help you do the same.

One last note: Marketing is a dynamic industry, and these interviews span the better part of the past five years. As such, some of the marketers you're about to hear from no longer work at the companies they did when I interviewed them. In such cases, the chapter titles typically identify the subject with his or her former company—the one where they performed the work that caught my interest in the first place.

May the insights and wisdom these sixty-four visionaries so generously share give you as many "Eureka!" moments in your marketing laboratory as they've given me.

Drew Neisser
September 2015

I. Basic Elements

Element one on the Periodic Table, in the upper left, is hydrogen.

Perhaps you've heard of it. Perhaps you're even made of it. It's the most abundant chemical substance in the universe. By atom count, it's two-thirds of water. Associated elements like carbon, nitrogen, and oxygen, or elements from the table's first two columns like sodium, magnesium, and potassium, are no slouches either. All are some of the essential building blocks of our lives.

Similarly, the Basic Elements of marketing are the building blocks of what we do. They're things like research, strategy, metrics, and branding. They're the concepts we've been studying and practicing since our first bright-eyed day on our first marketing job, and they're the concepts we'll be continuing to use and profit from until the time comes to ride off into the sunset and hang up our spurs.

Like hydrogen or sodium, the Basic Elements tend to keep turning up as essential components in many, if not most, of the "compounds" that comprise our efforts as marketers. Everyone from the fresh-out-of-school marketing neophyte to the most experienced and accomplished CMO needs to make study and review of the Basic Elements a regular, if not daily, practice.

Many marketers make the fatal mistake of neglecting the concepts in this section, particularly when they're in the seductive grip of some flavor-of-the-month marketing trend that has no real staying power. When the bottom falls out as the hot trend becomes

Se
Setting Expectations

P
Planning

R
Research

S
Strategy

B
Branding

Rb
Rebranding

M
Measure

Me
Metrics

Cy
Consistency

Np
New Products

yesterday's news, the fall is steep and painful for the marketer who hasn't kept the Basic Elements at the core of his or her thinking.

The Basic Elements are simple concepts but they take a marketing life-time to master. And as the digital landscape of our work evolves at an ever-faster rate, successful marketing initiatives will require constantly re-exam-ining these concepts and reformulating how we apply them. But what they are will remain the same, as they have since the dawn of modern marketing.

I was really excited to land every one of the interviews in this section. To truly understand these core concepts, it's critical to hear about them from a person who's truly nailed each one. And that describes every one of the marketers you're about to meet.

Starting with the dynamic, pull-no-punches Jeffrey Hayzlett, this sec-tion brings together nine leaders who show that once you have a strong grounding in the essential elements, there is no limit to where your cre-ativity can take you and your marketing.

We'll sit down with Colette LaForce, who shows how strategy is your greatest ally when you're a small company facing off against an industry super-giant. We'll check in with Visa's maestro of measurement, Antonio Lucio, and follow that up with a conversation about metrics with the innovative Dan Marks.

And a whole lot more.

From healthcare to fashion, from microprocessors to tequila, get ready to see how the most fundamental ingredients of marketing success are handled by the best in the business.

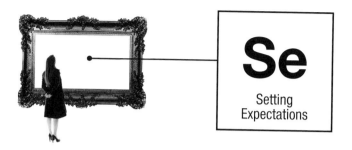

Making Sure Your CEO Gets the Picture

"A lot of CMOs fail because they forget to get conditions of satisfaction."

Jeffrey Hayzlett
C-Suite Network

Do you follow @JeffreyHayzlett on Twitter? If not, may I encourage you to join the 67,000+ who do? Another option is to join his legion of 36,000+ fans on Facebook.

Either way, keeping up with Jeffrey's regular online dispatches—every one of which bursts with sui generis energy and tell-it-like-it-is attitude—is a smart move if you're in the business of marketing. You can also sit down with any of his best-selling books, catch his show on C-Suite TV, or cue up episodes of his podcast *All Business* on play.it.

Anyway, I digress. Here's what you're going to learn from Jeffrey right here and now, drawing from his tenure as CMO of Eastman Kodak and currently as Chairman of C-Suite Network: In marketing, expectations are critical. For one, this means adjusting the expectations you and your team have of the campaign and of each other. It also means managing the expectations your client or boss has as a result of what you tell them…or fail to tell them. Before anything else, you have to get this right!

Our interview also covers mobile advertising, how the ever-changing economic climate affects marketers, and a long-overdue update to the famous "four pillars" of marketing.

Where do setting expectations with the customer figure into your marketing priorities?

A lot of CMOs fail because they forget to set conditions of satisfaction. I won't move forward until I know exactly what makes the customer (who, in some cases, may be my boss) happy. Business leaders need to set their conditions of satisfaction as soon as they take their position. Mine have always been the same: to make money, grow professionally, and have fun doing it. These remind me why I'm in business and guide each decision I make.

How does risk-taking enter the equation?

No one is going to die in marketing; we're not surgeons. If you want to grow, you're going to have to take risks. Risks may work or they may not, but you just won't know until you try it. The biggest mistake you can make in business is to do nothing. Marketers constantly need to adapt, change, or die.

What emerging trends do marketers need to be on top of…yesterday?

Mobile is the most personalized technology—which replaced the car as the more personal device. I would tend to say that at any given moment, most people know where their phones are—perhaps even more than they know where their children are. In fact, I question if most people lost their children or lost their phone in a mall, which one they would go looking for first. But mobile is still in its infancy stage and it's extremely complex. Like the early days of the Internet, and with varying browsers and service providers, we have the same thing with mobile today. While it's in the millions, it's not in the billions in terms of revenue with regards to advertising and marketing. With regards just to advertising, it's certainly become one of the best; it's become a place to go for search but it has not become a place to go for [great] advertising. But the good news is, the best is yet to come!

I was lucky enough to catch a panel appearance where you proposed an update to the famous "four pillars" or "4 P's" of marketing (product, place, price, and promotion). Can you explain that additional P here?

The 4 P's aren't going away, but it's hard to deny they've been joined by a powerful 5th "P": People. This is the social element of marketing, and it leads us to the fact that we can never, ever discount the power of one. Just one follower, whether they are an evangelist or a critic, will tell their friends and followers. Feedback from your customers is critical; in the past I've used that feedback to develop new features and products customers loved and bought like crazy. As marketers, it's critical we really listen and respond. That creates brand ambassadors for your company. On the other hand, don't ignore the critics. I call the ROI of social media "return on ignoring." You can't ignore the comments, whether they're positive or negative.

Tell me a little more about turning positive social media interactions into sales.

It's all about listening. When a consumer tweets something positive and mentions a company or product, chances are they're thinking about buying. If we're listening when that tweet goes out, we can point them in the right direction. When I was CMO of Kodak, I wanted to put a lot more emphasis on the voice of the customer. To that end, I created a Chief Listening Officer position to bring scale to all our social activities. The CLO did a lot to ensure that questions were answered, comments were addressed, and, yes, that complaints were addressed too.

You're widely viewed as a "maverick." How would you describe your attitude towards risk-taking?

I'm always open to trying new things and I love to take risks. But I also think it's important to continue to examine your company inside and out, drive change, and make tough decisions. In my new book, *Think Big, Act Bigger: The Rewards of Being Relentless,* I want to inspire readers to take risks and stop making excuses. It's about taking action and having an attitude to put oneself out there, steamrolling obstacles, ignoring perceived boundaries, and even being a little irrational.

I enjoyed your past books, **Running the Gauntlet** *and* **The Mirror Test,** *a lot. Tell me about your new book.*

Think Big, Act Bigger weaves together personal stories and anecdotes from my time inside both small and Fortune 500 businesses. In this book, I want to teach readers that the one value you need to succeed in business is true, hard work and to own your own persona.

KEY TAKEAWAYS

- *Before you take on a new job, make sure you understand and can achieve your boss's "conditions of satisfaction."*

- *While mastering the classic 4 P's of marketing (Price, Product, Promotion, Place), don't lose sight of the 5th P, People.*

- *Playing it safe is for accountants. Great marketers take calculated risks.*

Further reading:
Jeffrey Hayzlett, *The Mirror Test: Is Your Business Really Breathing?*

Planning

Better Planning, Better Pizza...Papa John's

"I am the type of leader who doesn't try to fix things that aren't broken."

Bob Kraut
Papa John's

It won't surprise you to learn that Papa John's is a busy place, from corporate headquarters all the way down to each individual oven at the mega-successful chain's 4,600-plus individual franchises. So how does it all get done? When it comes to marketing, the "special sauce" is the savvy planning of CMO Bob Kraut.

In the spirit of Papa John's "Better Ingredients. Better Pizza." tagline, Bob is a big believer in fundamentals as the basis of effective global and local marketing plans. These fundamentals include product quality being essential, customer satisfaction as the bellwether metric, employees as a critical ingredient of the brand experience, getting your message right, and (perhaps hardest of all) sticking with it.

It was my privilege to be on the receiving end of Bob's refreshingly matter of fact and commonsensical sharing of his insights on how he makes the fundamentals click at Papa John's. Of course, to paraphrase President Harry S. Truman, "If common sense were so common, more [marketers] would have it."

When it comes to putting together a plan, how long did you give yourself from your first days at Papa John's and what were the key steps in the process?

When I first joined Papa John's, I inherited a good situation. The company was doing well and was profitable as a result of their strong position of quality through "Better Ingredients. Better Pizza." It was not a typical situation where the new CMO comes in and changes everything. I had to transform surgically without breaking down the systems and practices that made the company great. I gave myself about sixty days to develop a plan. I did a lot of listening and analyzing.

My first task was to meet and listen to as many store operators and franchisees as possible. I went on a multi-city roadshow that was already scheduled and met over 700 people. Next, I met with our leadership team at Papa John's and our Franchisee Council to get a sense of where we wanted to go. Then I met with every team member in the marketing department. I did an extensive SWOT analysis and reviewed all the key customer data. This led to developing a plan that built upon our success and elevated everything that we were doing to the next level. The resulting seven-point plan included the following activities:

1. Elevate the quality of our advertising and better define the role of our founder, Papa John.
2. Redirect budget dollars to target fast-growing customer segments.
3. Maximize our media spending to gain more reach and impact.
4. Increase spending in digital and social media and institute a big data program to more precisely and effectively reach customers through eCRM and our Papa Rewards loyalty program.
5. Institute a premium pricing strategy to solidify our quality positioning.

6. Develop a winning marketing calendar process through a more data-based approach to promotion and product development.
7. Restructure the marketing department to deliver on the plan and to "execute with excellence."

The "brand renaissance" plan was introduced in 2014 and the results were very strong. Papa John's became:

- #1 eCommerce brand, with more than 50 percent of sales derived from online sales
- #1 in Customer Satisfaction according to the American Customer Satisfaction Index
- #1 loyalty program, according to Bond Customer Loyalty
- #1 recognized NFL sponsor

In addition, sales growth doubled and we launched our first-ever Hispanic campaign, resulting in a 43 percent increase in Hispanic sales according to NPD.

QSRs (Quick Service Restaurants) are notoriously responsive to media activity, especially promotional deals. Does this make it a little harder to have a long term plan? How do you resist the temptation to go from promo to promo...or is that just the nature of the beast?

Well, you have to do both in the QSR category. You have to make the sale every day, and you have to sell the brand long term. The QSR pizza category is in a state of maturity so it's very promo-driven. In my opinion, you have to be focused on your position but have a good blend of brand news, product innovation, and promos. At Papa John's, only half of the calendar consists of promos and value offers—in the rest we are very focused on better ingredients and recently announced to remove unwanted artificial ingredients. We focus on value when customers want that and create news through digital and product innovations.

As for the timelines, we are very "planful" for a retail business—we know what we are doing six to nine months out and we practice "optionality." If the market or customer preferences change, we have the ability to adjust in that we have multiple options that are in development. The key thing is to stay on task with the positioning because everything flows from there, but be flexible to make adjustments; so in the end, we "plan the work" and then "work the plan."

"Better ingredients. Better pizza." has been the Papa John's tagline for a long time. What has allowed you to stick with it for so long?

Papa John's is a textbook case on how to build a brand based on quality and consistency. Quality is the core value of the company. It's in our DNA and it's given the company the strength to resist changes over the ups and downs of the business cycle. And I think it's a testament to the leadership of our founder, John Schnatter. Great leaders have discipline. "Better Ingredients. Better Pizza." continues to work well for us. I am the type of leader who doesn't try to fix things that aren't broken. That said, we are making progress in enriching our brand promise and injecting a more contemporary currency to the brand.

How have you been able to impact the customer experience in your current role?

For us, the consumer is at the center of all we do. We always "keep our eye on the pie," so that the ultimate customer experience is bringing people together to eat great pizza at a great price with an exceptional ordering and service experience. As for marketing's role in the customer experience, we do the heavy lifting in creating emotional connections with our customers in our branding, online experience and social media, and engagement. The pizza business is dominated by heavy price promotion, which I don't think contributes to a sustainable customer proposition. At Papa John's, we have incredibly loyal customers and they love the brand experience. The American Customer Satisfaction Index has ranked us the #1 pizza brand in satisfaction thirteen of the past fifteen years.

Is employee advocacy a priority for you? How are you handling it?

When I came to Papa John's a little over a year ago, my biggest surprise was how happy the people are and how aligned they are with our vision and positioning. Simply put, when you are in the service and delivery business, "happy employees equal happy customers." So I think we count on all of them to be great customer ambassadors. One of the ways that our employees feel like an owner of the business is through our "open innovation" culture. We solicit and source product ideas and ways to make things better for our customers, and I think it shows up in customer ratings and in our business results.

How have you used social media to advance your brand's overall marketing efforts? Are there any networks/platforms that are working better for your brand than others?

We use social media to talk to our brand believers and to reach broader audiences in ways that are authentic, real time, and meaningful to them. Pizza is the perfect platform for social media. At its core, pizza brings people together. In 2014, we greatly expanded our social reach beyond Facebook and Twitter and are now active on Instagram, Google Plus, Vine, the publisher platforms, etc. And we have taken our highly visible NFL sponsorship into social media, especially on the local level—where we sponsor twenty-one NFL teams.

What have your experiences with mobile marketing been to date?

We run an eCommerce site, with nearly 50 percent of sales coming from online, and we have a greater share of customers accessing our brand online than any other pizza brand. So we're doing very well there. An increasing share of our sales is coming from mobile so we have increased our investment in all things mobile: advertising, apps, alternative payment, and localization. These are all working well so far.

KEY TAKEAWAYS

- *Get out into the field and listen firsthand to your customers and partners.*

- *Don't walk away from a successful campaign prematurely. Marketers tend to get bored with their campaigns long before consumers do.*

- *TV advertising remains a potent weapon especially for quick service restaurants.*

Further reading:

John Ellett, *The CMO Manifesto: A 100-Day Action Plan for Marketing Change Agents*

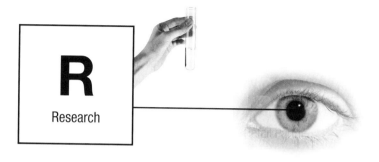

Research Is Great, Insights Are Greater

"We wanted to offer our customers and prospects some insights that they could use immediately to plan and execute increasingly effective events."

Eric Eden
Cvent

Steve Jobs and Henry Ford aside, few leaders can find their way through the marketing wilderness without using research as a guide. Whether to shed light on consumer behavior, gather feedback on customer experience, or figure out which landing page is the stickiest, nothing can substitute for going out into the marketplace and asking questions. Learning awaits the curious.

The questions of what research you need and what you do with it depend entirely on your marketing situation, so this chapter is by no means meant as a comprehensive roadmap. Instead, I want to share an off-the-beaten-path approach taken by Eric Eden, who served as CMO at Cvent, the leading event management software company.

Cvent's Global Event Industry Benchmarks Study, as you will soon see, performed multiple roles simultaneously. These included offering insights for product development, establishing performance benchmarks for customers, and creating all sorts of PR-friendly content, all of which reinforced Cvent's leadership role in the industry.

Research seems to be a very important part of Cvent's DNA as it is baked into your product offering, and you do a lot of other market studies. Can you talk broadly about the importance of research to your organization and how it impacts your overall approach to marketing?

Research informs every aspect of our business. As an organization, we are dedicated to constant improvement and as such we need research to help us figure out not just what needs to improve, but how to make those improvements. Usability research is an essential part of our product development process.

For the marketing department, research is fundamental. It helps us narrow our target and understand their needs. Research also helps us figure out what messages perform the best.

You recently conducted a global study on event marketing effectiveness. Why invest in a global study?

Let me answer the second part first. Cvent is a global company and events are a global business, so doing research on a global scale made tremendous sense to us.

Now to the first part—as the leading provider of event marketing management software, we believe it is imperative that we celebrate events as a highly effective marketing channel and help our clients make their events as successful as possible.

Put another way, as the category leader we have the opportunity, if not the obligation, to help grow the category by continuing to prove and thus celebrate event efficacy. To make this happen, we actually surveyed over

2,000 event planners, executives, and marketing professionals from all over the world.

What were you hoping to learn from this study?

We wanted to learn a lot of things about how events can be planned better, executed better, and ultimately measured better. We also wanted to establish a number of norms that event marketers could use to compare and evaluate their own event success. Finally, we wanted to offer our customers and prospects some insights that they could use immediately to plan and execute increasingly effective events.

Were there some findings that you expect could have an impact on product development?

Without revealing any trade secrets, I can tell you that some of the findings that were most interesting to us were where event planners spend their time and what causes them the most stress. Given the findings, you can expect us to develop a number of tools that will help planners do their jobs that much more efficiently.

How do you see this study being of value to your current clients and prospects?

This study helped establish a number of benchmarks that previously didn't exist in the event business. For example, we now know what the average conversion rate of attendees to leads is. We also have the average conversion rate of leads to new business sales. These benchmarks, along with facts like the average renewal rates of current customers who attended events and the average cost recouped through registration fees will be very helpful to the next generation of event planners.

One of the findings of the study was that 90 percent of event organizers conduct post event surveys, though more than a quarter of these folks still use paper or comment cards. Shouldn't manual surveys be a thing of the past?

Yes, that part of the research was quite surprising. First, the fact that 10 percent of event marketers don't bother to survey after their events is astonishing. But equally astonishing is the fact that the paper surveys and comment cards still account for roughly a quarter of all of the measurement at events. That said, given the fast growing use of mobile apps, we expect most surveying to be done digitally in the very near future.

I seem to recall that you work with a NYC-based agency called Renegade on a variety of projects like the study already referenced! Can you talk about that experience and the role they play?

Of course I can do that, Drew. Renegade played an integral part in helping us think through our overall social media and content marketing strategy. One of the many recommendations Renegade offered was the Global Event Industry Benchmarks Study. And happily for us, your work didn't stop there. You and your team helped us shape the questionnaire, field the survey, and draft the study itself. Oh, and you yourself presented the findings in a highly entertaining yet enlightening fashion at our annual user conference, Cvent Connect. In all honesty, Renegade has been a great partner.

KEY TAKEAWAYS

- *There are no good reasons not to conduct market research given the myriad ways of gathering useful data cost-effectively.*

- *Not only can research inform your marketing strategy, it can also provide provocative and compelling information for content marketing.*

- *If you embark on a research study by asking, "What info will help our customers?" you'll never go astray.*

Further reading:
Fred Reichheld, *The Ultimate Question 2.0: How Net Promoter Companies Thrive in a Customer-driven World*

S

Strategy

A Force to Be Reckoned With

"One critical trait I see in great leaders is an ability to simplify goals and objectives."

Colette LaForce
AMD

I don't blame people for being incredulous when I tell them that when I was growing up, my hometown boasted an oral surgeon named Dr. Gum and a plastic surgeon named Dr. Smiley. But I swear with my hand on any book you like that they were real.

Perhaps I naturally gravitate to people whose surnames are accurate descriptors of who they are, like Colette LaForce, currently the CMO at Cars.com. Colette, at the time of this interview in 2014, was the CMO of AMD (Advanced Micro Devices), the nimble microprocessor company that plays David to Intel's Goliath, and she is a true force of nature when it comes to strategy-driven marketing leadership.

Her bold determination and mastery of the big picture has exploded AMD's global presence and guided it through complex rebranding and (simultaneously!) corporate restructuring.

What's the first thing current and aspiring marketing leaders need to know about strategy?

One critical trait I see in great leaders is an ability to simplify goals and objectives. People can't remember ten goals, or even five. Great leaders, like great sports coaches, prioritize just one or two compelling goals for the team to commit to and focus on.

AMD is considered an "ingredient" brand, but you've said that your customers' relationship with your product is more emotional than with other such "ingredient" brands. How did you come to that conclusion, and how has that realization helped your strategy in sparking consumers' passions for AMD?

We consider AMD beyond just an "ingredient" and more of an "enabler" brand. Semiconductor technology powers the devices we use every day, giving people very personal, rich computational and graphical experiences that literally enable us to change the world. Our research with thousands of users echoed this sentiment, and we are actively building a more emotional connection with buyers.

AMD recently underwent a major rebranding. Describe that process and how you met the challenges it presented.

We recognized that our multi-year business transformation needed to start with a global brand transformation. Evolving a brand while simultaneously cutting costs, completing a corporate restructuring, and pushing into new markets with new competitors is quite challenging and might seem even counterintuitive to some. But without a baseline for purpose, values, and mission and an outstanding team to execute, we could not have effectively united 10,000 employees and millions of fans worldwide.

For better or worse, marketing budgets are a constant presence in a CMO's strategic planning, and they're getting more complex as new tools become available. How are you staying on top of budget allocation and optimization?

One of the first things I did when I came to AMD was create a Marketing Operations team. We now have centralized visibility to spending, metrics, and ROI. We have a great team that may not always have the fanciest new tools, but we are steadfast about how we measure and optimize marketing performance.

Did you make any major strategic changes to your budget allocation in 2014?

Like many marketing organizations, while our overall marketing budgets continue to shrink, we've protected funds for earned and owned media. We're also setting aside funds for what I like to call "innovation marketing." For example, we'll soon kick off a unique program in China, designed exclusively to engage with our Chinese fans. Too often, U.S.-based corporations pilot programs in North America and then try to localize further. We're starting in China and then will see where it goes!

On LinkedIn, you bill yourself as a "Transformative CMO." What does that mean?

For me, the word 'transformative' represents a desire to be a steward of change. Stewardship is really all about making lasting contributions that leave your environment in better shape than it was the day before. Couple that with a leadership approach that encourages meaningful change and an outstanding team that can drive execution and consistency, and you get true transformation.

What are the first specific steps to transforming an organization?

To drive transformation, a team must to be aligned on the organization's purpose, goals, and values. Why do you do what you do? What are you trying to do? And how will you do it? Once you get clarity on those points, true transformation can begin.

AMD competes in a market category dominated by Intel. How has this dynamic shaped your approach to marketing? Does it compel you to be innovative?

Innovation and creativity should always play a role in what we as marketers do, whether you work for an existing market leader or an emerging player. Many of us are drawn to challenger brands because of the "underdog" phenomenon. Being the underdog can be a great motivational tool that builds character, forces innovation, fosters creativity, and can be very rewarding.

KEY TAKEAWAYS

- *Great leaders strip the complexity out of business strategy.*

- *When crafting your brand strategy, start with the desire to transform, not just improve.*

- *Set aside a small percentage of your budget for experimentation to ensure your marketing never gets calcified.*

Further reading:
Rick Page, *Hope Is Not a Strategy: The 6 Keys to Winning the Complex Sale*

The Building Blocks of Branding

"We focus less on brand loyalty or retention than we do on positive health outcomes."

Dave Minifie
Centene

What is a brand, anyway? If you ask ten CMOs, don't be surprised if you get ten different answers. Yet that doesn't diminish the importance of branding to the work we do every day.

Building, coordinating, and maintaining a single brand can seem like a never-ending challenge. Now imagine juggling over twenty brands, each with its own "personality" and idiosyncrasies. That describes a typical day at the office for Dave Minifie, CMO of the St. Louis-based multi-line healthcare enterprise Centene.

Dave came to Centene after a distinguished 12-plus years at Procter & Gamble, where he was required to master the ins and outs of diverse brands and build strong relationships every step of the way. Here, he shares valuable insights on how to make sure branding always furthers a larger goal, and how a strong peer network is a linchpin of marketing success.

How did your tenure at Procter & Gamble prepare you to thrive as Centene's CMO?

P&G has a strong brand building framework which is key to its effectiveness in cultivating marketers and business leaders. It's certainly been useful to me during my career, whether I've been marketing toilet paper, dog food, or healthcare. It provides a reliable method for meeting challenges, especially in times of transition.

In short: Learn the culture of the organization; assess the landscape of the category and your competition; understand, articulate, and drive your point of difference; ensure you never waver when it comes to getting the basics done first and done well.

When you take on a new senior marketer role, what are your top priorities? Do you have a first 100-day plan?

I strive to execute a three-tiered 90-day plan as quickly as possible. First, I assess the internal and external landscape. What are the drivers of the business? What is our point of difference? Does my organization have the right culture, capacity, and capability to accomplish everything that needs to be done? Second, we strive to execute all the basics well. Finally, we can work on accelerating the business.

Several of Centene's subsidiaries have undergone rebranding under your leadership. Describe how you're managing these rebrandings.

The answer to this question highlights the importance of doing the basics well when it comes to branding. When I arrived at Centene, each subsidiary had a different name, different mark, and different look and feel. However, as we sought to drive scale efficiencies (we've gone from $5 billion to $15 billion in three years), we saw we could move to a common visual identity for each of our health plans, and this is what we're doing now: updating their look and feel while staying true to our company purpose, and incorporating consumer-driven insights to better connect with our members. In the end, all healthcare is local, and must be delivered locally.

Do all of Centene's subsidiaries have a common identity now? If so, how long did it take and what was the biggest hurdle in making this happen?

Yes, nearly all of Centene's health plan subsidiaries are working from a common visual identity, brand character, tone of voice, and common health literacy best practices. With almost two dozen health plans, it took over a year to update each brand's look and feel, even though we didn't meaningfully change any names. We needed to work with each state's regulatory bodies, and work within the parameters of each health plan's "plan year" to ensure we changed at appropriate times and didn't confuse members or providers.

How can you tell when a branding initiative is successful, especially when it involves a name change and a possible drop in awareness?

Although we took the opportunity to streamline some of our names, we didn't change any. Also, we performed A/B testing on before/after designs to confirm that all our new designs were better: easier to read on a billboard, easier to read in a handheld device, and more tightly tied to our corporate purpose visually.

We test brand awareness and brand equity on a rolling, iterative basis, and with multiple audiences. This helps us keep a grip on how we're doing in market with our names, identity, and overall brand experience.

When chatting with a fellow CMO about branding, what advice would you give them?

First, know your brand; own your brand. What do you stand for and why? How and why are you bringing this to life? What brand experience do you deliver across multiple touchpoints?

Second, do not constrict your brand. While you own your brand, so do your stakeholders. Learn what they feel about your brand and adjust where necessary. P&G does this by innovating on product. Google does this more literally by playing with their brand mark on the search page. Howler Bros innovates on product and plays with their mark (http://howlerbros.com). Depending on your business model, one of these may be more or less appropriate.

How do you drive loyalty in your category?

We focus less on brand loyalty or retention than we do on positive health outcomes. To drive positive health outcomes, we educate our members on proactive health management techniques and conduct outreach to members who may need additional assistance such as expectant mothers and people struggling with addiction. We believe if we can improve health outcomes for our members, they'll probably want to stay with us.

KEY TAKEAWAYS

- *New CMOs should have and implement a 90-day plan that starts with 30 to 60 days of intelligence gathering.*

- *Basic A/B testing of branding options is an easy way to make sure you're on the right track.*

- *If you identify branding as a problem/opportunity, make sure you involve your stakeholders in the research process.*

Further reading:
Debbie Millman, *Brand Thinking and Other Noble Pursuits*

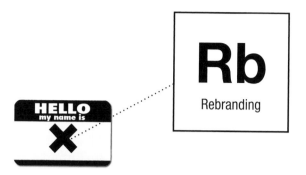

A Healthy Rebranding Process

"Rebranding isn't a one-time event."

Wendy Newman
AMN Healthcare

Rebranding is something most long-lived businesses eventually must do or at least closely consider.

And it's a nerve-wracking process. The stakes are high, there are many moving parts, and there's little room for error. A misguided or half-baked effort can sink the brand permanently.

Marketers who pull off effective rebrandings are deservedly hailed as heroes. A sterling example of a successful rebranding is the one Wendy Newman orchestrated at AMN Healthcare, the San Diego-based health-care staffing innovator where she served with distinction as Senior Marketing Executive.

The story of her rebranding initiative, which united diverse brands and subsidiaries under one coherent and appealing message, is a clinic in what to do and what not to do to maximize the odds of rebranding success.

Where did your rebranding journey begin?

The company started as a healthcare staffing company in the space of travel-nursing, and over the years evolved into the nation's leading healthcare staffing company. We went through multiple acquisitions and did not have a strategy to integrate these brands under the umbrella as AMN. In addition, there were missed opportunities to leverage all the service offerings of these brands to client stakeholders. Over time, the company also realized there was a lack of corporate brand awareness among prospective clients as a result of the fragmented multi-house of brand approach.

How did you lay the groundwork for AMN's rebrand?

We interviewed probably 3,200 current and prospective clients, healthcare professionals, team members, executives, and analysts and asked questions such as:

- What does our corporate brand stand for?
- How many brands do we need in our portfolio?
- What's the value of each brand?
- What are the key attributes of our client-facing brands?

We had to go through the entire positioning of the company. We went back and looked at our core values and made sure that all corporate strategy was aligned.

I imagine it was a time and thought-intensive process.

It got very complex and took us about a year to finish the entire project. We went through all of the decision-making criteria along the way, figuring out what the ideal brand architecture was. The bottom line was the realization that we needed to have one master brand that went out to our clients overall.

Did you have an outside partner helping you?

Yes. We worked with a partner on the initial strategy work, the brand architecture, and the design of the research. We involved an internal research person, so once our partner helped us with figuring out the right questions to ask, we conducted a lot of the actual research internally. There were some cost savings and efficiency with this approach. We used another agency to do all of our brand identity visual work.

What was the primary message of the rebranded AMN?

The two-second version was: "Inspiring connections." AMN is composed of numerous brands, each with their own team members, unique culture, and value propositions. But every single one of the brands importantly contributes to this successful organization. And while they all provide value to our customers in unique, non-interchangeable ways, there's a core message and set of values underlying all of them. They are all inter-connected. That's what we wanted to convey in the rebrand.

What was the response like?

There was an overwhelmingly positive, enthusiastic response. There were accolades from our investors, our clients, and our team members. And we received great blog coverage that said AMN did it right, and our method-ology set a great example for others looking to rebrand.

What are the three most important takeaways from your rebranding experience?

First, having the buy-in of the CEO and other executives is critical. You need your executive team as champions and advocates for the rebrand. Don't get me wrong—you're not going to achieve consensus on all aspects during this process. But the CMO has to do a stellar job getting executive team members engaged with the rebranding, and to continue that process along the way.

Second, you need to motivate every member of every team to believe in the rebranding effort and take ownership of it. Don't look it as some directive coming down from the top that everyone in the organization just has to accept whether they like it or not. Work with them to be sure they're truly comfortable with it and feel great about what it means for them and the company. The CMO needs to create a compelling value proposition for the rebrand and "sell" it company-wide.

Third, don't just go through the rebranding and then put it in your file cabinet and walk away from it. Rebranding isn't a one-time event. After it's "done," the company and the market are going to continue to evolve. You have to consider how each change ties into the brand and consider appropriate adjustments. And, don't just react to the present. You need to remain future-oriented, always thinking about what your brand is going to look like and how it needs to evolve.

KEY TAKEAWAYS

- *Bringing in experts for help with rebranding is often a good idea although you don't necessarily have to work with just one firm all the way through.*

- *If you can't get your CEO to support the rebranding initiative from the beginning, don't bother since it will be doomed to failure.*

- *Roll-out your rebranding campaign first to your employees and make sure the "inoculation" takes before sharing it with the outside world.*

Further reading:
Al Ries and Laura Ries, *The 22 Immutable Laws of Branding*

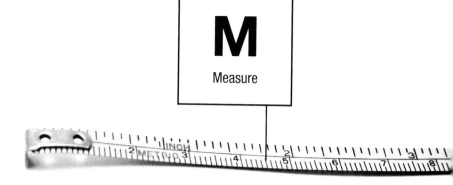

Measure Twice, Market Once

"Showing has a much bigger impact than just teaching alone."

Antonio Lucio
Visa

At Visa, a company that's been a household name for decades, staying ahead of the curve when it comes to customer engagement is more important than ever. This requires having a clear and accurate sense of what's working and what isn't in their marketing, and acting decisively on that information.

The man in charge of making all of this happen for Visa was Global Chief Brand Officer Antonio Lucio, who recently became the CMO at HP. At the time of our interview, we started off by talking about the why and how of measuring, and this led to a valuable discussion about marketing innovation and the future of social communications.

With the entire world watching, Antonio brought this all together in a seriously successful campaign that ran during the 2012 Summer Olympics—a gold-medal triumph we can all learn from.

How do you measure the success of your marketing?

At Visa the ultimate measure of success for our marketing is ROI—our ability to drive the business. We break that down to three components. First, reach. This is defined as how many people can recall our campaigns. Second, short-term impact, defined as the short-term usage lift of consumers. Third, long-term impact, defined as lift in our brand equity and our ability to influence consumer behavior longer-term.

Have there been any big surprises in terms of what's worked really well and what hasn't?

It's not really a surprise, but what I've learned is that showing, rather than telling, is the way to go. I've observed this whether it's addressing a question from our management by showing results and data or teaching the organization how to do social by putting a team in place to show them what a best-in-class social effort looks like—for example, our recent #goinsix social media campaign. Showing has a much bigger impact than just teaching alone.

Marketing seems to be getting increasingly complex in terms of ways to spend and ways to monitor. Has it gotten more complex for you and, if so, how are you dealing with that complexity?

While the media ecosystem is definitely becoming more complex, our approach of putting the consumers at the center has not changed. We strive to understand how our consumers are using different devices, where they are spending their time, and what they want to hear from us. And then we adjust our media mix and messaging accordingly. We want to ensure we are delivering unique and relevant experiences across all these screens by using the unique capabilities of the technology or platform the consumer is engaged with and delivering them a message that will interest them. Through technology we are better able to measure engagement with our brand and understand the impact of the experiences we are delivering to our customers.

A CMO has a lot of choices in where to invest time. Where have you been investing yours lately?

Given the increasingly complex media landscape, deepening Visa's focus and commitment to digital and social communications is a constant priority for my leadership team and me. The imperative has never been greater for us to better communicate the strengths, values, and mission of Visa to our full range of stakeholders in an integrated way. This meant that some structural changes were needed to set us up for success. We have made significant progress on this front, but it is a constantly evolving ecosystem. Our work is never done.

How do you stay close to your customers when you operate in so many markets and have so many different types of customers?

Social media is a great equalizer in so many ways. It enables global brands like Visa—and myself personally—to stay close to customers in markets around the world, including understanding what is important to them, what they are talking about, and what they care about, all while providing the ability to engage them directly.

Your "Go World" cheer campaign during the 2012 Olympics was one of the most successful examples of traditional and online marketing integration to date. What strategy did you use to integrate the various channels, and what were some of the biggest lessons from that campaign?

We used our "Audience First" approach to develop a global campaign framework that directly engaged consumers through a global social platform. That allowed fans to connect with the Go World marketing campaign by "Cheering" on athletes. London 2012 was heralded as the most social games ever, and our Olympic Games marketing campaign was the most successful in our history. It was a true game changer in the way we drove engagement. We're still applying the lessons learned from London, such as the benefits derived from engaging in social with concise, snackable content (which inspired our #goinsix campaign).

Have you been able to link your innovative marketing activities to the kinds of business metrics favored by CEOs?

Our key performance metrics evolve to address changing dynamics in the industry. For example, we recently added metrics to address social marketing, which enables brands to build direct relationships with consumers. We added social KPI goals that are part of a select few KPIs known to drive the business. We closely track our progress, and have timely and transparent accountability across leadership towards delivering against these business driving KPIs.

Visa has made a big push to integrate social media into their overall marketing efforts over the past few years. Can you comment on your current strategy and where you plan on taking the program in the future?

Visa believes we are in a social era that extends beyond any platform or community. Social is a mindset that empowers consumers and connects communities. We are incorporating social in the very heart of our marketing, not merely during the execution phase. We strive to develop social-at-the-core campaigns by designing for shareability and planning for conversations. We invite consumers to drive the conversation while structuring our ecosystem to make sharing frictionless.

KEY TAKEAWAYS

- *Professional marketers ALWAYS have measures in place to track progress and guide expenditures.*

- *These measures typically include short-term responses like direct impact on awareness and sales and longer-term reactions like brand perceptions.*

- *The arrival of social media has created the opportunity for new metrics AND "social-at-the-core" campaigns.*

Further reading:

Michael Porter, *Competitive Strategy*

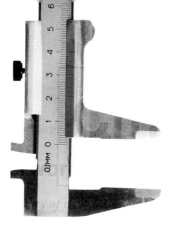

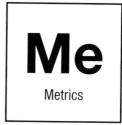

Me

Metrics

The Metric System

"My team still cringes when I say, 'You can't eat awareness.'"

Dan Marks
First Tennessee Bank

Dan Marks had a great idea…the sort of idea many CMOs would love to have fall into their lap. It was a new system for gathering and analyzing marketing metrics and it made a big difference for First Tennessee Bank, enabling them to look backwards at the impact of 84 percent of Dan's marketing spend and predict with reasonable accuracy what would happen when budgets change—up or down.

I'm not going to encapsulate his stroke of brilliance here because Dan—who recently moved to the CMO position at Hancock Bank—is about to explain it better than I could ever hope to, and also give a clinic in how to approach the overall question of metrics.

It's worth noting that the fact he's sharing this with the world is a testament to his intellectual generosity, which is also a key element shared by the most successful marketers.

One of the terms you used that I really liked is the notion that creating a metrics program is a journey. Talk to me a little bit about the journey.

The revolution really is in saying, "Let's not have a separate set of metrics," or "Let's, at the very least, connect the marketing metrics to the core bottom line revenue and costs and profit objectives." And so that's the journey. The measurement approach varies by type of marketing activity and channel. So the stages of the journey start with direct marketing, where the linkages and the science are the most developed. Even in B2B, if I can quantify that I'm helping create opportunities from introduction or helping move things along the pipeline, all of a sudden now you are speaking the same language as sales. One of the most elusive goals and one that's still not there yet is the overall full media mix impact—what's the cumulative impact of everything working together?

What's the difference between an outcome measure and a diagnostic measure? Can you put them in a priority order relative to job security and doing your job well?

Outcome measures have impact on revenue profits and margins. These are the key results that the CEO and board ultimately care about. And so those are the cardinal metrics. Diagnostic measures are important to understand outcomes. Diagnostic metrics are things that help us understand what the potential actions we should take are, and the prioritization of those actions based on understanding the customer, the customer and the marketplace, and the buying process and the competition.

So for example, we look at awareness. My team still cringes when I say, "You can't eat awareness." But it's important to understand that customers do go through this buying process of awareness, consideration, purchase, and then various levels of loyalty. That said, our goal is not to create awareness. Our goal is to get people to buy stuff and generate revenue. We have to understand the buying process. We have to understand if we're having trouble getting people to buy stuff, is it because the awareness is low? Do they not know about the product, or are they trying it but not repeating it?

Do you look at the various points of contact in the customer experience and measure each of those?

We look at it both overall and after a key experience point. So after you've had an interaction at a branch, after you've had an interaction with a business banker, after you've interacted with some of our online technology. So we do. We definitely understand how they are all different. And we've studied it. So we also know that our experience scores and our recommend scores strongly correlate/predict future changes in retention and revenue.

So when you see your experience score decline, you can go to the CEO and say, "Sales are going to be down next quarter"?

Well, maybe not quite that quickly! We know over time if scores are trending down or scores are trending up, that will translate into a strong probability of having lower or higher revenue in the future.

Give me a sense of how often you're looking at numbers.

Well, we do have an alert mechanism. So if poor scores are spiking, we know that pretty fast. But generally speaking, we look at our customer experience and customer buying metrics on a monthly basis, and that's where you see trends.

In a round of budget cuts, were you able to predict how the marketing budget cut would impact your business?

Oh, yes. And the level of prediction was pretty close. I mean, not a hundred percent. No model is completely perfect, but it's definitely useful.

What three pieces of advice do you have for CMOs about to start the metrics journey?

One, definitely have the conversation with your key partners, whether it's your CEO, CFO, or sales leaders. Figure out who is going to judge your performance and collaborate with you because most of the time CMOs can't actually sell stuff themselves. They're influencing sales activities. Have that conversation early on, and ask what metrics are important to them and what are the outcomes that you should focus on.

Two, I would definitely commit to a program of optimization and continuous improvement of marketing results.

Three, connect to and focus on giving back to the community. And there are a number of different ways to do that—The CMO Club is one example. There are also several great CMO-type organizations that exist to help CMOs share information. And you've got to do that, carefully. You don't want to give away trade secrets, but there are great resources out there to help talk about common challenges, common best practices. And every CMO has got something to add to the conversation, and what you give, you get back in spades.

Since we originally talked, using data to inform marketing decisions has become even more prevalent. What are you excited about now in the area of marketing metrics?

There are some really exciting advances in tools and techniques for marketing assessment and optimization. Two of the areas that show the most promising advances are in programmatic buying and full media mix optimization. Every marketer should be at least experimenting with programmatic buying because of the ability to more precisely target and track results. There is a very good chance that some of the big digital players will have a usable buying and reporting tool that lives up to the promise of an integrated cross channel dashboard at least for digital and potentially for both online and offline media buying this year or perhaps in 2016.

I hear marketers use the expression, "If you can't measure it, don't do it," which can favor direct response over other forms of marketing. Are you a subscriber to this notion? If so, are all forms of marketing really measurable? If not, have there been some components of your marketing plans that go into the "leap of faith" bucket?

Marketing has to be about winning the hearts and minds of the people in our target market. Ultimately, the buying decision makers, even in a B2B type setting, are people. People make decisions based on a mixture of emotion and reason. The marketer that errs in either direction will just not be as successful.

Markets also change, so marketers who spend all of their resources on "proven" tactics or channels will get left behind as the market moves. Therefore, experimentation is essential. In experiments some stuff will work and a lot of stuff will not. Edison said something like an essential part of creating the lightbulb was first finding ninety-nine ways that did not work. In the same way, proper marketing should always have a portfolio of experiments where some work and some do not, but you learn from both. Setting an expectation that everything should work just sets the team up for never advancing or learning. Measurement helps with that learning.

Also, the level of rigor and attribution will vary depending on what the goal is. I remember when we first got started with social media, we did not attempt to put a short term ROI goal on it. There was a high level sense that based on the millions of people engaging with social media, this was going to be an important communication channel and that we needed to learn. We decided to allocate a very small percentage of our overall spend to experiment and learn in the channel. The purpose was to gain a long term understanding and determine what the potential ROI could be in the future. The shorter term measurement was more along the lines of followers and engagement with the channel as indicators of potential relevance.

KEY TAKEAWAYS

- *Never stop refining your marketing metrics.*

- *Since marketing is rarely the only factor in closing a sale, make sure your marketing metrics are approved and respected by the head of Sales and your CEO.*

- *Buying decisions are rarely just rational, so make sure your metrics include emotional factors like brand perceptions.*

Further reading:

Shane Atchison and Jason Burby, *Does It Work?: 10 Principles for Delivering True Business Value in Digital Marketing*

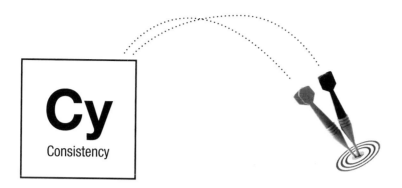

Cy
Consistency

Consistency Is the New Black

"At the end of the day it's not about what I think should work or is going to work, it's about how the consumer responds to the brand and product."

Louise Camuto
Camuto Group

I'll admit it: I'm not much of a fashionista, and I've never marketed a fashion brand.

But after talking with Louise Camuto, whose responsibilities as CMO of Camuto Group include such marquee brands as BCBG Max Azria, Jessica Simpson, Vince Camuto, and Arturo Chiang, it's clear to me that the top fashion marketer's success in the milieu is no accident.

Louise's insight on how Camuto Group provides a consistent experience for different demographics of women around the world contains lessons we can all use to market more effectively.

How do you infuse Camuto Group's values and maintain consistent messaging across all twenty of your brands?

We spend a lot of time thinking about how we can interpret each product—from footwear to apparel—in the most on-brand manner. As CMO, I emphasize the importance of image and brand consistency daily with my team. We work closely with our international partners to ensure that the way a brand is represented at every consumer and trade touchpoint not only reflects the brand's DNA, but also reinforces the message and aesthetic which allows for the brand experience to be omnichannel.

How does new product development work at Camuto Group? How do you ensure brand consistency without stifling creativity?

Our design process is extensive. We have a team of people who shop all over the world for inspiration and they bring ideas, concepts, and materials to the table for review. We sit as a team and determine what items are appropriate for each of our brands, and we spend a lot of time analyzing the marketplace for trend direction as well as what's happening at the consumer level. What I have found to be paramount is listening to customers. I make sure to spend time in our stores watching how the customer shops, how she selects product, as well as what her purchasing process is.

How are you using social media in your marketing?

We've invested heavily in a social media team to build the brand voice cross-channel. Today, a lot of looking at fashion happens online, and the Internet has really democratized the business, which is exciting. The influence of bloggers is a breath of fresh air to me. On a good fashion blog you can see how the customer actually wears and styles your product. Delving into the online space has also helped with the design process as it gives me so much insight into the women I hope to win over or keep as customers. I can learn so much about what she's looking for in the upcoming season. Online is also a great venue for sharing new product and immediately testing the response.

How do you evaluate/measure the success of your marketing? Are there some channels that work better for you than others?

I read all the selling reports and market recap reports daily. At the end of the day it's not about what I think should work or is going to work, it's about how the consumer responds to the brand and product. I also look at how our advertised styles perform versus the items that are not included in our campaign. That can tell you some really interesting and unexpected things.

I love analyzing our online business as well because it is the purest form of analysis in the marketplace today. With a few clicks you can get a deep understanding of how your direct mail, email blasts, print campaigns, celebrity support, and editorial credits impact sell-through, and in turn leverage the knowledge to further reach the customer and meet her needs.

What's the biggest marketing risk you've taken at Camuto Group? How did it play out?

Several years ago, we re-launched Vince Camuto footwear and invested in a broad-based marketing campaign that crossed all channels. It was important for us to get the message out and we immediately saw success through exponential growth in brand awareness as well as sales. The marketing investment also allowed us to expand the multi-category licensing program rather quickly as we became a more significant brand for our retail partners almost overnight.

The fashion business more than most seems to favor new, fresh, and different. How do you balance the need to remain au courant yet somehow maintain brand consistency?

We look at adapting the concept for our ad campaigns each season to evoke the tone of the product. We also look to highlight key trends while offering a consistent brand message by using models and photographers for multiple seasons to drive brand recognition.

Has there been a product or design that you thought might be "off brand" but was just so unique you had to introduce it anyway?

The recent culottes and crop top trends were quite forward but we made them wearable, put them in our campaign, and they sold out. I was excited to see the results as they clearly indicated that customers were responding to the product.

Have you "freshened up" the marketing of any of your product lines recently and, if so, what inspired the change and was there a conscious effort to be consistent with previous activities?

When we launched men's apparel, we shifted our ad campaigns and brand imagery to integrate the man within the total lifestyle. Since the launch of menswear, our campaigns have been shot with both a male and female model and this year we moved from a studio to a location as we wanted to create a more cinematic feel and give our customers a more intimate look inside the complete brand experience. The consumer is really responding to the connection between the man and the woman and the way the product is showcased as the hero of the images, complementing the mood of the entire campaign.

KEY TAKEAWAYS

- *When in doubt, listen to your customers!*

- *Find your element of consistency even if the market requires "newness" every year.*

- *Marketing done correctly will drive sales and create opportunities for brand extensions/new products.*

Further reading:
Sally Hogshead, *Fascinate: Your 7 Triggers to Persuasion and Captivation*

New Products, Shaken and Stirred

"Creativity and innovation aren't just about another page in a magazine or another billboard with clever imagery or copy."

Lee Applbaum
Patrón Spirits

When Lee Applbaum stepped on board as CMO of the iconic beverage brand Patrón Spirits, he took an admittedly conservative "stewardship" approach to his new duties. People around the world ask for Patrón by name when they want a fine tequila that conveys prestige and class, and they don't need much outside motivation to do so.

But as a relentless innovator honored by the CMO Club with their Creativity Award, it wasn't long before Lee was making his mark and showcasing his outside-the-box talents, all the while maintaining and amplifying what was already working for Patrón. The successful new product launches Lee has devised and overseen are an excellent reminder that the best marketers are always looking for ways to connect with customers by doing something that hasn't been done before.

In this interview, you'll see prime examples of the way Lee is driven to realize ambitious marketing initiatives that lesser CMOs might dismiss as logistically unfeasible, and consistently deliver a solid ROI.

How are you being creative in your current role, and how is that advancing Patrón's overall marketing efforts?

A lot of my team's creative energies are directed towards reimagining the conversation in our category, which is ultra-premium wine and spirits and, more specifically, tequila. Creativity and innovation aren't just about another page in a magazine or another billboard with clever imagery or copy. They're about what we can do that's disruptive in our increasingly digital, social, and mobile ecosystem.

Can you talk about a recent launch that showcases your approach to new products?

We recently launched a new line of artisanal tequilas called Roca Patrón. Historically we haven't launched new products very often or in a particularly strategic way. The traditional approach for this brand and for the industry would have been to splash it out in magazines, maybe advertise a little on TV, and see what happens. But we were very cognizant of the fact that a majority of media today is being consumed digitally, and we were determined to capitalize on that opportunity.

One of the keys to marketing in the spirits industry is the consumer's interest in sharing stories and experiences. We latched onto the insight that consumers in the luxury space now feel that it's not just enough to have a big bold logo. They want to know the backstory, and understand the authenticity and integrity of a brand. And importantly, they want to share this all with others.

So we rebuilt all of our Web assets, including building experiential mobile-optimized microsites for Roca Patrón to help consumers learn about the product. We explained the artisanal process that goes into making Roca Patrón through a series of vignettes, and we made it easy for the audience to curate and share the information. We created a tool for both consumers and the trade to streamline sharing and commenting on cocktail recipes featuring Roca Patrón.

Did you rely on organic discovery of the new Web assets, or did you "market the marketing?"

We did "market the marketing." We wanted it to be known that Patrón was very serious about making Roca Patrón a success. We marketed the marketing to our distributors, who in turn marketed our marketing to the retailers. Our objective was to inspire confidence that if they bought Roca Patrón, their efforts to sell it would be supported by an ample amount of media gravity owned, earned, and paid for by us.

And how has the response been?

The initial response has been nothing short of phenomenal. We launched it in July 2014 and we've already beaten our annualized sales goal by 50 percent. Now is that attributable to the digital piece alone? No. But our digital marketing initiatives were certainly a key driver of that great result.

It's interesting that you talked about this story becoming social currency. Can you explain this idea a bit more?

The focus for the launch of this particular product line was rooted in the handmade, artisanal, very traditional production process. We're talking to a very specific artisanal audience; the same people who follow the farm-to-table movement. This is a garden-to-glass movement.

We're unapologetic about the success of our marketing. There are cynics who believe that, because the core product can't deliver, they just have to be clever. But the truth is we don't. We've got a very honest, real, great artisanal product, and we developed really great marketing to go with it. We wanted to make sure that everything was really rooted in authenticity, and that we never got accused of just fancy window-dressing.

Is there one specific program you've created at Patrón to date that you're especially proud of?

Yes, "Roca on the Rails." Patrón owns a 1927 vintage railcar that Clark Gable and Huey Long and FDR rode on. We gutted and restored it in a very cool, very authentic style. This thing makes the Orient Express look like a New York City subway car. It's over-the-top opulent.

So we took the railcar into cities all over the U.S. and got leading mixologists and an iconic chef from each city to create beautiful, bespoke dinners and tastings on and off the car featuring Roca Patrón. And we harnessed our huge social media footprint to give consumers a "behind the velvet rope" look at these massively luxurious events. Roca on the Rails got wide media coverage from bloggers to big publications, and just created a ton of buzz within the mixology community and the consumers who follow it.

KEY TAKEAWAYS

- *New products warrant fresh marketing approaches—especially as a means of generating press coverage and conversations on social media.*

- *Sometimes it is necessary to "market the marketing" such that various stakeholders get excited about a new product/campaign.*

- *The medium is also the message, so make sure your media choices are consistent with your brand.*

Further reading:
Clayton M. Christensen and Michael E. Raynor, *The Innovator's Solution: Creating and Sustaining Successful Growth*

II. Internal Elements

A hard truth every ambitious marketer learns eventually is that creativity only gets you so far on your quest for the CMO's chair. For an organization to entrust you with the top marketing job, you need to prove—every single day—that you possess a certain skill set rooted in a different garden from the one that produces innovative campaign ideas.

The word "Leadership" is serviceable shorthand for this skill set, but there's much more to the picture. Marketers destined for the C-suite know how to get the troops excited to charge into battle. They know how to respond to internal changes without getting flustered. They know how to organize and reorganize as many times as needed to get the big wins, and they also know how to secure the buy-in of their bosses and team members every step of the way.

These are the Internal Elements of marketing. For the most part they're the things consumers don't see. They're the behind-the-scenes beating heart of a marketing campaign, and they're the cause of some very tense, high-stakes moments in our world…moments that could end with a breakthrough or with a disaster.

So it's very important to hear about the Internal Elements from the men and women who have a track record of success with them. I'm pleased to offer you this "fly-on-the-wall" access to ten conversations with CMOs and other marketing leaders who have proven they can be counted on when the Internal Elements must be handled with perfection or something darn close to it.

Bt
Building Trust

O
Organizing

Ro
Reorganizing

Ga
Global
Agendas

Re
Retooling

Lc
Leading
Change

C
Cohesion

Cs
Consultative
Selling

Cu
Culture

E
Empowerment

I like to think of marketing pros who have mastered the Internal Elements as mechanics who specialize in high-performance automobiles. Upon popping the hood they can take a quick look, tap a couple of "sweet spots" laypeople don't know exist, and quickly know exactly which tools they need, which bolts to tighten, and which parts to replace.

Then they work their magic, close it all up, and send the sleek, humming Maserati out of the garage as the rest of the world oohs and aahs, beholding the machine in action.

If you're still with me on this analogy, consider this section an apprenticeship with the world's best mechanics. These wizards of the Internal Elements know what makes a marketing department hum and can be counted on to keep it running...which is precisely why they are counted on by major national and international brands to do just that.

We "start our engines" in this section by chatting with Kawasaki's Chris Brull, who pulled off a small miracle across two very different business cultures by speaking the universal language of trust.

We'll check in with ultra-successful Silicon Valley veteran Jonathan Becher as he takes us through an internal shake-up he oversaw at SAP, and with great candor discusses how he corrected course after one of his initiatives had unexpected consequences.

We'll also hear from marketing leaders for a pair of industrial titans, namely 3M and Dow Chemical. At these companies, Raj Rao and Snehal Desai are using forward-thinking techniques to keep the fresh, profitable ideas flowing.

And that's just a taste of what's ahead. It's time for us to go "under the hood" and learn what keeps the world's best marketing engines humming.

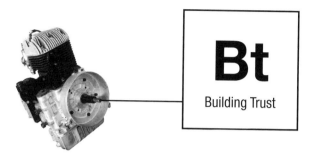

Revving the Trust Engine

"Our goal is to push authenticity to the point where we're almost like a family member."

Chris Brull
Kawasaki

If conducting consumer and product research by revving up and riding motorbikes, ATVs, and Jet Skis sounds like a fun gig to you too, then join me in holding a bit of envy (and a lot of respect) for Chris Brull, Head of Marketing for Kawasaki. Chris is a man on a mission to reinforce the "wild, unrestrained, amazing fun" that his customers have while using Kawasaki products.

This might make you assume that Chris has always taken an equally wild, unrestrained "full-throttle" approach to his career at Kawasaki. And while his marketing certainly reflects a sense of fun and fearlessness, the reality is that Chris's rise at the company has been fueled by a very methodical and careful process of building trust with his bosses (who were over in Japan) before going for the sexy stuff.

Chris and I also covered ground on Kawasaki's impressive online presence, which was zooming at top speed way before everyone else was doing it.

What were some of the strategic considerations that went into the way you started and built your career at Kawasaki?

When I started, I saw that trust needed to be built between the factory team and the U.S.-based marketing team. At that point, the U.S.-based marketing team didn't find out about a product until six months before launch. There was an inherent distrust.

So I set about building an internal coalition within Kawasaki that proved the U.S.-based marketing team was able to work with and add value to the home office in Japan. The Times Square launch of the Ninja in 2012 was a turning point that showed this was working. It was the first time the Kawasaki message was the same globally, and the content was the same globally, for a product launch. To be able to pull that off and get people to work together and trust each other as part of a global coalition was an accomplishment, and now I get to be team leader of that global coalition.

Author's note: See for yourself what the Ninja launch was all about at ninjanyc.kawasaki.com

Have there been any big surprises in terms of what marketing has worked really well for you?

We started testing our online tools on customers via trial and error, and this was before online bandwidth was widely available. And there was skepticism from within the company. But it worked! We were giving fanatic customers their Kawasaki fix. They wanted to see the next big thing from us and we were giving it to them online. Our strategy was to give them just a little bit, and so we delivered the content in bite-sized pieces that gave customers a reason to buy. The videos were engaging, educational, and exciting. I like to think our content strategy was ahead of the curve at that time.

Tell me a bit more about how you use this sort of content to keep customers interested and engaged.

We think that content related to "how the product works" is critical to our audience. Then there's the "what it is" content—this is about the physical product, how it's supposed to perform, etc. Then you get to the most important piece: Why. Why do you ride? Is it the wind in your face? The escape? Leaving friends and family behind? Or is it riding on the open road in a big pack of other riders? We want to tap into the inspiration.

So our content is saying: "Let me show you what goes on at Daytona Bike Week." "Let me show you what happens in Europe at the Isle of Man TT." "Let me show you what's going on inside the Ninja ZX-14 when it's actually in a drag race." Our fanatics are hanging on to every morsel. They want to connect. They want to belong. The content is the hook, but it's the product itself that's almost like a ticket to the Kawasaki party.

It must be great to have such fanatical customers.

It is, but that puts the obligation on us to be very authentic with them. We respect them as true enthusiasts and we know they can spot a fake in an instant. We really have to know what we're talking about to have a chance at connecting. This means being very targeted and direct. No one-size-fits-all campaigns. It may sound like I'm exaggerating here, but our goal is to push authenticity to the point where we're almost like a family member.

Kawasaki has huge presences on Facebook and Twitter. Can you talk about this a little? Are you set up to handle customer issues on social platforms?

We were the first in our industry to have a social presence, which we're proud of. And we've never bought a single fan or follower on social.

The easy thing to do with Kawasaki on social would be to just post a bunch of cool shots of cool bikes. Of course, that wasn't going to cut it. We're sharing riding tips, riding locations, history of the brand, dealership locations, and a lot more. This is what gets the deep conversations with our customers going. Social for us has always been about the voice of our customers before anything else.

So yes, we have our social team set up to respond almost 24/7. It's critically important that we're sensitive to what's going on with our customers. These hyper-enthusiasts are very much our "friends" well beyond the fact that they clicked "like" or "follow" on our pages. And so they expect Kawasaki the brand to respond to them in real time.

One of the things we talked a lot about in our interview is the importance of building trust with management. Can you offer any words of advice to new CMOs on how they can build trust within the organization, especially if the executives happen to be from another country?

Be trustworthy. Trust comes from being reliable, delivering on time, and having an open and collaborative nature. It is also putting the mission, the direction, the strategy, the company, and the team before yourself. People are always watching the leader—are they in it for themselves or for the betterment of the group/team/company? No one wants to follow a dictator "into the wall."

Be refreshing. Be for the cause.

Be empathetic. To the customer, and to the person in the "back" who may indeed be too shy to share but just needs the safe haven opportunity to share what could very well turn out to be the solution and the amazing insight.

A boss is someone we have to listen to and obey because of rank and power but they may not necessarily be trustworthy. People will not follow them passionately and at all costs.

A leader is a person we truly trust—a person we would run through the wall for at nearly any cost…passionately.

Ownership, colleagues, staff, and outside partners desperately want to be part of something bigger than one person. They want someone in a leadership position who people will trust and rally around, and who will lead the business forward.

Be a leader. Be passionate. Be trustworthy. It will get you where you need to go!

Is there one thing CMOs should try to avoid when trying to build trust internally?

Don't put blinders on and only look at yourself.

It is much like being in a pitch black room where you can't see a thing. But you have a flashlight. What fool would point that flashlight on themselves? If they did, they would never get out of the pitch black room! Point that flashlight forward, away from yourself, and find your way out. Point the focus on others, not yourself!

But even more importantly, be sure to spend as much time (and recognition) with your team, the very group of people who are "doing the work." Make sure the person who "does the work" presents the work and is given ownership and recognition for doing the work.

No one wants to work for someone who gives orders, receives the work (without doing much of it on their own), and then takes the limelight for the success of the work—and even worse, doesn't take ownership if the work fails and passes the buck punitively.

You can never build happiness/success on other people's sadness.

Be a leader. Walk point and be sure to encourage those in the back.

KEY TAKEAWAYS

- *As a new CMO in a large organization, look for quick wins to build internal trust.*

- *Trust is earned through your everyday actions.*

- *Share full credit for success with your team and accept full responsibility when things go wrong.*

Further reading:

David Allen, *Getting Things Done: The Art of Stress-Free Productivity*

O

Organizing

High-Def Organizing

"Any organizational structure that puts customers and prospects at the center of its efforts should be successful."

Stephanie Anderson
Time Warner Cable Business Class

No one ends up CMO as a result of gravitating towards the easy things. The demands of a successful marketing career are relentless, the barriers to success—inside and outside the company—are steep, and getting consistently outstanding results in the expected time frame requires the CMO to be at least a little bit of a superhero every single day.

Hopefully this sheds some light on why I'm so impressed by Stephanie Anderson, CMO of Time Warner Cable Business Class, who has repeatedly demonstrated her ability to survive and thrive under these high-pressure conditions. Her secret is her mastery of organization, which enables her to accomplish more in the span of a day than most can in a week.

One of the big challenges a CMO faces is organizational, given all the different marketing channels. How are you addressing your organizational challenges?

I'm going for best-in-class in this area. We've implemented what I call an "outside in" structure that takes into consideration all the customers and competitors in the segments we serve. I have a lead GVP of Small Business, a lead GVP of Mid-Market and Channels, and a GVP of Enterprise and Carrier Business. They run the marketing end-to-end for their segment. (This includes offers, competitive, and lifecycle strategy.) And then I have two functional teams that are shared resources. One is mass & digital, and the other is customer experience and knowledge for all of the database, research, and retention. It's a new design, but I believe any organizational structure that puts customers and prospects at the center of its efforts should be successful.

Often a CMO arrives with a department already staffed and has to make some tough choices regarding who stays and who goes. How much time would you advise a fellow CMO to give the current team before deciding a reorg is necessary and what are the steps to take, if it turns out that significant changes need to be made?

A new leader has to consider other organizational designs and issues within the company and "assess and address" pretty quickly. Sixty days for most decisions is a good benchmark. I have never wished I wouldn't have moved so fast, always faster. When you know changes need to be made, get the wheels in motion. A quarter means a lot in business and marketing. You're not getting any newer and changes don't get any easier, really. If it's a tough one, it's always going to be tough. Trust your gut a bit as well. That's what great leaders do.

When you implemented your departmental reorganization, did you run into any surprises? How did you address them?

As you know the effort to begin the formation of our now more than $3B division was marketing driven. We looked at our market opportunity and built a team from the "outside in." The toughest part was giving market-ers permission to focus on a specific segment, but for a bigger footprint.

Our team got deeper on customer and prospect knowledge and broader on reach/geography. It's hard to dabble in all things marketing when your goals and objectives are really specific and defined. That took some getting used to for some of the creatives!

Once you've completed your reorg, how do you as a leader make sure that the new structure "takes" and the team functions in sync?

Communicate like crazy, measure results, hold teams accountable, and did I say communicate? We have monthly leadership meetings, 1:1 calls, all associate Web conferences with the whole team every six weeks, and a monthly marketing scorecard report. We also implemented a continuing education program for marketers, which had never been done in our company before—focused on our self-identified weaknesses. This consisted of monthly live, Web-based training delivered by our Customer Executive Board and Marketing Leadership Board. I think this gave us all a chance to grow into our roles quickly and learn along the way without fear.

A CMO has a lot of choices in terms of where they invest their time. Tell me a little about your top priorities.

I use my boss's rule: 1/3, 1/3, 1/3. A third of my time is spent with my peer group, making sure they all understand the strategy, focus, and priorities for Marketing, Advertising, and Offers. The next third is spent with my direct reports (three GVPs and two VPs), helping them with priorities and people/budget issues. The last third is spent out in the market, with customers, suppliers, vendors, events, continuing education, etc.

Big data is a big part of the CMO conversation these days. How are you tackling it?

We're revamping our database to not just be more encompassing, but also more searchable and friendly. The data is useless without the ability to pull together the storyline and make decisions based on what you find out. That's an ongoing challenge.

How do you stay close to your customers when you operate in so many markets and have so many different types of business customers?

We serve very small, small, medium, and large enterprises. It's easy when you're dealing with a national customer to be responsive and available. But in the world of small and very small customers, it becomes harder. The danger is that your relationship ends up boiled down to email and a monthly bill. We're trying to counteract that with things like newsletters and a value-added benefits program for small businesses. It's getting better as we use campaign and lifecycle management tools, but there's always room for improvement. Our job is collecting and keeping customers and helping them thrive and grow.

KEY TAKEAWAYS

- *Focus: Build your marketing organization from the "outside-in" by focusing first on your target audience and their needs.*

- *Execute: Once you have your organizational plan, execute it as swiftly as possible.*

- *Communicate: Constantly communicate with your team and encourage continuous education.*

Further reading:
Neil Smith, *How Excellent Companies Avoid Dumb Things: Breaking the 8 Hidden Barriers that Plague Even the Best Businesses*

Ro

Reorganizing

Tearing Down Those Walls

"Incremental changes will not be sufficient; we need to innovate the discipline of marketing."

Jonathan Becher
SAP

There's a sometimes-frustrating air of mysticism around the word "innovation." It's fun to think about and inspiring to talk about. But how does a marketer tap into it on a consistent basis and translate it into real initiatives with real results? It can't just be a matter of waiting around for the "muse," right?

Right indeed. While a later interview with Beth Comstock of GE will deep-dive into the nature of innovation itself, this one with Jonathan Becher, CMO of software pacesetter SAP SE, focuses on a single internal tactic that can spark innovation amidst any rut: Reorganization.

Jonathan's long and distinguished track record in Silicon Valley—where either you produce game-changing innovations on a regular basis or you hit the road—proves he's one of the rare marketers who truly walks the walk.

In your words, why is innovation so important, particularly for CMOs?

For all good business leaders, there comes a day when you realize, "What got us here won't get us where we need to go." We all know that the way customers consume information, products, and services has completely changed. It follows that the way we need to engage with customers must also change. However, incremental changes will not be sufficient; we need to innovate the discipline of marketing.

Real innovation requires organizational change. Can you talk about the changes you made to your marketing organization to institutionalize innovation?

A few years ago, I created a group called "Innovation Marketing." The charter of that group was to try new things, break rules, make people uncomfortable, and change the status quo. The team generated tons of ideas, many of which were very interesting and impactful. However, it didn't accomplish what I expected, as we were essentially segregating innovation to one small group. People who weren't in it felt left out. And in fact, it created some resistance to change and new ideas.

So we disbanded the group and focused on creating a company-wide culture of innovation instead. We made it everybody's job to innovate. Now, we highlight efforts throughout marketing that push boundaries and embrace change, even ones that are not completely successful. We're reinforcing our corporate motto, which highlights our quest for relentless improvement: "Run Better."

Marketing seems to be getting increasingly complex in terms of ways to spend and ways to monitor. Has it gotten more complex for you and, if so, how are you dealing with that complexity?

Luckily for me, I run marketing for a company that specializes in using technology to solve complex business challenges. For example, I have a mobile dashboard where my leadership team and I have real-time visibility into all parts of our marketing business. We can see what's working and what isn't, then redeploy resources and budget as necessary.

SAP seems to be in the midst of a brand transformation. Can you describe that transformation?

I'm not sure whether you should call it a transformation or a brand expansion. For many years, our approach was talking about how big, successful companies run SAP. You didn't know what exactly we did for the companies, but you knew we were somehow linked with their success.

Now we're taking a much more human approach that's closely linked to our company mission: to "help the world run better and improve people's lives." We're telling stories of how we create value, not only for our customers but for our customers' customers. For example, rather than talking about how a big bank benefits from an SAP deployment, we talk about how a man in a very rural area who can't physically get to a bank is now able to bank on his mobile phone. This access to banking opens up entirely new economic possibilities that weren't previously an option to this man and improves his life. SAP makes that possible.

It's not just "business runs SAP"; it's also "life runs SAP." You can sum up the change as moving from B2B to P2P—people to people.

Author's note: The remaining questions and answers are from a follow-up conversation I had with Jonathan right before this edition went to press.

You are in a new position since we last spoke. Did you need more reorganizations to foster a culture of innovation?

We did have another reorganization but not specifically for innovation; that one was more for efficiency. On the culture side, we adopted "change is the only constant" to remind ourselves that we always have to be innovating. Today's innovation is tomorrow's standard practice which must in turn be disrupted.

*One of the things I'd admired about your presentation to other CMOs
a couple of years ago was your admission of trying something and then
course correcting. In other words, you were remarkably honest about a
reorganization that didn't quite worked out as planned. When it comes
to reorganizing your teams, how important is trial and error?*

Trial and error requires a testing/learning mindset that is critical in marketing and, yes, can apply to reorganizations. But reorganization doesn't
require a structural change to reporting lines. You can create special-pur-
pose temporary project teams that test theories and then bring them back
to standardize and scale.

*How did the brand transformation, or as you called it, an expansion,
go? Any lessons learned there?*

Better than expected but also in a slightly different direction than we
expected. You and I talked about how marketing is getting so much more
complex. All of business is experiencing the same thing. Conquering that
complexity turned out to be the major theme in our brand. We now
stand for "Run Simple."

KEY TAKEAWAYS

- *Reorganizing can lead to unintended consequences so don't be afraid to
  course correct.*

- *It is possible to test new structures by creating temporary project teams.*

- *Reorganizations tend to be more successful when they are aligned
  around a newly defined or refined brand purpose.*

Further reading:
Simon Sinek, *Start with Why: How Great Leaders Inspire Everyone to
Take Action*

Ga
Global Agendas

Scoring a Global Goal

"I want to create a global dialogue around what I think is the best profession in the world."

Phil Clement
Aon

Smart brand managers for global companies would never dare attempt a one-size-fits-all approach to marketing a brand across different countries and regions. They know each nation's customer base has a unique set of needs and pain points that must be specifically addressed for an international brand to thrive.

So imagine the responsibility of coordinating a marketing effort across not just a few but 120 countries! Welcome to a typical day at the office for Phil Clement, Global CMO for insurance and risk advisor Aon. Aon has a presence in nearly half the world's territories, and it's Phil's job to set the global agenda and ensure the brand's message rings loud and clear in every one of them.

Here's how he does it…with an "assist" from arguably the world's most famous sports team: Manchester United.

As CMO of Aon, what do you hope to accomplish in the immediate future?

Over the last eight years we've done a really good job of developing an awareness of our brand. Now I'd like to develop the world's understanding of what, exactly, we do. Most people understand the word "insurance" as straightforward consumer insurance, which misses the mark when it comes to Aon.

Internally, I would like to be more connected with my colleagues across the globe. I want to create a global dialogue around what I think is the best profession in the world.

How does Aon's sponsorship of Manchester United Football Club fit into your go-to market strategy?

Manchester United is "understood" in all 120 countries where we operate. Aon's sponsorship of them makes my job much easier because it means we can use the same team, same language, same sponsorship material, same explanation for what we're doing, how we're doing it, and why we're doing it across the world.

Besides Aon's sponsorship of Manchester United, tell me about some of your other marketing initiatives.

One of my favorites is our "best employer survey." What we do in about 100 countries is identify who are the best employers. It's a two-part process. The first is to identify what the local economy believes are the best qualities of an employer and then rank the companies against that criteria. The process of doing the survey, doing the ranking, emailing the report and having a media partner distribute it is very affordable. It's difficult for us to move the needle if we do one good idea in one geography. When you're sifting through $11 billion in revenue in 120 countries, one percent improvement in one country can get lost. Getting something like the best employers program to work globally has been wonderful for us.

Similarly, rather than producing 100 reports on benchmarking and data, which we may have done in the past, we pick a few that cut through the noise. One would be our risk map, where we publish a map color-coded based on equivocal risk. What's the likelihood of a change in regime? If you're doing business around the world, this map becomes an important tool, and it also suggests that we're experts in understanding risk. Those are two of my favorite ideas.

What metrics have you used for tracking the success of your programs?

To use the Manchester United sponsorship as an example, we have a unique points system for that focusing on three objectives. First we looked at employee engagement via surveys asking: Do our employees believe we have an important and engaging brand? Are they proud to work at the firm? We did extraordinarily well. The surveys revealed that our people were very proud to be part of Aon and felt the brand was very strong.

The second way that we measured it was in marketing equivalency. We took some of the sponsorship fee and applied it against that. Then we used third party, almost public domain-type measures on the value of the advertising on television and in media, PR, online, and in chat rooms.

The third measure was client engagement. We looked at renewal rates, new business, and crossover efforts. We counted the margin on that business, divided it by half, and did a calculation on whether or not it was a better investment than stock buyback. Everything else—like the fact that our recruiting lines in India went from 25 to 1,000 people, wrapping around the block—didn't go into the calculations. The fact that employees were wearing jerseys to work, you can't count that.

Does corporate have to approve local activities?

I have to approve any sponsorship that is above $25,000. But anybody that's good at their profession doesn't try to make big sponsorship decisions without the help of others, so I'm not really in a "brand police" role with these. If I'm getting involved in the decision, I want to make sure it's consistent with our messaging and that we can talk about six pillars that we use in all sponsorship activity: Risk, Talent, Health, Retirement, Data & Analytics, and Access to Capital.

Does social play a role in your business?

It does, but not in the straightforward direct-to-consumer way it does for most companies. This is because people generally prefer not to talk about the details of their health and benefits policies on social media.

Social does play a big role for us internally. We've found that the most effective way of connecting a 22-year-old colleague in India with his counterpart in the U.S. is to provide a forum on Facebook or our internal platforms. We did a program a couple years ago called "Pass It On," which focused on getting our colleagues to pass on their knowledge. We had three teams; one flew to Australia, one to Africa, and one to South America and we handed off footballs through three routes back to England. Every time a ball came to your city, you did things to celebrate the culture with clients, colleagues, and the community.

KEY TAKEAWAYS

- *A CMO for a multinational corporation must establish and communicate 4 to 6 brand pillars in order to gain consistent execution across borders.*

- *Global branding can be facilitated by global sponsorships—assuming a relevant and universal message can be built around the sponsorship.*

- *Maintaining budget approval for large local sponsorships is a smart way for CMOs to manage global teams.*

Further reading:
Jim Collins and Morten T. Hansen, *Great by Choice: Uncertainty, Chaos, and Luck—Why Some Thrive Despite Them All*

Sometimes Simpler Isn't Better

"Improving customer trust has always been my single most important goal."

Mark Hanna
Richline

The easy thing for jewelry giant Richline would be to group all its offerings under one tidy brand umbrella.

Thankfully for their bottom line, CMO Mark Hanna saw that it would also be the less profitable thing to do. So he segmented it all into thirty-one (and counting) retailer-specific jewelry collections. Yes, it created a lot more work for Mark, his entire team, and the other departments who suddenly had a lot more file folders to juggle. But good marketers—and especially CMOs—are nothing if not diligent, and the Richline squad stepped up to meet the challenge.

Not only did sales increase, but key intangibles like customer satisfaction and trust showed exciting improvement. While simplicity is generally a virtue in business, Mark's success retooling Richline's brand structure shows that—if and only if a rock-solid strategy and bulldog work ethic underlie the entire process—"complicating" things a little can lead to great results.

Can you talk a bit about the structure of Richline and your role at the company?

We have four independent divisions or business units within our larger company. These include Richline Brands, Inverness Corporation, Rio Grande, and LeachGarner. There are synergies among them but they are very independent of each other and, since I'm corporate, they all fall within my purview.

I've been CMO of Richline for eight years and see myself as chief business catalyst, which means that I carry the marketing responsibilities for everything from outbound to services. I also carry the responsibilities in terms of ecology and social responsibility issues, and I have significant influence on our operations.

Can you describe the decision to split Richline's offerings into many more collections than previously existed?

In 2009, we identified our biggest weakness as not having control of the consumer touchpoints. We were a company presenting our wares to a buyer and had very little influence over how things were packaged, how things were displayed, or how they were advertised. So from 2009 onwards, we made it our priority to gain that control. We identified twenty key customer touchpoints for each of our brands. And it became the single best focus decision that we ever made, as well as the most important strategy we've developed over the last few years.

The first thing we did was look at our market and our customers, which are the major national jewelry chains, shopping networks, mass merchants, and department stores. If we sell a branded product to one of them, we can't sell it to another. So the strategy became going from national label to private label and creating very specific multiple private labels within that category of products. In karat gold for example, we have fourteen retailers carrying assortments of products within a reasonably small range of innovation, all under different names.

What that did for us was take away channel conflict. It multiplied the marketing stress because we had to create everything from brand guides to color guides for fourteen instead of one. But it absolutely shot our sales through the roof because we took away channel conflict and allowed each retailer to create their own margins and positioning. It got us on this track of being very in control of this vast number of private label collections of which we now have forty-two.

So now you manage four divisions and forty-two different brands in retail. How do you set the big picture for everyone involved, since you obviously can't have your hands in all the day-to-day sales?

Firstly, we have a strong marketing team led by an exceptional VP and key directors. However, it's not all on our marketing department. Each of those brands is associated with a retailer and a retailer-specific internal team, which includes a product development team, an operations team, and a customer service team. Ultimately, we become the organizer of that team and the catalyst for them to walk in the customer's shoes. There might be occasional conflicts, but for the most part everyone is focused. At one given point in time, everyone is focused on one brand and one customer. We honestly have so few sales and marketing conflicts; we work side by side with the sales teams for our customers and it creates a bond, not an antagonism.

The world is about trust and transparency. At some point in time there'll be a day where we can say: "We're Richline, these are all of our brands and you can trust them." To do that, we need to be socially conscious and able to live in a glass house. That's why improving customer trust has always been my single most important goal.

How do you keep things straight and get down to who controls what between both your marketing department and the marketing departments of the retailers?

We're very careful, and it's all proprietary. Everything is done on a project basis together with the internal sales and product teams of the store we're working with. Most of our customers have a single sales team associated with them, so we can keep it pretty straight. Collaboration at all levels with the retailer follows the same path.

How do you measure your own success as the corporate CMO?

One term I use to think about this is "return on relationship," because all of my goals are based on the growth of our business and the growth of our profitability. My goal is that we become the biggest go-to jewelry company among retailers. Growth of business over time is really about how strong our relationships are, which is about how strong the trust is between Richline and the retailers. So improving that trust every year is my single most important goal.

KEY TAKEAWAYS

- *If you are constantly running into the same conflict with your big customers, it is time to retool.*

- *Retooling starts with a clear-eyed appraisal of your customer's needs and how you can adjust your products/services to get a higher "return on relationship."*

- *The constant push for economies of scale can blind marketers to customer-specific opportunities that ultimately can provide competitive advantage.*

Further reading:
Ted Rubin and Kathryn Rose, *Return on Relationship*

Charging Towards Change

"Find those who are your toughest critics and turn them into advocates."

Elisa Romm
MasterCard

Payments and technology industry juggernaut MasterCard is in the upper echelon of brand recognition around the world—a position many companies (and their CMOs) would love to occupy. So why would its EVP of B2B Marketing Elisa Romm be so focused on change?

For starters, MasterCard went public less than ten years ago. That event sparked a cultural transformation that—as anyone who's been at a big company during its IPO knows—takes a long time to become comfortable for the whole team. As you'll see in our interview, Elisa's leadership through that period and beyond has been a cornerstone of its success.

Today she continues to drive a change agenda, innovate new ways to engage employees, and lead by example. In this interview, Elisa covers the fundamentals of MasterCard's "culture of change," including how she created it, how she maintains it, and how she overcomes resistance to it. Whether or not your business operates on the same scale as

MasterCard, the same principles apply for making your company culture stagnation-proof.

What does it mean to lead a culture of change? Can you discuss some of the ways you made this happen at MasterCard?

When MasterCard went public we shifted from banks as owners to banks as customers. We needed to sell where we didn't sell before, when we were solely relationship managers. I speak about the broader business, not just marketing, because marketing must be part of leading the change. Marketing had to help the rest of the company define product and service differentiation to customers and to consumers. I helped drive this change agenda by working with our sales teams for our largest customers to drive differentiated communications, and then the sales team endorsed the approach because the metrics proved it worked. From that point, the company bought the approach.

How have you overcome the naysayers who are resistant to change?

When I first took a role of running the marketing division within MasterCard for our advisory services, I had one of my peers, a non-marketing person, teach me the 4 Ps of Marketing. Three years later this "peer" is a general manager for some of our international markets, while I run B2B. We have the tightest alignment and relationship to the point that we are aligning on a new agenda together.

The idea is to find those who are your toughest critics and turn them into advocates. They will then sell your platforms to their peer group. Having my new projects filtered through this "peer" gives me a gateway to the international markets. Of course, the proof is in the results. There must be metrics for success to show that your strategy was correct.

Is culture change something that is measurable? What are the key metrics you use to measure it?

At MasterCard we measure culture change internally and externally. Internally, we run an employee engagement survey every year, with action plans designed to address the culture shift we want. For example, owning decision-making at middle management. We want everyone to feel empowered, so we measure how middle managers perceive their ability to make decisions, and then we measure their managers via 360-degree surveys on how they demonstrate empowering their teams. For external demonstration of change, we run customer satisfaction surveys to determine if we've progressed on things such as "easier to do business with." Everyone at the company owns these ratings.

Given that the MasterCard brand in many ways is in the hands of others, does this have an impact on your approach to driving change?

Yes, your path to market is through others, who sometimes have similar goals, other times competing goals. It is a balancing act, because you have to influence your distribution network, which we do through our insights, expertise, and superior knowledge of the future trends, and you have to have a sound strategy that differentiates you from your competition; otherwise your distribution partners will level the playing field. "Priceless" is our differentiator, as is our knowledge and innovation.

For CMOs new to their jobs, when should culture change become a priority? Is this something to tackle in the first 100 days?

Culture change is necessary to achieve your marketing goals, but absent firing everyone and starting over, there always must be a culture shift. But 100 days is not long enough for the journey. You can identify the changes that need to take place and find folks within that represent the new way of thinking. But moving too fast, you risk leaving too many behind and not having a team to back you up. That said, your leaders/direct reports had better be aligned with your vision and sign up to make the culture shift happen.

What are three key things—let's say, two "Do's" and one "Don't"— ambitious CMOs need to think about when approaching change?

Do: Lead by example. The culture change must permeate beyond marketing to the company, but marketing must demonstrate it first.

Do: Show, don't tell. Treat the sales team like consumers, let them experience Priceless surprises, and they become advocates instantly. No PowerPoint presentation or video can produce that effect.

Don't: Create a siloed culture for marketing. Marketing must be seen as integral to driving business results, and culture clashes are often a reason that marketing isn't internally perceived as a business driver.

KEY TAKEAWAYS

- *Leading change at a large enterprise starts by understanding the current culture and how it needs to evolve.*

- *Change doesn't happen overnight and requires constant reinforcement to become deeply embedded.*

- *Since the Marketing department is often the agent of change, it must ingratiate itself across the organization.*

Further reading:
Jeffrey Hayzlett, *Running the Gauntlet: Essential Business Lessons to Lead, Drive Change, and Grow Profits*

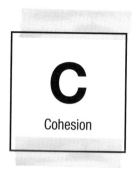

C

Cohesion

The Glue that Holds 3M's Marketing Together

"Our marketing strategies are to promote user engagement and strengthen our insights so that we can drive focused commercialization programs."

Raj Rao
3M

Look around your home and I bet you'll find at least one product created by 3M. Chances are you own many. The brand isn't just an American staple—it's made its way into marketplaces across the globe and is part of the Dow Jones Industrial Average as well as the S&P 500. From Post-it Notes and reflective traffic signs to epoxy and your dentist's preferred cleaning tools, 3M's products are essential to daily life around the world.

Competing in so many categories and spaces also means that 3M's marketing has to be meticulously organized to be effective. If not, the brand's many innovative campaigns will inevitably step on each other's toes, launch awkwardly, and land with a thud. The eCommerce initiatives headed up by Raj Rao, 3M's VP for Global eTransformation, are essential to laying that foundation of careful, logical organization—the foundation that enables the brilliant marketing innovations of Raj and his colleagues to flourish for one of the world's most ubiquitous brands.

What are your top responsibilities at 3M? I love that your title suggests forward movement and innovation.

My role in the organization is to use social and digital channels to strengthen 3M's product innovation and eCommerce commercialization programs to roadmap activity for multiple brands in several global locations. As a marketer, my responsibility is to drive digital excellence through the adoption of world-class cloud and on-premise services that enable our marketers to get to real-time engagement and strengthen the competitiveness of 3M brands in industrial, professional, government, and retail channels.

How are you making sure that all of the internal stakeholders are working together cohesively, both on a planning and execution basis?

We have developed an integrated model for customer engagement management across several high value business models in our Industrial Safety, Dental, Automotive Aftermarket, and Personal Protection business lines. These models enable us to manage search, social blogs, communities, tradeshows, mobile, eCommerce, and channel touchpoints in a cohesive way. At each interaction, we have two models at play: One where the customer or user has no previous record of interaction with 3M and chooses to remain anonymous, and a richer interaction based on known, high touch collaboration engagement where the customer is seeking to obtain a sample, retrieve "how to" videos, or make a product or service purchase. Getting all stakeholders on the same playbook is done through best practice simulations and storyboarding, which are led by eTransformation subject matter experts and eLeaders in international hubs.

What tools are you using to enable your marketers to get real-time engagement?

We have developed some proprietary algorithms to understand customer and channel opportunity and competitive insights. These are real-time capabilities that include Collaboration Command Centers, which are key for new product launch activity or campaign activation. Our architecture combines on-premise platform for data management and back office customer management, with front office applications which are cloud based like CRM, Social Engagement, and Analytics. Our key challenges are transforming legacy process to contemporary digital engagement models, and re-talenting our sales, marketing, and service teams so that they can be fluent with these new technology-enabled capabilities.

Is this latest wave of marketing tools actually driving productivity?

The most significant driver for success is understanding the need state of our customer, and enabling them to be productive in a relevant way at every stage of their engagement with 3M channels or touchpoints. We need to make sure that the workshops and customer optimization models are well understood, and that we have content automation capability in local languages and across the portfolio. Once that is in place, we are seeing strong ROI for MarTech investments and high sales conversion through eCommerce channels. The specific improvements are search performance, sample-to-order conversion, and customer market basket growth. We are also measuring digital share-of-voice and leveraging the generation of tools to drive actionable insights.

How do the boundaries of your position extend beyond the typical purview of a CMO?

My perspective is that the CMO needs to have strong operational knowledge of sales and customer service. Customers no longer follow a linear path to purchase, nor are they tied to any single channel. They are using digital tools like never before, amplifying brand experiences without any relationship boundaries, and demanding more service options as part of the product purchase. So, the role of CMO needs to have that broader perspective on the customers' experience journey and be prepared to generate appropriate content for that diversity. The big challenge is designing learning experiences for different levels of the organization that foster a new level of understanding, yet challenge us to break free from current channel or buyer/persona silos that are no longer relevant. To achieve this, we need to have courage and be prepared to risk losing some of the cultural heritage that has become embedded in our operational DNA. 3M is very well positioned for this change and has already taken big steps in several business teams to make the leap forward.

What roles do technology and innovation play in your marketing strategies?

We strive to create extended product experiences through digital channels. This has been evident in the cloud library service that we have successfully launched, in the custom car wrap business, and in our health care brands. The digital channels play a key part in providing a differentiated user experience in all these businesses. Recently, we unveiled an innovative partnership between our Post-it brand and Evernote. We have an exciting pipeline of innovative solutions that exemplify the inherent technology strengths in diverse 3M markets and channels. Our marketing strategies are to promote user engagement and strengthen our insights so that we can drive focused commercialization programs.

KEY TAKEAWAYS

- *Since consumers no longer take a linear path to purchase, marketers need to make sure the entire customer experience is consistent and differentiated.*

- *Marketing automation tools are making it easier for brands to have a cohesive presence across multiple messaging channels.*

- *A cohesive approach does not mean setting things in stone—adjustments can and should be made along the way.*

Further reading:
Pat Fallon and Fred Senn, *Juicing the Orange: How to Turn Creativity into a Powerful Business Advantage*

Cs
Consultative Selling

The Trusted Advisor
Always Beats the Salesman

"We have the best people in the business and the most expertise. Our customers rely on that."

Snehal Desai
Dow Chemical

Focusing on the customer is one thing, but truly becoming their trusted advisor and a source of profound value for them is another. When you've reached that stage, making the sale requires minimal huffing and puffing from the marketing end. This is the goal of consultative selling, of which Snehal Desai is a master over at Dow Water & Process Solutions, a division of The Dow Chemical Company.

What Snehal has to say about how marketers can deliver overwhelming value to earn trust and, at the end of the day, drive sales is indispensable. You'll see how his team pours their energy into creating educational content like seminars, white papers, studies, and models to drive the perception that they are service-minded experts, not parts manufacturers.

You also don't want to miss his insights on the subtleties of marketing a sub-brand with multiple product lines, aimed at multiple verticals with multiple constituents, all while remaining true to the parent brand's vision. (And keep in mind, he's marketing highly technical things like reverse osmosis systems to separate salt from water.)

Can you talk a little bit about how your brand—Dow Water & Process Solutions—operates relative to the parent brand of The Dow Chemical Company?

That's a good question because Dow's integrated, market-driven, industry-leading portfolio of specialty chemical, advanced materials, agrosciences, and plastics businesses delivers a broad range of technology-based products and solutions to customers in approximately 180 countries and in high-growth sectors such as packaging, electronics, water, coatings, and agriculture.

In 2014, Dow had annual sales of more than $58 billion and employed approximately 53,000 people worldwide. The Company's more than 6,000 product families are manufactured at 201 sites in thirty-five countries across the globe. We are continually leveraging the large company presence and the understanding of Dow's capabilities and history. But we don't lose sight of the fact that we have customers who are and have been buying the suite of Dow Water & Process Solutions products for years. So, our first thoughts are focused on our customers and what they want most from us.

If you were to define the Dow brand, and then you were to define the Dow Water & Process Solutions brand, would there be differences?

We are the same brand. Slightly different when you get right down to the specifics of the solutions and markets. Obviously every division in Dow has its own specific products but I think we pivot off of a lot of the same things. It's a strong technology base and innovation focus. It's the ethic around reliability and consistency, and, of course, a global reach. So I think we have a lot of similarities.

How important is consultative selling to what you do?

It's the way we do business. We did some brand study work here three or four years ago which showed one of the things people recognize about us was expertise—they were buying the knowledge of the people that they were working with. So consultative selling is the way our sales team and our technical sellers do things in the marketplace. We conduct seminars, and we have technical projection programs that allow us to model treatment systems for customers to help them make choices on what options they might have, the tradeoffs, and that sort of thing.

Our customers rely on us to give them good answers and to help them solve problems that aren't always directly related to the product that we sell. In fact, this is a core value proposition and our biggest differentiator against our competition. We have the best people in the business and the most expertise. Our customers rely on that.

With the person who's buying your product and essentially reselling it to someone else, is there a combined branding activity?

If you consider a water treatment system integrator, they can buy pumps, valves, and fittings on the market, so the question becomes one of differentiation: How do they differentiate themselves in a crowded marketplace? One of the ways they can do so is to communicate the fact that the components in the customer's system are components that the industry knows and everybody trusts as the best on the market. So when they put their bid in, and highlight the fact that they are using Dow components, that's a way of saying: "Look, my bid with this technology is really the winning, reliable, and trusted solution."

But some companies are more collaborative—they'll ask us for help. They'll ask us if they can come in and jointly sell or help answer questions for the customer and give them confidence that technology will work. And we do that. But that's the industrial sector. We also sell into the residential market which is very different. That's more about brand owners putting good appliances into your house. So in that case, you're talking about a consumer story. Building the confidence that these products are good and healthy for you, and they're going to deliver what they say they're going to deliver.

Do you feel like you have a luxury that other brands don't have in operating within a well-known and highly respected parent company? Maybe as though Dow Chemical takes care of the "story" or the "saying" component, allowing you to focus more on the "doing" part?

You're absolutely right. And yet by "doing," as you say, that becomes the basis of the stories of what the company wants to "say." As long as we continue doing well and enabling changes and differences in the market, we are giving our parent company the materials to tell those stories in creative and inspiring ways.

KEY TAKEAWAYS

- *Consultative selling requires a deep understanding of the customer and knowing where they could use your expertise.*

- *Be prepared to offer counsel that goes beyond product specifications.*

- *Share the right expertise at the right time and you'll make a customer for life.*

Further reading:
Kit Yarrow, *Decoding the New Consumer Mind: How and Why We Shop and Buy*

Setting the Table
for Company Culture

"Make everything the customer touches a reason to love Black Duck."

Phil Granof
Black Duck Software

Perhaps you're familiar with Peter Drucker's observation that "culture eats strategy," which highlights how the best-laid marketing plans can be undone if they don't jibe with the corporate culture. For a prime example of it playing out (in a positive way), look no further than Black Duck Software and its former CMO Phil Granof, now the CMO at NewStore.

Phil's work at Black Duck proves that from the product to the placement to the people, every fiber of your company has to be consistent with your marketing campaigns. If it is—as it is at Black Duck—great things seem to just keep happening. And if not? Your entire marketing effort is a house of cards with a hurricane approaching.

When Phil took over at Black Duck, he quickly began to execute on a culture strategy that was a perfect fit for the company. Then, five months in, a massive shake-up resulted in a new CEO and a new direction. Lesser CMOs might have thrown in the towel, but Phil wasted no time changing course and reorienting Black Duck's marketing and culture to be better than ever before.

When you arrived at Black Duck, what did you see as the biggest culture-related challenge facing you and how did you meet it?

The reason I joined Black Duck Software was that I saw huge potential for the brand. To elevate the meaning of Black Duck, I had to begin internally. Culture eats strategy, and as with many successful software companies, Black Duck has a thriving engineering-driven culture. The challenge was to elevate the meaning of Black Duck by injecting a new perspective into that paradigm rather than overturning it. My message was simple: Products, patents, and people come and go, but the brand can outlast them all. I worked closely with the VP of HR to underscore the connection between corporate values and brand.

Then I went to product management and engineering and aimed to help them understand how future value could be created within engineering through a shared vision of the company. I slowly introduced the word "brand" as the idea took root that we needed a shared heuristic for product development. And I ended every single presentation with the same three slides. The first was a slide that read, "Think Like Apple." The second read, "Act Like Disney." The final slide was a mantra: "Make Everything the Customer Touches a Reason to Love Black Duck."

Five months into your tenure at Black Duck, the company brought in a new CEO, Lou Shipley. How did this affect your approach to the company's culture?

More than anything, the brand embodies a CEO's vision for what he believes is the future of the organization. When Lou arrived, we had just begun to rally around a new big idea created by marketing and were days away from launch. Lou quickly evaluated the previous CEO's vision, which had more to do with the social aspects of coding with open source software (OSS), and saw a different future. Lou's vision was to see Black Duck as an integral part of how every modern enterprise develops software. Marketing not only had to start over from scratch, but also there was the not-so-surprising senior management turnover that often comes with the arrival of new leadership. My only advantage was that the organization had already taken the first steps toward integrating a brand-driven mindset, and so we were much further along culturally than when I first arrived.

Handling organizational change can be tricky particularly if it involves reorganizing or replacing long-time staffers. What advice do you have for fellow CMOs when it comes to handling reorganization?

First, determine whether or not the long-time staffer is a "tipping point" in the organization, that is, a person with a great deal of influence on the culture. Not every long-time staffer is a tipping point, but many are. If the one you're considering reorganizing or replacing is, all I can say is to be extremely careful. Don't just treat it as an item on your to-do list—treat it as a major decision that will have far-reaching effects (at least some of which you probably won't anticipate) on the culture and, by extension, on the whole business.

Second, on a more positive note view reorganization as a treasure hunt. I personally found three hidden gems in the organization that had been overshadowed and overlooked for various reasons, and now they are thriving. Had we blindly seen quiet people as underperforming, it would have been a big loss. Outside of the business world, my favorite example is David "Big Papi" Ortiz on the Red Sox. When he was with the Twins, Ortiz battled inconsistency in field and at the plate. However, in a new context with the Red Sox? Well…the rest is baseball history.

Can you talk a little more about what you did to adapt culture to the sudden shift in the company's direction when the new CEO took over?

Lou asked me to think differently about how to approach the market, more in alignment with his view that Black Duck should be as integral as SAP, Salesforce, or Oracle. While he shared my intention of elevating the brand, he was seeking a way to make Black Duck a necessity, not a choice.

The first step was where I had begun all assignments in my past life as a brand consultant. (All CMOs need to be their own brand consultants, at some level. If you totally outsource this, it is hard to embody a brand vision.) I took a deeper look at the language we were using that was successful in driving subscription revenue. Having some background in the science of metaphor analysis, I uncovered a surprising aspect to the Black Duck brand. If one stripped away the Black Duck name from all of our spoken and written communications, what remained was a company story that sounded more like UPS and Amazon than HP and IBM. We were using the language of logistics: selection, scanning, approving, cataloging, automating, securing, and delivering. We even produce a bill of materials.

It seemed there might be an entirely new way to reposition not just Black Duck, but also the whole industry. As trial balloon for the concept, I wrote an article that appeared in Wired called "Think Like Linux, Act Like UPS, and Smile Like Amazon." In the article, I offered up a concept: For companies to successfully incorporate open source software (OSS) into their applications, what they really needed was an OSS Logistics solution and not another application development solution. With this novel combination of recognizable terms, we instantly elevated ourselves from a mere software scanning solution to a business process solution that allows companies to build software faster, better, and cheaper. To expand on the UPS slogan, "We love logistics, too."

Once the article drew positive attention, we tested the OSS Logistics concept among analysts, customers, employees, supply chain experts, and even Jim Zemlin, who runs the Linux Foundation. He saw OSS Logistics as a way to manage a company's "external R&D," a concept he has been promoting for a while now.

With validation under our belt, internally and externally, the marketing team developed programs around launching OSS Logistics, from an easy to comprehend video that we integrated into our nurturing campaigns to a sweep of every word of content from the past three years. Finally, we undertook training with sales and channel partners, and surprisingly the universal reaction was, "Yes! Finally, we've captured what Black Duck does!"

And what about tangible results?

OSS Logistics launched in the beginning of 2014. By November of that year, marketing had produced a 30 percent increase in qualified leads over 2013, a 44 percent increase in unique Web visitors, an across-the-board increase in social media stats, and more importantly, it completely changed the internal discussion around product improvement and new product development.

One interesting note: We decided explicitly not to trademark the term OSS Logistics. As the market leader, we have the greatest interest in seeing broad comprehension of the value our industry produces. We would like everyone to use it, from analysts to competitors. A longstanding frustration with past leaders at Black Duck has been poor market comprehension of exactly what is meant by open source governance, compliance, and risk mitigation. "OSS Logistics" has swept that away.

The CMO Club recently recognized you with their Leadership award. What are some lessons about leadership as pertains to culture that you'd share with aspiring marketing leaders?

I think successful leadership requires a simple and easily overlooked aspect: Quality people must want to work for you. Talent is free to move where it will, and technology fuels this mobility. So as a leader, my goal has always been to win the hearts and minds of the most talented team I could find. That means trading value for value. Leaders must provide as much value back to their people as they provide the organization, or the best talent will sense an imbalance and move on. In the final analysis, talent is the final arbiter of culture.

KEY TAKEAWAYS

- *Ignore your company culture at your professional peril.*

- *If you get a new boss, determine his or her priorities ASAP! Give to get.*

- *If you don't invest in your employees, they won't stay invested with you.*

Further reading:
Jim Collins, *Good to Great: Why Some Companies Make the Leap...and Others Don't*

Empowerment

The Foundation of a Beautiful Brand

"Mary Kay is about empowering women, helping them discover their inner beauty, their confidence, their passion, and their special gifts through the opportunity of becoming an Independent Beauty Consultant."

Sheryl Adkins-Green
Mary Kay

Most CMOs pride themselves on their ability to rally the troops when a massive, coordinated company effort is required to create a desired result. But I only know one CMO for whom rallying the troops means marshaling an independent army of 3.5 million Independent Beauty Consultants around the world, and that's Mary Kay Inc. CMO Sheryl Adkins-Green.

For Sheryl, being an effective CMO is less about the conventional marketing approach of driving demand from end users, and more about empowering every one of Mary Kay's Independent Beauty Consultants to be confident, self-motivated entrepreneurs and inspired champions for Mary Kay products. By working to gain genuine insights into the Independent Beauty Consultants' dreams and aspirations, Sheryl taps into their potential to improve their own lives while improving the lives of their customers.

Mary Kay as a company does not recruit or hire the Independent Beauty Consultants. How do you ensure the Beauty Consultants believe in and represent Mary Kay's culture and values?

Our values are "viral" in a sense. Many if not most Independent Beauty Consultants were Mary Kay® customers first. And in their interactions with the Beauty Consultants who sold them Mary Kay products, they learned about the company history, values, and what the company is doing in the community. Our core values go far beyond just cosmetics. Mary Kay is about empowering women, helping them discover their inner beauty, their confidence, their passion, and their special gifts through the opportunity of becoming an Independent Beauty Consultant. The customers with whom this message resonates are often the ones who decide to start their own Mary Kay business and see it through.

Mary Kay's Independent Beauty Consultants are the "face" of the brand worldwide. How do you ensure they represent the brand well?

It all ties back to the strong values that Mary Kay Ash herself built into the company and into the culture. Those values are based in the Golden Rule… treating people the way you want to be treated. Mary Kay Independent Beauty Consultants provide "Golden Rule Service," the kind of service that we would want for ourselves. When you ask how we manage the customer experience that individuals might have, I really credit the value system and the Independent Beauty Consultants' commitment to those values. Inspiring that commitment in each of them is my and my team's responsibility, and so I strive to make my interactions with the Beauty Consultants reflect how I hope they'll interact with their customers.

Do you spend time with both the Independent Beauty Consultants and their customers?

Actually, the Mary Kay independent sales force is our only customer. Each independent Mary Kay business has its customer base, the end users. I connect with the independent sales force in larger forums such as our annual Leadership and Seminar company-sponsored events. When I travel to international markets, I also attend company-sponsored events for the independent sales force and solicit suggestions from the independent sales force. We include the independent sales force in any research that we're doing on major new products and new promotion concepts. The goal is for them to always feel beautiful, confident, and connected.

I'm always "listening" to the independent sales force via our social media channels. In addition, we have an intranet where we're receiving input from the independent sales force. Certainly, on the public social channels such as Twitter, Instagram, and Pinterest, we're in touch with what they're interested in and what they're talking about. It's valuable insight.

Can you talk about a specific marketing program you've spearheaded where you were especially proud of the results?

Yes, we developed a campaign to commemorate the company's 50th anniversary, and our mantra for the anniversary year was "One Woman Can." It not only paid homage to the accomplishments of Mary Kay Ash, but it also represented our empowerment message. One woman can do amazing things, and one woman can do anything that she sets her desires on. The marketing program, specifically, was centered on a global makeover contest. It kicked off on March 8th, which was International Women's Day. Our goal was to complete the highest number of makeovers ever, and we completed 44,000 makeovers within a 24-hour period.

By engaging the independent sales force all around the world, it kicked off a global contest where women not only participated in makeovers and agreed to have their picture posted in a gallery, but more importantly they had an opportunity to tell a story about a cause that they cared about. The winners of the contest also had an opportunity to win a grant for the charity or not-for-profit of their choice. The specifics varied a little bit, but in the United States the company awarded fifty $5,000 grants on behalf of the fifty women who received the most votes in the makeover contest.

Mary Kay Ash started her company with her life savings of $5,000. This anniversary marketing initiative, therefore, celebrated what Mary Kay is about—inner beauty showing through as outer beauty. It was an opportunity to engage the independent sales force not only with their current customers but also to connect with potential new customers. A lot of women shared that they typically wouldn't be interested in a makeover, but because there was an opportunity to support a cause that they care about and possibly earn a grant, they would be willing to "lend" their faces.

KEY TAKEAWAYS

- *Empowering employees (or independent sales consultants) begins with a comprehensive listening strategy.*

- *Having clear performance values like "Golden Rule Service" is essential to empowerment.*

- *At the heart of empowerment is a company with a heart (i.e., values that speak to the purpose and mission of the organization).*

Further reading:

Chris Malone and Susan T. Fiske, *The Human Brand: How We Relate to People, Products, and Companies*

III. Transitional Trends

Now we find ourselves moving into the low-rise center of the CMO's Periodic Table. In chemistry we'd be embarking upon the Transition Elements (also known as "Transition Metals").

In our marketing journey, we're also in a place of transition. Then again, aren't we always? Transition is a constant in this industry. While the fundamental goals of service, brand-building, and increasing sales are eternal, the techniques and tools we use to get there are in constant flux. Like it or not, trends are as much a driving force behind marketing as they are behind, say, pop music. (Though it's a coincidence that the CMO in charge of marketing The Grammys landed in this section.)

The term "trends" gets a bad rap. Somehow it's become associated with flash-in-the-pan gimmicks and jargon that are light on substance. Granted, too many such fly-by-night fads do exist, like mosquitoes whining around our heads, thirsty to suck away our precious time and attention.

But then there are the good trends. The ones that catch on because they suddenly obliterate marketing inefficiencies and churn out ROI at an unprecedented rate. The ones that transition into their destiny as the new normal. These are the scouts that lead the armies of change.

Now, I'm not guaranteeing this is the case with every topic the eight superstar marketing leaders and I cover in this section. If I could predict the future with that kind of accuracy I'd get a whole lot more respect

Ma
Marketing Automation

Bb
B2B Content Marketing

Bc
B2C Content Marketing

Ug
User-Generated Content

In
Influencer Marketing

Gm
Grassroots Marketing

St
Storytelling

Sm
Social Media Success

in my NCAA March Madness pool every year. The aim here is to capture a snapshot of the most exciting trends dominating today's marketing conversations. Will they still be front-and-center in the mix next year? In five? Quite possibly. And even if not, the changes they're effecting today certainly will.

Spotting and tracking trends can be fun, albeit exhausting. But as marketers, I think we should be less concerned with identifying them and more concerned with leveraging them—whether that means consciously rejecting them (and perhaps incorporating that rejection into some branding effort) or wisely utilizing them, never losing sight of the real value we intend to get from doing so.

Not all of these Transitional Trends are brand new. Storytelling? I have it on good authority that our hunter-gatherer ancestors were doing that around Pleistocene-era campfires long before anyone was stressing over their content marketing strategy. But we sure are hearing more about it nowadays. And if you're an acknowledged master of storytelling (like Belkin's Kieran Hannon) you're in high demand as a marketer.

Then we've got more modern innovations like marketing automation, influencer marketing, and of course, social media. Are they all here to stay, or are some just keeping a seat warm for the next trends? That's not for me to say here and now. But what visionaries like The Weather Channel's Scot Safon and Viking River Cruises' Richard Marnell have to share about their success with these trends will make smarter marketers of us all, whether or not the trends themselves are destined for immortality. In the end, that's up to us.

High-IQ Automation

"And because Sales has better quality leads, they close at a higher rate, allowing for higher quotas and fewer sales reps."

Jon Miller
Marketo

Jon Miller, who co-founded Marketo and served as its VP of Marketing, is what you might call a "numbers guy." Whether snagging a Harvard physics degree magna cum laude or growing Marketo into a software-as-a-service colossus and an industry leader in marketing automation, he's always brought a razor-sharp analytic mind and a data-driven laser focus to the task at hand. A little vision (by which I mean a lot of vision) hasn't hurt either in securing over 1,000 clients who pay Marketo around $30,000 per year to supercharge their marketing.

Companies considering engaging Marketo and its eponymous software rightfully have a lot of questions about whether they'll secure a return on that big investment. And while there are case studies galore suggesting they will, none is more compelling than the fact Marketo conducts its marketing with…any guesses?

That's right, Marketo. While the popular expression describing a company powered by its own product is to "eat your own dog food," I think it's more accurate to say the team over at this classy, top-of-the-line marketing system are drinking their own champagne.

Jon recently left Marketo to found Engagio, where it's a safe bet he'll further cement his legacy as a breakthrough marketer. In this interview you'll get a look into one of the industry's brightest minds.

Marketing Automation is essentially a new model. Can you talk a bit about what it is replacing?

In the old model, almost half of the salesperson's time is spent on unproductive activities. This includes educating prospects on the category and the product. But today buyers want to manage the buying process on their own schedule and terms, not the sales rep's. Assuming you are providing information that is relevant and resonant, then you too can optimize the demand chain by only giving Sales leads that are already engaged with your brand.

Why was there such a fundamental need for Marketing Automation?

For most companies, a lead is a lead, entered into a CRM system like Salesforce and treated with equal urgency. The result is that few leads ever close and only half of the salespeople make their sales goals. Marketing automation separates leads into two buckets, the 20 percent who are ready to engage, and those that require nurturing. If somebody downloaded our webinars or thought leadership [documents], we know they're at the early stage. However, if you go to our website and see the detailed pricing pages or register to watch a detailed demo, you're more likely to enter a buying cycle with us. And if you show buying signs, we're going to be dialing your phone in 3 to 4 minutes!

So suddenly marketing is more effective. How did this impact your business structure?

At most companies, marketing generates about 30 percent of the leads, which means the sales force needs to be heavily incentivized to not just close but also to find the leads themselves. At Marketo the marketing team generates 80 percent of the sales pipeline allowing the company to radically reduce the salesperson's risk and change how the marketing department gets compensated. And because Sales has better quality leads, they close at a higher rate, allowing for higher quotas and fewer sales reps.

You spent a fair amount of time explaining the problem—is this an important part of your sales process?

Companies typically get a mix of potential customers that are aware of the problem and are looking for the right solution, and those that know there is something wrong but haven't defined it just yet. For the prospects that have yet to define the problem, content becomes an integral part of the sales process, because you need to know what is broken before you can go about fixing it. Again, this is where vision, thought leadership, and content marketing play a key role in engaging with the customer, as they come to see the company as trusted advisors.

How have you integrated social media monitoring into the overall process?

Social media is a vital component of a marketing offering. As the number of channels continues to proliferate, businesses need technology that allows them to listen to a prospect's online body language, no matter where they are, online or offline. You can use marketing automation to listen, score, and segment prospects based on what they say.

Talk to me about content marketing and how it works at Marketo.

Marketo invests heavily in marketing, spending as much as three times the ratio of most companies—but because of the conversion rate, the overall model is more efficient and profitable than these other companies. A huge portion of that investment goes into content development including things like webinars, white papers, blogs, and social media. In addition to creating a lot of inbound leads and SEO, [this content] also helps to build trust and credibility with buyers who are starting to perceive us as innovators and thought leaders.

I know you've started a new company since we spoke originally. Can you tell me a bit about it and how you are applying any of the lessons you learned while at Marketo?

I've learned that as powerful as marketing automation can be, it isn't always a sufficient solution—especially for companies with complex, six- and seven-figure deals. For those companies, a new concept has emerged: account-based marketing (ABM).

ABM focuses on the whole account, not just individual leads; it reaches out to target companies, instead of just waiting for them to respond to a campaign; it supports land and expand models, not just new business; and it measures engagement and penetration with an account, not just leads and conversion rates.

KEY TAKEAWAYS

- *Marketing Automation can dramatically improve lead quality and closing rates.*

- *To be effective, Marketing Automation requires a sizeable and ongoing investment in content (such as blog posts, videos, research studies, brochures, etc.).*

- *Social media activities can be integrated into your Marketing Automation campaigns and enhance the outcomes.*

Further reading:
Brian Halligan and Dharmesh Shah, *Inbound Marketing, Revised and Updated: Attract, Engage, and Delight Customers Online*

B2B Content
Marketing

Beyond B2B Blogging

"Our goal with content two years ago was to build our reputation as a small business advocate and influencer."

Judy Hackett
Dun & Bradstreet

Content Marketing has arrived. Gone are the days of shoving ads down the consumer's throat until they submissively open their wallets. To win new customers and nurture existing ones, businesses need to do something useful for the consumer first, before expecting any transaction—whether it's the first one or the fiftieth one—to take place. Content marketing, that is, offering valuable information via live events, webinars, seminars, audio, video, or text, is an ultra-effective way to perform this quintessential example of Marketing as Service (which has been the cornerstone of Renegade's philosophy for seven-plus years).

I was delighted to catch up with Judy Hackett, now the CMO of Dun & Bradstreet Emerging Businesses, a recently acquired division of D&B that provides credit and credibility solutions to small businesses. Judy and her team are noteworthy for their ability to build an integrated, multichannel content program that extends from events to research studies, and from blogs to personalized videos. As you will see, Judy is particularly proud of the videos, which deliver "one-to-one" content based on multiple variables. This individualized approach should (in my humble opinion) become the standard in the near future for B2B companies.

Author's note: If you're in a B2C business, you'll still want to read this. And you'll definitely want to read the interview that follows this one with Richard Marnell.

Is content marketing a new thing for Dun & Bradstreet Credibility Corp?

As a conscious marketing strategy to drive sales, yes. As an ongoing marketing tactic, no. We've been producing content from the start and have a resource center filled with loads of evergreen content geared towards small businesses. Early on it was all about authoritative content to drive SEO, but it evolved. We developed our blog. We launched a monthly one-hour livestream event called Credibility Live. Our goal with content two years ago was to build our reputation as a small business advocate and influencer. The difference today is we are now carefully crafting a more integrated and meaningful content strategy to drive customer acquisition and upsell.

Do you approach content creation differently than ad creation?

Yes and no. For larger content projects, we draft a creative brief with the usual considerations: Target, language/voice, call to action, marketing objectives, etc. Where it differs is in its ability to engage a prospect for longer and to tell a larger story. Infographics, videos, and links within an article can take a prospect deeper than an ad that is limited by time and/or space.

Is your company increasing its investment in content? If so, why?

Absolutely. The need for quality content is increasing rapidly and keeping up with that requires investment in the people who create it, as well as the technology to publish and syndicate it. We are investing in more dynamic content to speak to prospects and customers on a one-to-one basis for the purpose of upselling and cross-selling. As an example, we're creating some pretty innovative one-to-one video content with multiple variables that will be delivered starting in September. It's highly customized to their businesses and what's happening in their credit reports.

It's interesting to me that you've taken your content program offline to events. What are the benefits of this approach?

The most obvious benefit is the content creation and marketing of that content that takes place before, during, and after the events. Panels of experts on traditional, alternative, crowdfunding, and start-up capital share their words of wisdom as do the business owners sharing their funding stories. All of these participants from businesses to banks and panelists to moderators become content generators for us. Attendees share their experience via social, and I could go on and on. It's probably the single best way to create content!

Are you finding some content types more effective than others?

Video content is the clear leader in effectiveness so far. Also, our active corporate blog has been able to engage hundreds of thousands of people on a range of topics including educational material for small business owners, relevant opportunities for small business owners, and informative posts that help tell our story.

With content, is it as simple as "If you build it, they will come?"

Definitely not. It takes a village. You need collaboration between social, marcom, online, sales, etc. Also, we do extensive outreach to our employees—we send out an email to all our corporate employees each week that includes relevant events, interesting articles, new employees, and, most importantly, one "ask" at the top of the email. Through this "ask," we've been able to increase our employee engagement and generate substantial social interactions around targeted campaigns.

Since we last talked, has content marketing continued to play a profound role in your marketing activities? If so, can you share a recent example of what you did and how it worked?

This past year we launched a new content initiative designed to help small and medium sized suppliers learn from the companies with which they hope to establish a supplier relationship. We developed a supplier content site intended to give businesses interested in supplying to large companies the edge they need when trying to secure a supplier relationship with a larger company. We hosted educational online events with the leaders and decision makers at these companies and tied into these events the role that strong business credit plays in securing these relationships. The content is meaningful in helping businesses make the business credit building decision, as it plays a significant role in their success. Without certain scores they are eliminated from consideration. The next step is a live event at which we can create speed dating-type meetings with suppliers and the companies they want to supply.

Is it getting harder to cut through with content given that so many brands have decided to become publishers? If so, what advice do you have for your fellow CMOs when it comes to developing new content programs today?

Yes. Articles, webinars, newsletters, education centers…there's a proliferation of content. We are just as guilty as others in likely creating too much of a good thing. We recently inherited the Hoovers brand as part of the sale of our company back to Dun & Bradstreet. Talk about a content-rich property. Hoovers produces an amazing amount of quality content and they were doing a nice job of distributing the content but it wasn't necessarily impacting subscriber counts. In a B2B environment, success should ultimately be defined by subscribers or customer acquisition. This doesn't necessarily mean paid subscribers as long as you are addressing the complete marketing funnel. One of the best pieces of advice I can give to marketers is to work closely with the product and digital teams to think about developing a unique "free-mium" acquisition strategy. What content can you create that will add subscribers and provide ongoing opportunities to engage them? Is there a data component that can be updated monthly, or alerts that can notify them of a change? This creates the funnel needed to engage meaning-fully. This is what we did for business credit in creating CreditSignal. We now have nearly a million free subscribers. This is what we hope to do to unleash the true power of Hoovers. Check in with me in a year to see how we're doing.

We didn't talk much about how your content program integrated with your marketing automation activities. If you are using a Marketo or Eloqua type service, can you talk a bit about how your content fits into this?

Marketing automation tools have become quite sophisticated over the past few years and have made it much easier for us to manage the sub-scriber/customer relationship. D&B has been utilizing Eloqua. Our customers can sign up for free products that both educate and guide them deeper into the sales cycle. We've also built cradle-to-grave mar-keting automation tools that allow us to send targeted messages to these businesses. The system captures every source of a prospect/subscriber/paying customer and every single touchpoint through sale. Because the value of D&B products can cover so many different areas from securing lending opportunities to getting better contracting terms to getting into supplier programs to sales and marketing solutions, we're in the process of expanding these efforts to encourage prospects to self-identify early in the process so that we can do an even better job educating them about how to leverage our product set.

KEY TAKEAWAYS

- *B2B Content Marketing has evolved from a nice-to-have offering to a must-have essential.*

- *To get maximum impact from your content, develop multichannel campaigns versus isolated pieces.*

- *Content programs can work without marketing automation software but are easier to manage and measure with these tools.*

Further reading:

Mark W. Schaefer, *The Content Code: Six Essential Strategies to Ignite your Content, your Marketing, and your Business*

How Content Marketing Keeps Consumer Brands Cruising

"Good content turns awareness into consideration, and consideration into intent."

Richard Marnell
Viking River Cruises

At a glance, B2B and B2C content marketing look similar enough, but from the CMO's perspective the inner workings of each are substantially different. The path to a buying decision for a consumer is not the same as it is for a business, and a winning content strategy needs to take this into account.

For a clinic on how to nail B2C content marketing, look no further than Viking River Cruises CMO Richard Marnell. With over 6 million minutes of video watched and a robust user-generated content base, Richard's efforts at Viking are skyrocketing customer engagement and propelling forward the discussion of how to effectively market content to consumers.

Can you give me a quick overview of your current content marketing strategy?

We started really digging into digital content marketing about three years ago in three very focused areas:

1. Videos about our destinations that focus on history, culture, food, and experiences—things that travelers want to learn about;
2. Recipes that tie into the product because they're for regional foods from the destinations we travel to; and
3. Social media on the platforms that are either relevant to our guests, business partners, media partners, or all of the above.

How is this approach working?

It is increasing brand awareness. Videos such as language lessons, or meeting the cats of St. Petersburg's Hermitage Museum, or a recipe for Vienna's Sacher Torte, are things that our audience wants to share with their friends. And on Facebook, for example, when our audience engages with our content, it is then spread to their other Facebook friends. Plus, travel is something they naturally talk about on social media anyway.

Our product has a somewhat long purchase cycle, so content marketing keeps our guests engaged throughout the customer journey. Most valuably for us, it has filled a hole that was previously there for a segment we refer to as Booked Not Departed—meaning those who reserved their cruise a year in advance and are excited but no longer receiving marketing messages from Viking. Now they receive content marketing that is relevant to the product/itinerary that they've purchased. This content amplifies their anticipation, continues to connect them with the brand, and builds a base of knowledge and enrichment from which to further enhance their actual product experience when they do travel.

Content marketing seems to be a slow build versus a quick win as a company builds up its library and proficiency. Was it a challenge to sell this to your management and, if so, what were the key points that made the sale?

New initiatives can be a hard sell, and investing in video and social media wasn't necessarily intuitive for the entire management team. So we ran a lot of tests and gathered data that showed it was a smart move—for example, visits were much longer on website pages that had video versus ones that didn't, emails that had "recipe" or "video" in the subject lines had much higher open rates, Facebook sweepstakes consistently generated lots of new leads, and more things like that. Presenting that data did a lot to break down internal resistance to investing in content.

From a purchase cycle standpoint, what is content marketing particularly good at?

Good content turns awareness into consideration and consideration into intent. This is especially true of user-generated content because people are more inclined to believe their peers—even the anonymous online reviews of others like them—or a third party expert such as a journalist, than to simply trust advertising alone. Also, the content that we produce ourselves is very useful in the re-engage stage of a long purchase cycle.

Our passengers may not take a trip every year, so maybe they don't always latch onto our promotional marketing, but even if they're not ready to start planning their next trip, there's a high probability that they'd like to test out the recipe we just emailed them, or answer a question we posted to Facebook. It keeps us in their consciousness and adds value to their day. Our content marketing helps create a "brand halo."

Will we still be talking about content marketing a year from now?

Yes. I read once that content marketing began in the 1890s when John Deere published *The Furrow* magazine to inform farmers of the latest trends and technology that they needed to know about. Today, as marketers, we're still using content marketing to grow our businesses, attract the attention of new customers, and maintain relationships with current customers. Digital has only made it more important as a long-term strategy.

A year from now I suspect we'll be discussing how, through content curation, brands are becoming both publishers and broadcasters for the best content relevant to their customer and their brand. I suspect we are heading toward competition between brands and traditional broadcasters and publishers.

If I'm a CMO and I'm late to the content marketing party, what are the big mistakes I should avoid in getting started?

Focus on digital, not print. Accept that there will be a lot of trial and error. And most importantly, resist the urge to have all your content be directly about your products and services. If it's not truly valuable and/or entertaining to your consumer, it's going to work against you in the end. No one likes a one-sided conversation, so don't be the guy on the first date who only talks about himself. Be the guy she wants to tell her friends about. Ignore this and you'll find yourself in a frustrating and never-ending cycle of first dates that go nowhere.

KEY TAKEAWAYS

- *Content marketing can be a potent tool for customer retention and referral generation.*

- *Finding the right balance of quantity versus quality is tricky but important especially for premium brands.*

- *Content marketing is not a new idea but understanding how to become an effective publisher is a new requirement for just about all marketers.*

Further reading:
Joe Pulizzi, *Epic Content Marketing: How to Tell a Different Story, Break Through the Clutter, and Win More Customers by Marketing Less*

Ug
User-Generated
Content

Giving Music Fans a Voice

"It's all about content."

Evan Greene
The Recording Academy

Perhaps The Recording Academy isn't a household name for you, but I'd wager the Grammys is. The Recording Academy is the organization that puts together music's biggest night every year, and the man who's in charge of keeping the world captivated by its spectacle is CMO Evan Greene. I've had the privilege of interviewing Evan several times over several years, which has yielded a great birds-eye view on how marketing the ceremony changes every year, and how Evan—supported by longtime agency partner Chiat/Day—unflinchingly meets his goal of outdoing his own efforts from the previous go-round.

Over the course of our robust interviewer-interviewee relationship, I've been especially struck by how Evan has gotten Grammy fans and even celebrities to excitedly generate shareable content on behalf of the program. Another masterstroke was to stretch the spectacle and buzz about the telecast itself across a longer timeframe—getting us amped up about "Grammy Week" to build anticipation for the big night.

Anyway, enough from the opening act. Ladies and Gentlemen: Evan Greene of the Grammys!

When it comes to user-generated content, what's the biggest mistake marketers need to avoid?

Don't copy others just because they did something successful. Find your own true north—your own authentic voice and perspective.

It is important to recognize that all content is not good content, and not all good content is sharable. The objective is shareability, and people only share if they care and are invested. People love discovery, and discovery leads to shareability, which ultimately helps to build an engaged community. Consumers are more jaded than ever before, and in order to trust, they demand both authenticity and respect.

Can you talk about the evolution of the Grammys from a once-a-year TV show, to Grammy Week, to nearly a year-round presence?

The 4:00 a.m. epiphany was that if we have built this brand by virtue of a single 3 ½-hour television event held once per year, how powerful and impactful a brand could we be if we built a proactive 365-day-a-year strategy.

When trying to scale a brand that in many people's minds exists as a one-day-a-year event, we need to build a longer runway…a deeper relationship with music fans. So the over-arching strategy is to create a connection throughout the year, become a relevant, credible voice in music the other 364 days. Ultimately, while the Grammy telecast is the payoff, and the culmination of an engaged, respectful, daily two-way dialogue we have with an engaged social ecosystem, it is a continuation of how we celebrate music throughout the year.

How important is content in marketing the Grammys? What's an innovative way you've created or leveraged it?

It's all about content. Granted, we're a not-for-profit trade organization, so we don't have the budgets that you probably think we do. But we've made a sizable investment in our content infrastructure because we want and need to be creating a lot of content. For example, we want to be creating engaging, short, episodic video pieces that are easily digestible and easily shareable.

In a lot of ways we're fortunate because music overlaps and enhances so many different areas. A good example is the intersection between music and sports. So six years ago, at the Beijing Olympics, the biggest story was what's on Michael Phelps' iPod as he's mentally pumping himself up to win all those gold medals.

So we thought since there's always been that overlap between music and sports, we created a content program called "Champion's Playlist" where we talk to professional athletes and say, "What's on your iPod? What do you listen to while you train, to get motivated before the big game?" This became a really fun, shareable thing for music fans, who got to see how the playlists of some of the world's biggest athletes overlaid with their own musical taste.

Could you talk a little bit about your planning process on social media or elsewhere?

We've hit on what we think is an important insight over the last couple of years that guides our planning. People are generally looking for two things: discovery and community. So if we can enable the idea of discovery and empower the concept of shareability, then we are, by default, going to be leading to a greater, more robust community.

Our campaigns need to engage people. If they don't, then social media is not going to help and we usually abandon it. We're always looking to create a very respectful two-way dialogue with our viewers and really all music fans. We're not presenting ourselves as the authority or the expert who's going to tell you what music to listen to. We just want to be where the music is happening and be a credible voice in that conversation.

*What can marketers in more "traditional" companies marketing
products and services learn from what you're doing with the Grammys?*

It goes back to the idea of realizing there's an ongoing conversation which
you need to get your voice into in a credible, trustworthy, and respectful
way. You need to be where your customers are and not just expect them
to come to your website one day. You need to seek to create evangelists.
So if your business is photography sales, you go to a photography forum
where people are talking about a new camera. From a social media standpoint, don't try to sell people with a link to your website and a price.
Rather than talk about this new camera, utilize the buzz that is already
happening organically, and retweet or repost other credible voices in your
community. Trust and credibility are powerful tools toward acquisition.

KEY TAKEAWAYS

- *One key measure for user-generated content programs is the degree to
  which content is shared by others ("sharing is caring").*

- *Brands can encourage fans to share content by helping them "discover"
  things they really like or care about.*

- *Look for opportunities to engage influential communities (like celebrities) to increase the reach and impact of your UGC programs.*

Further reading:
David Meerman Scott, *The New Rules of Marketing and PR: How to
Use News Releases, Blogs, Podcasting, Viral Marketing, and Online
Media to Reach Buyers Directly (Your Coach in a Box)*

The Power of Positive Influencing

"It's not a one-shot event—it's a strategy that will evolve over time."

Tami Cannizzaro
IBM

One evening, a CMO whose name I'll omit asked me: "So, do you think all this influencer marketing stuff is overhyped?" I felt like I imagine Derek Jeter did in his Yankees days when he expected a curveball low and outside and then the pitcher threw...a curveball low and outside.

I didn't take a caveman uppercut swing and scream "NO WAY!" Instead, I channeled Jeter and "went with the pitch," letting the conversation ebb and flow until it landed in just the right spot to convince my interrogator that influencer marketing is very much for real.

That spot is the influencer marketing program conceived by Tami Cannizzaro for IBM when she was a VP of Marketing (she's now a Senior Director for eBay). Tami's program worked so well for a lot of reasons, foremost—in my opinion—because it involved key IBM people (including Tami) investing time to build individual relationships with influencers and actively participate in the conversations.

Just in case you are unfamiliar with this marketing approach, the basic concept is that brands focus on building relationships with specific individuals whose opinions hold sway with broader groups. These programs can take many shapes. And for full disclosure, I am not just a fan of IBM's approach, I'm also among the folks they designate as an influencer.

Tell me about the origins of the influencer program and what your expectations were in year one.

I recall speaking at a CMO Club Summit event in New York about two years ago, and Ted Rubin and Margaret Molloy were sitting in the audience. They both actively tweeted my session and it received lots of great pickup by influential people in the marketing community. It hit me that we could scale this phenomenon and invite prolific social influencers to our events to extend the reach of the content beyond the four walls of the conference. In year one, my objective was simply to drive a robust social conversation that would amplify all of the great content coming out of the conference.

If you had one piece of advice for a brand starting an influencer program, what would it be?

If you're going to start an influencer program, take the time to think through the process of choosing the right brand sponsor within your organization. The program needs to be nurtured by someone who will invest the necessary time and personal investment. It's not a one-shot event—it's a strategy that will evolve over time. Ted Rubin has coined the phrase "Return on Relationship." I agree with his thinking here. Social business is not about making a business transaction. It's about building a network of business relationships that will yield results over time. You'll get as much out of the program as you put into it.

What are the factors that guided you in putting together a list of influencers for the IBM Smarter Commerce Summits?

My social media team monitors social channels and measures those influencers with the most "signal" in our industry. Tools like oneQube can help you navigate, measure, and manage social relationships. We wanted to field a group of influencers who were prolific at generating content and who also had a very engaged following.

Are there any pitfalls to avoid when putting together a program like this?

The hard part is that you have to depend on good faith that the investment will yield. If you have a CEO focused on ROI, it may not be immediately evident how it's returning back to the business. I liken it to a relationship with the analyst community. Nurtured over time, these relationships help you to build traction in the market and drive momentum for your brand. The pitfall is that it takes faith—and a lot of times, that isn't enough to garner support for the program in the first place!

Could a marketer try to run an influencer program like yours without being personally involved?

Outsourcing the program completely to a staff person or an agency is missing the point of an influencer program, which is to make these people part of your overall brand strategy, to treat them like VIPs and give them insider access to your strategy and brand. Sharing your passion for your business with them and asking for their help to accomplish this is perhaps the secret ingredient of a successful influencer program.

Can you describe the costs—monetary or otherwise—involved in assembling a program like this? What kind of metrics/KPIs do you use to rationalize this investment?

The time investment is significant, but it's one of the best parts of my job. Becoming a member of the influencer community has enriched my knowledge of the industry and paid me back in a number of ways. There are also measurable success factors. We actively measure the increase in engagement for our properties. For example, years ago, we were seeing limited pickup and reach from our social efforts. Today we have surpassed over 2 billion impressions, and we've seen a significant increase in engagement on our owned properties.

Looking back at your work at IBM on the influencer program, what outcome was the biggest surprise to you?

The biggest surprise for me was the scale and reach of the influencers we engaged. I was a bit skeptical that we could move the needle but in reality the influencers blew away traditional PR. The biggest surprise was that a powerful group of individuals could truly move the needle for a major brand. The technique of finding influencers and using them to drive hype is not a new idea. The movie industry was the first to use "nodes" to launch a good buzz around a new movie. It's a powerful way to drive word of mouth across a set of consumers.

KEY TAKEAWAYS

- *Be prepared for the time commitment required to build personal relationships with the influencers.*

- *Not all influencers require monetary compensation though all expect some benefit like special access to people/information or added exposure.*

- *These programs can be an incredibly cost-effective means of generating PR coverage BUT don't expect to mandate the details with your influencers.*

Further reading:
Danny Brown and Sam Fiorella, *Influence Marketing: How to Create, Manage, and Measure Brand Influencers in Social Media Marketing*

Gm
Grassroots
Marketing

The Power of Positive Influencing

"Show them you're listening."

Kyle Schlegel
Louisville Slugger

Great brands become prominent, but only a select few reach the point where they define their product—think of Heinz 57, Harley-Davidson… and Louisville Slugger. The mere words evoke generations of baseball excellence. They evoke pine tar-smeared lengths of elegant wood in the powerful hands of batters like Babe Ruth, Ted Williams, and Derek Jeter, spraying singles and launching homers in all directions with that unmistakable *crack* sound.

So the precarious task of relaunching Louisville Slugger into the modern baseball world called for one of marketing's clutch hitters. Rather than opt for a grizzled veteran, parent company Hillerich & Bradsby went with an exciting young talent: Kyle Schlegel, who was fresh off a successful re-staging of several long-standing brands with new competitors (Old Spice, Wella, Herbal Essences, and Aussie) while at Procter & Gamble.

Though he was no longer working with a king-sized P&G marketing budget, Kyle stepped to the plate in his new role as VP of Global

Marketing armed with novel strategies, a commitment to grassroots marketing, and a willingness to take bold risks.

Most recently, Kyle became Global Marketing Director, Racquet Sports, at Wilson Sporting Goods. A rookie no longer, Kyle generously shares his evolved perspective on grassroots marketing and more in the latter part of this interview.

How did you have to change your marketing approach when you arrived at Hillerich & Bradsby from P & G?

The significantly smaller budgets led to a reduction of touchpoints (for example, TV wasn't possible) but the introduction of a robust grassroots focus comes with new challenges and decisions. So far as grassroots are concerned, we are a part of nearly 400 individual events but we limit this complexity by working with partners in the space that work closely with our team to pre-plan, execute, and track.

You faced a similar challenge with Louisville Slugger that you faced with Old Spice: Younger, "hipper" brands looking to grab some of your market share. How did you overcome this with Old Spice, and how do you plan to do the same with Louisville Slugger?

With Old Spice, we realized there were a few critical dynamics to the future success of the brand. It had to be rooted in the past in some way. It had to be forward-looking, which is to say we had to focus on entry point consumers who would be the lifeblood of the brand for decades to come (rather than the "lost" generation of consumers from the prior generation). And we had to identify programs that would reach those consumers. One of the successful ones was distributing samples to middle school boys.

These same principles are at work with Louisville Slugger. We did deep analysis of the brand's history and chose which elements to leave untouched and which to evolve. We created a 3- to 5-year plan for growing the brand's relevance, consumer by consumer. And we had to make the tough choice not to try to regain "the lost generation" but rather gain the next generation of players.

You operate in a relationship-based business. How do you improve loyalty among your customers?

Quite simply, show them you're listening. We are working more and more with young athletes and reaching them in more channels. Each time, this gives us an opportunity to cede some control for where the brand is going and give them a say. When we show them we've heard them by baking their ideas into our brand, loyalty comes with it. This will be a bigger focus for us going forward.

Author's note: The remaining questions and answers are from a follow-up conversation I had with Kyle right before this edition went to press.

Looking back on your time at Hillerich & Bradsby, what are some of the biggest lessons you learned about grassroots marketing?

The biggest lesson was that, to change the course of a brand, we had to start with the consumer. The one place we know they have their mind focused on the sport is at the ball field. It's the one place where the "noise" of their world is quieter and baseball/softball are the things that matter most. In that environment, we could expose them to products and innovations in a way that is more effective than any other marketing touchpoint. In sports, especially with equipment, players need to be able to touch and feel the product and even demo it if possible. We also needed to show them that we were just like them, passionate about the sport, able to walk it and talk it.

Big brands often forget about grassroots marketing. Is this a mistake?

I think the thing that brands that don't have grassroots in their mix miss is a personal connection with the consumer. We need to create programs that intersect our consumers' lives in all aspects but, in my opinion, nothing is more powerful than a face-to-face conversation. If done correctly, the brand can literally come to life for the consumer in those moments. There are so many factors that dictate success though.

You must be on tone; the staffing must be direct representations of the brand while being someone completely relatable to the consumer. You must be approachable and not try too hard. You don't have to have the biggest and most expensive presence in grassroots…you just have to have the one that the consumer would like to engage with.

KEY TAKEAWAYS

- *Grassroots marketing is particularly effective when a community of consumers are involved (like Little Leaguers).*

- *Like so many other "elements," this one should start with listening to your customers.*

- *Grassroots marketing is a hands on affair—you can't just talk the talk.*

Further reading:
Chip Heath and Dan Heath, *Made to Stick: Why Some Ideas Survive and Others Die*

Once Upon a Modem...

"That is the power of a brand—how its story resonates and gets shared amongst its customers."

Kieran Hannon
Belkin International

I didn't think anyone could get me excited about a story featuring the "Linksys WRT1900AC" until I met Belkin CMO Kieran Hannon. Then he deployed the storytelling acumen that's led to his success at Belkin, and I was instantly spellbound. Even for the most tech-heavy companies, storytelling has become the gold standard for engaging audiences and enhancing the customer experience.

Granted, it's not a new thing. As mentioned in the introduction to this section, people have been telling stories since time immemorial. But it's also been a cornerstone of effective marketing and advertising for some time, with perhaps the most notable early example being Procter & Gamble producing radio soap operas as early as the 1930s. The audience was so drawn in by the intrigue and scandal of the stories, they hardly realized they were being sold P&G products at the same time.

Today, storytelling is back in the spotlight as brands face more pressure than ever to be interesting if they are to stand a chance of cutting through the information overload that defines the Internet Age. Additionally, the rise of social and real-time interaction between consumers and brands gives CMOs an unprecedented chance to foster a strong ongoing dialogue where the brand voice is at once "interested and interesting."

At Belkin, Kieran has this all figured out. Learning about storytelling from him is an opportunity any smart marketer should be glad to have.

What is your "big picture" approach to storytelling at Belkin?

Finally, storytelling is back. Hallelujah! That is the power of a brand—how its story resonates and is shared amongst its customers. There's such a joy in illuminating how technology can help make people's lives better and more engaging.

When it comes to the art of storytelling, what are the most important things a CMO must pay attention to?

Authenticity and empathy, especially when it's necessary to acknowledge a product shortcoming. The proliferation of channels for consumers to learn about brands and products requires a high degree of agility. The best way to evaluate success is when consumers become evangelists themselves in further amplifying the conversation. That's utopia.

And what are biggest pitfalls a CMO should avoid in storytelling?

Being prescriptive. It's very important for the team to understand the brand tenets and let that be the guardrails for engagement. The road will be sometimes straight, sometimes windy, but never at a dead end. That's the death knell. Be willing to take risks as that will help in refining the engagement strategy.

What role does the customer experience play in how you craft a brand or product story?

The voice of the customer is always front-and-center for us. We have an on-site focus group for in-depth customer engagement, and active listening to customers across social media and our customer care teams is huge for us. All this is an absolutely essential piece of product development itself and how my team and I begin to craft the stories we'll be conveying. Recent successes of this approach include the highly regarded and reviewed Linksys WRT1900AC router (supporting the "Performance Perfected" brand positioning), the Belkin QODE keyboards, and the WeMo Maker launch.

What advice do you have for other senior marketers who want to impact the customer experience but aren't necessarily responsible for it from end to end?

You must have total empathy for your customers, understand their needs and wants, and recognize how your brand(s) fit into their worlds. More importantly, engage with them in multiple ways for a better-rounded experience. Whether in-store, online, or via other research methods, keeping constant tabs on the sentiment is a must. I personally enjoy engaging with customers on Twitter. I encourage all to be very active on one of the social media channels.

Tell me the story of the WeMo Home Automation system.

Technology has disconnected people. WeMo is reversing that unfortunate trend by allowing people to "be in the moment and enjoy what they're doing." It opens the door for serendipity to come back into their lives. Why should you be worrying about how you're going to get dinner together when you're still at lunch with your friends or associates? Well, WeMo has taken care of that with the Crockpot. Dinner—WeMo That! WeMo is setting itself apart by understanding how the brand benefits people's lives today and in the future.

Looking ahead, what marketing "nut" would you like to crack in 2015 and beyond?

Ah, if I had the genie before me now, I would wish for instant mastery of data. There's so much data and there's going to be so much more, but which of it is meaningful and which is trivial? Many people use different methodologies—so what are the best practices and what really works? We're using data well at Belkin, but like everyone, we need to use it better.

KEY TAKEAWAYS

- *Storytelling is yet another skill marketers need to master in the digital age.*

- *Authenticity is storytelling bedrock. Great stories reveal an emotional truth, even those involving a product or service.*

- *Listen to your customers carefully enough and stories worth retelling will emerge.*

Further reading:
Ann Handley, *Everybody Writes: Your Go-To Guide to Creating Ridiculously Good Content*

Sm

Social Media
Success

Walking the Walk on Social

"Social 'listening' is critical, but you have to listen carefully… and guardedly."

Scot Safon
The Weather Channel

Have you thought about your social media strategy yet today? If you're a marketer, the answer is most likely yes. Whether you're a skeptic or a true believer, social media is here to stay in the marketing world, and mastering it will serve you, your company, and your customers very well.

To increase your social savvy, you could do a lot worse than to closely examine the work of Scot Safon, former CMO at The Weather Channel, which—with over 5 million Facebook fans—occupies an enviable space in the social media universe, able with a single click to communicate any message they choose to many millions of already-interested fans.

A media veteran who served as marketing chief at CNN and Headline News before The Weather Channel, Safon saw early the powerful role social media could play in driving site traffic and generating conversation among viewers about a network's programming. Safon's success in this area was based on a keen understanding of the importance of listening with "guarded" ears, constantly producing highly entertaining content, and boosting that content with paid social media.

Can you talk about the role of social in the marketing mix at The Weather Channel? What were your primary objectives?

Social was always an important part of the mix when I was at The Weather Channel, especially since weather has always remained such a popular topic on social platforms. People love to share weather pictures and video, and much of that video is critical to weather news coverage, where The Weather Channel excels on every platform. In terms of audience driving, though, it seemed to help us drive people to severe storm coverage, long-form editorial content, and storytelling. Local forecasts, which are a huge part of the company's business, were—then, at least—less driven by social.

A lot of what TV networks do on social is sharing content (or "talking" to use the marketing parlance.) How important is "listening" to what social users say in response?

Social "listening" is critical, but you have to listen carefully…and guardedly. If something generates only a few comments or shares or citations, it likely didn't inspire any meaningful feedback and you shouldn't probably look at specific comments too closely. If something generates numerous comments, that indicates you might have touched a nerve. But it's important not to weigh the most extreme comments too much—I've seen executives at many networks get very, very concerned about one or two very negative comments…or get too enthusiastic about a few very positive comments. It's like when you attend focus groups—you can't weigh the outliers too heavily or you'll start making some bad decisions. But there are many forms of "social listening," and sometimes it's good to listen in to get some early warnings that sentiment might be shifting, new relevant topics are emerging, and things you've overlooked might actually be important.

What were some of the more effective social campaigns you developed at CNN?

The first time I saw social really emerge as a critical force in media was during Hurricane Katrina coverage in 2005, which many would describe as "pre-social." But we still saw people trying really hard to use any digital platform imaginable to try to connect with other people, and many were using CNN as the 'connector.' We tried very hard to respond to that need for information, connection, and help by creating all sorts of micro-sites, aggregators, and user-generated content gathering points. CNN iReport emerged from that. During the 2008 presidential election campaign social media started coming into its own, and we embraced it very enthusiastically, even bringing in YouTube as a debate presenter and Facebook as our partner in presenting the live streaming of the inauguration (at that point it was the largest live streaming event in history).

Since they're already in the content business (with writers, editors, etc.), don't media channels have a real leg up on social content development versus other types of companies?

I think that media companies are probably more comfortable and more nimble with developing social media content—mainly because they are prepared to make quick adjustments and tweaks to whatever they put out there. These companies already have producers, writers, editors, graphics folks working on content and promotions all the time, so A/B testing two content approaches is not daunting….and revising something that isn't working is also fairly simple. If you are having to reach back out to an agency to get that done, it's sometimes cumbersome and sometimes expensive. But agencies and clients are getting increasingly tight with each other on these efforts, and more agencies are acting as virtual in-house departments. And there is more in-house staffing going on too.

Social media has been great for other TV networks like ABC's Thursday lineup. Why is that?

ABC—and the brilliant Shonda Rhimes—have done an incredible job creating must-see-live-TV shows like *Scandal* and *How To Get Away With Murder*. They constructed the shows so that their core audience can have fun on social media throughout the show, and they've created a situation where half the fun is watching Twitter throughout ABC primetime. The comments are funny and intriguing…and they drive you right back to the show. I know a lot of people time shift those shows, but lots are watching and loving them live. And Fox is doing the same with *Empire*.

KEY TAKEAWAYS

- *Listen guardedly on social, and don't overreact to outlier negative (or positive) comments.*

- *Sharing timely, informative, and entertaining content on social channels can reinforce this connection.*

- *Social media success, especially on Facebook in recent years, is rarely built without paid media support.*

Further reading:

Bryan Kramer, *Shareology: How Sharing is Powering the Human Economy*

IV. Volatile Factors

If you're far enough along in your career to have found this book, you already know that marketing isn't for the faint of heart. We can apply all our smarts and experience to predict outcomes and anticipate surprises, but sometimes we just need to throw it all into the pot and stir it up.

Sometimes a million-dollar breakthrough bubbles to the surface, and sometimes…the whole thing goes boom. Hope you remembered to wear your safety goggles.

This is the volatility inherent in marketing. This is how we play with fire (or, if you prefer, Pop Rocks and Coke). And let's be honest, this is a big part of what makes our jobs so much fun. No, there's nothing fun about your campaign blowing up in your face. But once you've tasted the intense satisfaction of one of your big "mad scientist" bets paying off, you know it's a risk worth running.

And there's a big upside: Like any risk, this one can be mitigated. How? Step one is identifying the Volatile Factors that are part of modern marketing. Identifying the elements that have high potential to precipitate trouble makes you much more able to handle them like a pro and nip disasters in the bud. Step two is listening to what today's most intrepid and level-headed marketing leaders have to say about turning the elements' volatility from a cause for fear into a competitive advantage.

That's what this section of the Periodic Table is about. Get set to make the acquaintance of eight folks who don't waste time in their comfort zones, nor do

Ap
Agency as Partner

Ca
Changing Agencies

Rp
Retail Partners

Rt
Risk-Taking

Bd
Befriending Data

Mm
Media Mixing

Tb
Tiny Budgets

Cm
Crisis Management

they succumb to panic when things start to get hairy. These are men and women who are energized and inspired by Volatile Factors, as we all should be.

These natural leaders don't shrink from the challenges presented by tiny budgets, retailer relationships, sharing creative control with agencies, and crisis management. They know that change is natural and good in marketing, and it's also inevitable despite the potential disruption. To see this brought to life, look no further than this section's no-holds-barred conversation with Barbara Goodstein on the whys and hows of changing agencies, a quintessentially volatile reality of our business.

Perhaps the embodiment of Volatile Factors is the topic that closes this section, crisis management. Doug Duvall's cool head and deep, quiet confidence in the face of potentially brand-destroying chaos is something that we should all aspire to, no matter how big the crises we face day-to-day. And he's very forthcoming with his methods in our interview.

But if you're not staring down a crisis right now, please don't skip to the end of the section. Because then you'll miss my conversation with Terri Funk Graham, longtime CMO of Jack in the Box, who faced down a branding nightmare and won…with the vital help of an agency partner. Nor should you skip the insights of Julie Garlikov who truly did more marketing with less money at Torani, and shares how this elusive goal is possible for all of us.

Of course, there are more volatile factors than just these eight. But the mindsets and transferrable techniques you're about to discover will equip you to manage them all with the poise a CMO needs for success.

A Pairing as Perfect as Burgers and Fries

"Approval by committee is the death of a campaign."

Terri Funk Graham
Jack in the Box

For most CMOs, sharing creative control with outside agencies requires putting ego aside for the sake of the best final outcome…not to mention shouldering a share of the risk should the chosen agency miss the target. Often, it's a less-than-appealing proposition.

But a big gamble was practically required when, over two decades ago, fast food chain Jack in the Box was facing a potential branding apocalypse in the wake of a nationally publicized E. coli outbreak. Looking to turn things around, the marketing team, along with the help of creative director Dick Sittig, who spun out of Chiat/Day into his own agency (Secret Weapon Marketing), brought back the beloved smiley-faced "Jack" character—who had been "killed off" in the 1980s.

Sparking a renewed engagement between customers and the brand, the "Jack" campaign endured for nearly two decades, much of that under then helm of CMO Terri Funk Graham, whose partnership with Dick Sittig remains a model for highly productive client/agency collaborations. Here's how they did it.

Can you describe how the Jack Campaign came about?

Well, it came out of the E. coli crisis back in 1995. The reality was the company needed to do something to revitalize the brand and make the brand relevant again in the marketplace. So it came from a crisis. When you're in a situation like that, you're willing to put a lot more on the line. I think it actually drove the ability to take more risks.

How did the campaign launch?

The very first spot had some controversy around it because it showed Jack coming back. He'd had plastic surgery and he blew up the boardroom, because the folks from the boardroom are the ones who blew him up in the '80s. So Jack reintroduced himself in the marketplace as coming back, better than before, and he was going to be a big advocate for the consumers.

What was Dick Sittig's role?

Dick was really the creative mastermind behind the Jack campaign. We constantly challenged him to keep Jack relevant, and because he used this sense of humor that was a bit unconventional and irreverent, he kept rising to the occasion. Of course, he's Jack's voice in the ads. He had done the voice for the initial pitch, and then we hired an actor to do it for the ads. But there was this gradual realization that everyone liked Dick's voice more, so that's what we ended up sticking with.

What does it take to keep a campaign like this together for so long?

One is that I was always willing to take a risk and be unapologetic about who we were. Dick Sittig would present things that would make us feel uncomfortable. But we knew that it wasn't going to hurt the brand as long as we were true to who we were. I am not a believer in dealing with any sort of pretesting of advertising, and we never did anything of that nature. One key reason I don't like to pretest is that we live in a politically correct world where you're always guaranteed to upset someone, which can hold you back from developing great creative work. I also think that approval by committee is the death of a campaign. You end up with mediocre work that way. Dick and I truly trusted and respected each other in our work, and we would constantly challenge each other to keep it relevant.

Were there any other factors instrumental to this relationship?

The account director at Secret Weapon Marketing—Joanne O'Brien—was a critical, integrated part of my leadership team. Joanne and her team spent two or three days every week at headquarters.

What do you think were some of your most risky efforts?

Running Jack over…that was a trying moment. We were essentially taking the biggest brand equity that the company had, Jack, and putting him on the line to see if people cared. Because if they didn't care that he got hit by a bus, we were going to be in trouble. So we took a chance and introduced "Jack Gets Hit by a Bus" in 2009. It proved to be quite a success.

How did you develop that campaign?

We only showed the ad one time and it was on the Super Bowl. And then everything went digital and social from there. That was our way of stepping into the whole social media arena. So all of a sudden it got millions of views on YouTube, and it was talked about all over the place. We had amazing press and impressions on that. We had people sending cards, teddy bears, and flowers for Jack's recovery. Then we created a storyline. Multiple ads followed up that talked about how he was doing. It became a campaign within a campaign.

So what about the hallucinating kid who sees Jack on his dashboard? That must have stirred things up.

Yes it did. We really wanted to focus on selling our 99-cent tacos. There is a real following to those tacos. Young people, after they've gone to the clubs, tend to head to Jack's for their tacos. So we played off of that, if you will. We had a young guy in a van come up and he wanted to order as many as 30 tacos. Needless to say, that got quite a bit of attention.

You took a rather unique approach to handling the protestors, right?

Well, that's true. We had heard that these protestors and media were going to show up at our corporate headquarters. At that time, we had grass all around the building so that afternoon I suggested we turn on the sprinklers! I thought it was a good way of stalling their activities and sure enough, after we became a "water park" no more protestors showed up the rest of the week.

KEY TAKEAWAYS

- *If you are lucky enough to find a creative partner that truly understands your brand AND is capable of producing advertising that cuts through year after year, stick with them.*

- *Treat your agency as a critical strategic partner because that is what feeds truly great creative work.*

- *Challenge your agency to challenge you. If you don't ask for it, you'll only see the safe stuff.*

Further reading:
David Ogilvy, *Ogilvy on Advertising*

Reviewing the Review Process

"If the relationship isn't working, there are many, many agencies out there and it's in your best interest to make a switch, as opposed to tolerating underperformance."

Barbara Goodstein
Tiger 21 Holdings

If you're reading this book in a linear progression, you just heard from Terri Funk Graham about the intricacies of working with an outside agency. (If you're not, be sure to check out Terri's interview immediately preceding this one.) In any case, you must understand that forging a strong, profitable relationship with an outside agency takes significant time and effort invested from all sides.

So changing agencies, thereby starting the whole process over again from the beginning, is not something a marketing executive can take lightly. To understand why such a change can become imperative and how to get the most out of the process, I reached out to Barbara Goodstein. Currently the CEO of Tiger 21 Holdings, Barbara led agency reviews during her recent tenure as CMO of Vonage and before that as CMO of AXA Equitable.

You've initiated agency reviews a couple of times. What are top reasons for needing to change agencies?

In the case of AXA, we didn't have a full-service advertising agency. We had a small promotional firm that was doing brochures and sales information, but they were never doing a complete positioning and they didn't take us through a full process to understand what we were trying to accomplish. So, I upgraded the whole process by bringing in a very sophisticated agency with loads of creative talent.

So this was not about replacing as much as it was upgrading, right?

I identified that there was an upside opportunity if we improved the quality of the creative and the advertising. So nobody said, "We need to bring in an advertising agency." I just said, "Oh my gosh, think about how much better things would be if we brought in a strategically sound creative agency."

What was the reason for the switch at Vonage?

At Vonage there were multiple agencies. When I arrived, it was clear that the CEO was frustrated by the lack of strategy and planning at the primary ad agency. We would have quarterly business reviews and the CEO was miserable with what he was getting back. I said to him, "If you're that unhappy, let's start an agency search." Initially, he was very reticent to do so because he thought it could derail our whole program and he really had no confidence that it was going to work. He was most concerned about there being horrible switching costs. But, as it turns out, there weren't any. The handoff between agencies was completely smooth. Absolutely nothing bad happened.

What were the keys to making a switch like that work?

Because we did a whole review process, we had basically identified the creative that we wanted to move to. As part of the agency review process, multiple agencies prepared very well-thought-out, deliberate strategies. The pieces that we were missing with the incumbents were delivered even in the pitch process. And as we were buying into the strategy, we were being led down the road to buy into the creative, simultaneously. By the time we made the decision, we had strategy and creative ready to go. What also helped was that the future agency started working for us for about a month while we were winding down incumbents, and we did the same thing with both the media agency and the creative agency.

When managing reviews, how helpful to you was it to have a search consultant involved? What value did they add to the process?

I used Dick Roth Associates and he was fantastic. I used him both with AXA and at Vonage because we had such a good experience with him at AXA. He was able to identify all of the potential agencies that could help us. We then narrowed it down. We said we wanted an agency of a certain size because we wanted to be important, but not swamp the agency. Then we pinpointed what experience they needed to have. He also did a scan for the ones that had account conflicts. In the case of Vonage, it was particularly difficult because phone companies spend so much on advertising that it's hard to find an agency that's not already booked.

What are some of the lessons you learned about managing the review process that other CMOs might want to do (or not do)?

I think we did it the right way. I think that the "don't" is don't hesitate. If the relationship isn't working, there are many, many agencies out there and it's in your best interest to make a switch, as opposed to tolerating underperformance. That really became clear after we switched and we were getting everything that we previously wanted. People were thinking why didn't we do that sooner. It just wasn't as painful as people had anticipated.

How did you persuade these agencies to invest so much during the pitch process before you'd made your decision?

In the case of Vonage, there was so much value and so much upside to them that they were all willing to make the investment. Vonage was a very significant size opportunity for the agencies, so everyone did it on spec.

Would you recommend including creative development in the pitch process? Does seeing actual ideas make a big difference?

Yes. Because I think that if you don't include the creative you don't really know who you're "marrying." That's a big part of what you're buying. And in both cases we ended up running the creative that was developed during the pitch process.

At what stage of the review process would you recommend including the financial negotiations?

We started in each case with multiple agencies, then narrowed it down to about five, then from five to two. Once we got down to the two, that's when we would start pushing them on costs. Because at this point we knew who we wanted to hire and we had to make sure that the costs worked. It's just a lot easier to negotiate the cost down before anyone knows the final decision.

You've done the review. You've hired the agency. How do you make sure that the new relationship takes?

I think that you have to have a rapport with the people that you're working with and you figure that out during the pitch process. And then you have to stay close to them during the creation of the first round of advertising. Everyone needs to be connected at the hip when you start because you still don't know each other. You've only been dating for a while. So I think it's mainly about time spent.

Agencies are notorious for bringing out all of their senior people for the pitch who never show up again. Has this been the case for you?

We pushed on that during all of the upfront conversation. Are you the people we're going to be working with going forward? And we cemented it. So they were on our account until they left the agency. But, while they were at the agency, they were the people that we worked with.

Once the decision is made to go into a review, all parties involved want to speed things along. Are there some steps that you think could be eliminated in the typical process?

Not really. The first step was the comparisons—the capabilities presentation and knowing who you're dealing with. The next step was explaining our business to them. Then we had multiple rounds of reviews with them. I don't think that there's anything in this process that you could or should cut out.

As part of this process, I think that every client would love to hold their agency accountable based on performance. Is that possible?

I don't know if it's really possible because there are so many things that are happening concurrent with advertising. Let's say measures like awareness and Net Promoter Score go up with the new campaign, yet sales went down. Sales might have gone down because a competitor introduced new functionality.

You're not going to give your agency a big round of applause as sales are collapsing nor can you blame them since the competitive activity was out of their control.

So let's flip this and go back to the AXA situation in which the "800-Pound Gorilla" campaign you introduced was super-effective by just about any measure. At that point, could the agency have been rewarded more?

We didn't specifically reward them but we were winning awards and so were they. So the reward was that everyone was getting external recognition. In this case, the sales were going up and it was partially because of the Gorilla campaign, but then the question becomes, how do you attribute it to the agency?

So here I thought the agency was driving the sales, but others within AXA felt they deserved the credit. Which is predictable. At AXA, I think it was truly the advertising campaign that drove a lot of the success.

Sounds like the agency just can't win!

The advertising agency is always at the short end of the straw. When they're successful someone else takes the credit, and when they're not successful, they're responsible, even when it's out of their control.

KEY TAKEAWAYS

- *Changing advertising agencies is a time-consuming process but made easier by hiring a search consultant.*

- *Make sure you meet and bond with the team that will actually lead your business, especially the strategic and creative heads.*

- *Even with all the sophisticated data tracking available, it is still very hard to hold your agency 100 percent accountable for sales results.*

Further reading:
Fred S. Goldberg, *The Insanity of Advertising: Memoirs of a Mad Man*

Shining Up Your Relationships

"Build on what is proven, optimize what we know should work, and always test new efforts in small ways."

Colin Hall
Allen Edmonds

High-end men's shoe brand Allen Edmonds pulls off a precarious balancing act with elegance and style. On one end, they sell their product directly in their own retail shops. On the other, they make their premium footwear available through major third-party retailers like Zappos and Nordstrom.

If you take a moment to think about all the conflicts and other difficulties that could arise in this system—if, for instance, there weren't a top-notch team, including the CMO, holding it all together—you'll be properly impressed by CMO Colin Hall's ability to keep the entire marketing machine running like clockwork.

In addition to his success ensuring AE stores and third party retailers aren't stepping on each others' toes, Colin's shrewd integration of cutting-edge digital content and old-school media such as catalogs continues to pay off in double-digit growth numbers for Allen Edmonds.

Allen Edmonds sells directly to the consumer via your own stores as well as via large brick-and-mortar and online retailers. How do you balance supporting your own stores and supporting your retail partners?

As a manufacturer based in America, we can easily react to customers' desires and needs. A big advantage for us is the ability to fill in orders with our partners as needed. Competitive brands that warehouse inventory from overseas are forced to do exactly what you imply: Choose between their own needs and that of their retail customers when inventory is low. From a marketing perspective, we make our marketing materials available to our partners so that the brand is, ideally, presented in a cohesive fashion across all sales channels. Sharing creative assets allows the work to be seen by more eyes than just those shopping our company-owned channels. Customers can determine where they want to shop based on their unique tastes, experiences, and geographies.

One of the advantages of having your own retail stores is that one can control the entire customer experience, and—in theory—elevate it to the point that you engender brand love and loyalty. What kinds of things have you done to achieve this?

Our strategy is pretty straightforward, and it amazes me that executing the straightforward well differentiates our in-store experience from competitors. First, we have a terrific presentation of product including styles, colors, and sizes. Customers who have feet outside the "norms" know that Allen Edmonds has shoes to fit their needs. Second, our store and call center co-workers are incredibly knowledgeable and helpful. We refer to our longest tenured in-store co-workers as Master Fitters. They will measure your foot and help solve your style and fitting needs. Customers have a lot of confidence knowing our co-worker has fitted literally thousands if not tens of thousands of feet in their career. Third, we don't stop at the sale. Our co-workers will also service a customer post-sale, ensuring the fit and performance of the shoe. Fourth, we present the customer with an outstanding value proposition. Our shoes last a long time based on our 212-step manufacturing process, higher quality materials, and our legendary recrafting service. We recraft roughly 60,000 pairs of shoes a year making us one of the world's largest cobblers as well as a manufacturer. This "hug your customer" mentality is why we have so many loyal customers and why they choose to recommend Allen Edmonds to their friends, colleagues, and sons.

How do you ensure the customer experience with your retail partners meets Allen Edmonds' standards?

Each channel we sell through has unique attributes, so we don't dictate to them. But we try to help them whenever they need it. Our brand guidelines are well-documented and they help partners present the brand consistently. We also ask that our partners try to present our core brand pillars of American Made, size and style availability, Recrafting (a strong value proposition versus cheap shoes), 212-step handcrafted process, and highest quality leathers as much as possible through imagery, copy, and video content as examples. We will supply the content, although the partners may interpret and personalize the manner in which these pillars are portrayed based on the channel and target (e.g. millennials vs older businessmen).

How does working so closely with retail partners impact your marketing priorities? Do you focus on sell-in or sell-through?

We focus on both, but place more emphasis on sell-through. Sell-through means our wholesale customers are succeeding and our product is turning. Sell-through success leads to more confidence in our brand and ultimately stronger sell-in. We support our wholesale accounts with various co-op materials including digital photos, in-store signage, catalogs, videos, in-store appearances by reps, trunk shows, and recrafting services, just to name a few.

What are some recent new marketing initiatives you've rolled out?

We initiated two new marketing efforts. The first was an old-school approach based on ramping up our paper catalogs by leveraging co-operative big data for prospecting. We match back to our database and these efforts are driving sales of existing customers and new customer acquisition.

The second was more new-school, and included display network advertising targeting new customers. We've enjoyed huge increases in sales through digital media including retargeting, affiliate, email, and other channels, but DSP allows us to serve ads to those who look like our primary customers but have never been to our site. We're seeing a $5 revenue return for every $1 we spend on DSP customer acquisition.

How as CMO are you staying on top of the increasingly complex landscape of budget allocation and optimization?

This is one of the biggest questions year in and year out. Our approach is to build on what is proven, optimize what we know should work, and always test new efforts in small ways. If I had to put an allocation on it, I would say we allocate 70 percent on proven media, 20 percent on optimizing and 10 percent on testing new ideas. As a private equity-owned company driving by EBITDA, we never bet the farm on anything unproven. We stair step our way through testing, optimizing, and then investing in media.

KEY TAKEAWAYS

- *Retail partnerships are becoming increasingly difficult to manage since so many brands also sell directly to consumers.*

- *Managing these relationships means providing clear brand guidelines along with all the assets they need to make your brand shine in their particular environment.*

- *Good old-fashioned paper catalogs are still remarkably effective.*

Further reading:
Bernd Schmitt, *Happy Customers Everywhere: How Your Business Can Profit from the Insights of Positive Psychology*

Rt

Risk-Taking

Risks and Sky-High Rewards

"For about $10,000 in spend, we generated almost $10 million in impressions. We had captured the moment in a fun, creative way."

Marty St. George
JetBlue

The air travel business is risky on multiple levels, and seeing the numerous mergers and disappearances of once-proud airline brands in recent years shows that certain worst-case scenarios have been realized. But relative newcomer JetBlue shows time and time again that a bold marketing and service philosophy based on that never-gets-old principle of putting the customer experience above all else can still keep an airline brand flying high.

EVP of Commercial and Planning, Marty St. George pilots JetBlue's efforts to reach new passengers and retain loyal ones, and wise risk-taking is a cornerstone of his continued success. The result is one knockout promotion after another. We focused on that in this interview, and I also capitalized on the chance to ask him about some of the other factors keeping JetBlue in the upper stratosphere relative to their competition.

What is the biggest marketing risk you've taken at JetBlue? How did it play out?

I've taken a lot of risks, but I think the biggest was the "Election Protection" promo we ran in New York during Fall 2012. It went out to the folks who say things like: "If my candidate loses I'm moving to Canada." The promo revolved around JetBlue giving away 2,012 free tickets out of the country. It was risky because election promos are inherently risky; voting is a sacred duty, and there are many examples of brands commercializing the election to their detriment. Luckily, we played it perfectly and got more buzz than we ever imagined, and zero blowback.

Any others you're particularly proud of?

We did a promotion called "Carmageddon" when the 405 Freeway was closed in L.A. We flew for a day back and forth between Burbank and Long Beach. I need to give my team a lot of credit for this one. When they brought the idea to me, I said: "I can't imagine this getting buzz but feel free to do it, if you can do it cheaply." The result? For about $10,000 in spend, we generated almost $10 million in impressions. We had captured the moment in a fun, creative way.

JetBlue CEO David Barger famously posed the question 'How do we stay small as we get big?' to the JetBlue team. As CMO, how do you take on this challenge?

Every leader at JetBlue takes full ownership of that challenge. There are elements of the JetBlue experience that naturally lend themselves to helping us stay small. We don't ask our people to do anything that we wouldn't do. For example, when leaders take a JetBlue flight and the plane arrives at the gate, we become a full-on hands-dirty part of the cleaning crew alongside the flight attendants and pilots. On the holidays, many of us work at the airport helping customers during the busiest days. But specifically as CMO, I am focused on making sure that our mission and values come through in every communication we do, both internal and external. When we start looking like a faceless conglomerate to our people, we'll have lost the battle.

What steps do you take to better understand and communicate with your customers?

I'm very lucky in that our founders gave us a mission and a set of values that are core to our DNA. Our mission is to inspire humanity, and part of what we try to accomplish is that personal connection between the brand and our customers. Our customers feel personal ownership of the brand, and they're very vocal about the things they love and the things they want us to change.

How do you evaluate/measure the success of your marketing?

On a macro level we look at brand metrics for ourselves and our competitors. On a micro level, we measure every dollar we spend digitally and translate it into a cost-per-booking. We share our metrics with our media partners and expect them to help improve campaigns and targets to get our CPB lower.

Has marketing become more complex for you? How are you dealing with that complexity?

We deal with it by keeping up with technology, and by finding partners in that space who can help keep us current. In fact, every year we have a "digital day" where we invite current and potential marketing partners in to pitch our entire team. We've found several exciting new technologies and channels that way, just through an open "casting call."

Do you agree with the notion that marketing is everything and everything is marketing? If so, how have you extended the boundaries of your job beyond the normal purview of the CMO?

Absolutely agree, and luckily at JetBlue we all recognize that the experience is the ultimate manifestation of the brand, and our people learn this on day one. How? Every month we hold an orientation for new crewmembers at our training center, and many senior leaders attend. When I speak at orientation, my first line is to welcome everyone to the marketing team, since everyone who touches a customer owns a piece of the brand.

KEY TAKEAWAYS

- *Creative risk-taking can dramatically increase brand exposure.*

- *Stunts like "Carmegeddon" work so well for JetBlue not just because they are timely and clever. They are also relevant to what JetBlue does and consistent with the brand's friendly personality.*

- *Lean on leading vendors to keep you on top of the latest digital opportunities.*

Further reading:
Seth Godin, *The Big Moo: Stop Trying to Be Perfect and Start Being Remarkable*

Data, My Dear Watson

"We are engaging a consumer who is living in a massively digital world."

Mayur Gupta
Kimberly-Clark

The sheer volume of data that flows in and out of consumer goods giant Kimberly-Clark every day could make even the most diligent bean-counter quake in his loafers. But with the perspicacious and prescient Mayur Gupta as Global Head of Marketing Technology, this flood of information becomes the fuel for a powerful marketing machine. My interview with Mayur will make clear to all of the data-phobic marketers out there that it's time to welcome it with open arms.

The way Mayur observes data and deduces action plans from it reminds me of Sherlock Holmes, digging for hidden clues no one else can see and reassembling them into a cohesive fact-based narrative that concludes with a major breakthrough. In our interview we also had time to touch on Mayur's exciting data-centric work with program-matic marketing.

What new technologies have you leveraged recently, and did the results of using them meet your expectations?

We have tried to keep it simple. We orchestrate the entire marketing technology ecosystem at Kimberly-Clark across four overlapping bubbles—media, content, data (context), and commerce. We strongly believe that the ultimate seamless consumer experience occurs at the intersection of these bubbles. Underneath these, though, we have enterprise, tactical/localized, and innovative capabilities. Enterprise capabilities that need to be globally scaled. Tactical and localized capabilities that need agility and speed and pertain to local market and consumer needs. Lastly, technologies and startups that we need to partner with to drive innovation. While we have brought on a number of technologies across these buckets, a huge focus has been on connecting context, content, and commerce capabilities and constantly ensuring that we establish a connected ecosystem and not isolated technologies.

I'm paraphrasing here, but your CMO Clive Sirkin has said something along the lines of "We don't believe in digital marketing; we believe in marketing in a digital world." What does that mean, and how is it part of your work?

That's correct and through Clive's leadership we now have that as a foundational mindset and behavior across the organization. It's quite simple if you think about it. We are engaging a consumer who is living in a massively digital world. She is dependent on digital technology, which is now part of her daily life. She no longer differentiates between the analog and the digital world in her expectations from brands and how they engage, she expects the same value and experience seamlessly across the board. However, on the flipside, brands continue to consider digital as a "thing" or a "silo" which breaks and fragments that experience. We at Kimberly-Clark believe in breaking these silos by driving convergence across functions and capabilities that eventually builds legendary brands in this digital world. It's a shift from being multichannel (channel focused) to truly becoming "omnichannel" (consumer focused). We all have a single mission to deliver seamless experiences in a complex omnichannel world.

What's next for your leveraging of data?

Data is massive; it's the oil, it's the currency for the industry. I think most of the industry has a big "small" data problem and not so much of a "big data" problem. It's not so much the volume or size of data but how well connected and harmonized it really is. Do we really understand "her" universally as a human, and that's been our biggest focus. We call it data convergence, by which I mean an ability to stitch the fragmented data ecosystem across first-party, second-party, and third-party data. In order for us to drive relevant, personalized, contextual, and seamless consumer experiences across channels and touchpoints, we need this universal data and view of the consumer just in time, and an ability to make decisions and predictions relevant to her as she hops from one touch point to the other. Ultimately it's converging her context (consumer data and insights) to influence content (her experience) which will ultimately inspire the ideal behavior (commerce). These are the three "C"s of modern marketing.

How has programmatic marketing helped you reach your overall marketing objectives?

It has helped us become smarter as well as more relevant and personalized from a media buying and consumer engagement standpoint across paid channels. Having utilized and scaled the obvious benefits of programmatic, we are now on the next horizon, where we are starting to leverage the impact of programmatic across the rest of the ecosystem, including our owned and earned channels as well as our retailer partnerships. The early horizons of programmatic have helped us optimize our media buying efforts and maximized the ROI, but the subsequent horizons will include leveraging consumer data and insights in driving stronger consumer engagement and inspiring behavior across the board.

This, arguably, is the most underutilized and ignored benefit of programmatic buying.

What were some of the challenges of adopting programmatic? What advice would you give to another marketer who is just getting started with it?

Programmatic has been at Kimberly-Clark for a few years now, and was there before I joined. So the credit goes to our media leadership and our CMO. We were clearly one of the early adopters and pioneers in the space. The challenge for us now is to go beyond the obvious and scale the capability globally. We have already seen tremendous success with our current trading desk and programmatic buying capability; we are now challenging ourselves to take it to another level and impact the broader marketing ecosystem, smartly leveraging consumer data and insights that will drive seamless experiences and inspire consumer behavior across paid, owned, and earned.

KEY TAKEAWAYS

- *Understanding how to find, analyze, and use data are now mandatory skills for CMOs.*
- *The three C's of modern marketing are context, content, and commerce.*
- *Programmatic marketing is quickly evolving beyond paid channels.*

Further reading:
David L. Rogers, *The Network Is Your Customer: Five Strategies to Thrive in a Digital Age*

Mm

Media Mixing

Media Mixing Keeps Allstate in Good Hands

"People still watch TV—a lot of it."

Sanjay Gupta
Allstate

In an age of constant brand refresh, companies like Allstate are increasingly rare. Allstate stands firm on one message ("You're in Good Hands with Allstate") delivered via two main campaigns: one featuring Dennis Haysbert's comforting, iconic baritone delivering the familiar slogan, and the newer "Mayhem" advertisements utilizing "worst case scenario" humor to drive home the need for top-notch insurance coverage.

How does Allstate keep managing to find new angles on one theme while other brands are perpetually pivoting? The answer exists somewhere in the brain of Sanjay Gupta, EVP of Marketing, Innovation, and Corporate Relations for Allstate. One element is simply the strength of the message, combined with the adage of "if it ain't broke don't fix it." Another is Sanjay's deep understanding of media mixing: utilizing a variety of methods for delivering the message in order to keep it engaging year in and year out. We also discussed some of Allstate's most successful recent initiatives and what all marketers can learn from them.

What role does TV play in your marketing mix? Do you see that changing in the near term?

TV allows us to tell our brand story. For example, we debuted a powerful brand ad titled "We Still Climb" that helped us launch our new brand idea that Allstate doesn't just protect people when something goes wrong, but also helps them to live a good life every day. As part of that effort, we're leveraging our TV advertising to highlight Allstate's innovative products and features. These include proven ones like our Safe Driving Bonus Checks, as well as new ones such as our QuickFoto Claim and Drivewise smart phone apps.

As far as our marketing mix goes, people still watch TV—a lot of it. Though we continue to increase the percentage of our digital media as consumer media consumption evolves, we've found that a combination of media types usually yields the best results.

You have two very different campaigns with the Mayhem and Dennis Haysbert ads. What is the strategy behind these two initiatives?

The good news is they work very well together, each campaign complementing and working off one another. Mayhem disrupts and reminds people that all insurance is not the same, so they need to be careful in terms of who they choose for their protection needs. Dennis reinforces why Allstate is the compelling choice to protect everything that's important to you. While we know that each campaign continues to work very well individually, collectively the effect is even greater.

A lot of marketers change campaigns every couple of years. This doesn't seem to be the case in the insurance category and certainly not with Allstate. Why is that? Are there specific signals you look for to determine if just an ad or an entire campaign has worn out its welcome?

If you have a campaign that continues to prove successful, and becomes even more successful with time, then changing for change's sake is not what's best for the brand and the business. Of course we measure and constantly watch for wearout and diminishing effectiveness. But part of the reason "You're in Good Hands" has remained one of the most recognized taglines in America is because we haven't changed it in fifty years. And while the message remains consistent, we are constantly introducing new features and different ways in which we tell our story about Allstate while also leveraging the equity that Dennis and Mayhem have built.

What are some recent ways you've innovated the core message to build the Allstate brand?

Our most recent accomplishment that I'm most proud of—and it's actually still a work in progress—kicked off in September when we launched a breakthrough program and accompanying ad campaign to reach consumers and customers who represent what we're calling "New Households." These are people who are contending with life "firsts," such as a new car, house, baby, or combination of these. With these things come new uncertainties—car repairs, home maintenance, questions about financial security, etc.—that today's young families are typically not prepared to address. These consumers typically turn to a trusted inner circle of friends and family for advice. Yet, faced with bigger dilemmas and decisions than ever before, they're finding these "experts" sometimes lack the resources or skills to help solve them.

So Allstate is offering tangible solutions, expertise, and savings to help New Households get things right the first time. Things like a free one-year membership to Angie's List, assistance finding reputable real estate agents, discounts on infant and child car seats, and more. The campaign includes a combination of national and local TV, radio, digital media, print, social media, and PR, and it leads with real life, not insurance. It depicts the reality of being a young family versus the perception you may have had of how perfect life would be.

How important is mobile marketing to your brand and what does it encompass?

More than 50 percent of people are now accessing the Web through mobile phones, so clearly you can't ignore mobile. We do extensive work not only in terms of mobile optimizing our Web presence and our applications, but we also do quite a bit of marketing on mobile platforms. And we also leverage mobile to create new product features such as our QuickFoto Claim app and our Digital Locker home inventory app.

KEY TAKEAWAYS

- *TV advertising continues to reach large audiences and can be particularly effective when a brand has "news" about innovative features.*

- *Getting the media mix right for your brand is a continuous process of testing and learning.*

- *Once the media and the message are working, don't be in a rush to change them.*

Further reading:
Jeanne Bliss, *Chief Customer Officer: Getting Past Lip Service to Passionate Action*

Tb
Tiny Budgets

Making a Mouse-Sized Budget Roar

"...Trying things out small scale, proving that they deliver, and then expanding."

Julie Garlikov
Torani

It's easy to look at the marketing output of a Fortune 100 company and sigh, "If only I had a marketing budget that big..."

It's also very lazy! For proof of this, look no further than Julie Garlikov's work at Torani, maker of flavored syrups for coffee and other beverages. Torani, started in San Francisco by two Italian immigrants, has become the go-to flavoring brand in coffeehouses of all sizes. But the success of its growth as a brand hasn't been a result of dumping ever more cash into marketing. Rather, it's been the result of squeezing the maximum effectiveness out of every marketing dollar.

Julie's insights here show how for a product like Torani, which relies on retailers to establish the first relationship with customers, it pays to keep tabs on your consumer base not just by touching base over social media but also by adding to their daily lives in a fun, relevant way.

Has the fact that Torani does not have a huge multimillion dollar budget forced you to be more innovative?

We have to find the right partners to work with us who believe in our brand and who want to work with a great, local, family-owned business. And we need to focus more on things like PR and creating social buzz to get the word out. We can't do a lot of mass tactics, so we look to build really high loyalty with our business and consumer users, turning them into uber fans.

Have you been able to link your innovative marketing activities to the kinds of business metrics favored by CEOs?

I use a lot of test/invest methodology, trying things out small scale, proving that they deliver, and then expanding. It's the only way to ensure the best ROI on limited budgets like ours.

How do you stay close to your end users when the relationship with these folks is mainly owned by your retailer partners?

We get a great sense from social media and listening of what's important to our user. We've also been doing a lot of event marketing and mobile tours the past two years so we can hear more directly what our users like. Between our retail partners and our foodservice distributors, we can be one step removed. So we have to create opportunities to engage regularly and we do a lot of research like ethnographies to really understand what our consumer wants and needs.

Has social media played much of a role in driving your brand? If so, how has it helped or how do you see it helping in the future?

We have a very active, loyal fan base that we engage with daily on Facebook, Pinterest, Twitter, etc. We've also done a lot of blogger outreach and we engage with various bloggers on a regular basis, sending them new products, etc. This helps get the word out on a small brand and it forms a big part of our acquisition strategies.

Are you increasing your content marketing investment?

Yes, this is a huge area for us. We've developed videos and will be producing even more as the year wraps up—everything from how-to videos to funny content. We also continue to create enticing inspirational photos and editorial, almost like what you see in a food magazine. We've found that inspiring people with seasonal recipes and super on-trend ideas generates significant sales lift, so content is key for us.

Author's note: The remaining questions and answers are from a follow-up conversation I had with Julie, now VP of Marketing at Nuvesse Skin Therapies, right before this edition went to press.

Looking back on your time at Torani, what do you think was the key to making the most of your modest marketing budget?

Much of it comes down to people. If you pick the right partners, you have agencies and others who are really invested and do great work and are an extension of your own team. I often choose partners where the owners are very seasoned marketers, designers, etc., who have been well trained and are very experienced, but now have a smaller shop and want to work with smaller, more nimble companies. And I also select my own team carefully so that some of the work can be done in-house to make sure that I'm utilizing outside resources very carefully and supplementing with my own talent when appropriate.

Are there any other lessons you learned while at Torani that you are applying to your new position?

I'm applying the same lessons on budgets and sourcing the right people to help me that I learned at Torani. I just don't have the same internal resources to rely on given that we're a start-up, so it's mission critical to bring in partners. Many of the people I'm working with are relationships I built while at Torani or in other roles. It's sometimes hard to convince great talent to work on a start-up, but when you've nurtured the relationships over time, people will help or work on tighter budgets because they want to work with you personally again or they know what amazing work you can create together.

Are you seeing any marketing tactics right now that are particularly good at stretching your budget?

I think there is a lot that can be done in the digital realm that is more cost effective than in the past. As well, you can actually build a brand through online influencers and social word of mouth and this is a proven strategy, allowing independent brands a real chance to compete against the big guys and their huge advertising budgets.

KEY TAKEAWAYS

- *When faced with a small budget, look to PR and social media to help spread the word cost-effectively.*

- *Find nimble partners who can help you multiply the impact of every dollar.*

- *Event marketing can serve the dual purposes of gaining brand exposure and gathering essential consumer insights.*

Further reading:
Jay Baer, *Youtility: Why Smart Marketing Is about Help Not Hype*

Marketing's Emergency Room

"What happened? When did it happen? What did you do once you found out it happened? How can you assure the public that it won't happen again?"

Doug Duvall
Sprint

Crisis management: It's one thing to go through the motions of damage control when your social media team tweets an off-color joke that triggers a few hours of online outrage. It's quite another to protect your company's reputation while facing down a media tidal wave involving things like murders, suicides, bombings, hurricanes, and other true disasters that they don't prepare you for in business school…or anywhere else.

These situations are marketing's equivalent of when a heart attack patient is rolled frantically into the emergency room, requiring an immediate quadruple bypass. The surgeon in charge must be experienced, sure-handed, and unshakably confident in his or her ability to save the life that hangs in the balance.

With that in mind, meet Sprint's Doug Duvall. For crises large and small, every company should be lucky enough to have someone like Doug, Vice President of Corporate Communications, playing quarterback when the you-know-what hits the fan. Crisis management is a very specific expertise, one that requires someone like Doug at the helm for everyone to sleep well at night. But it's also something every marketing professional should have a working proficiency in, and internalizing Doug's insights here can make that happen.

What types of crises have you experienced at Sprint?

Most of the routine crises involve our network. Our nationwide network is the backbone of our company and it's the infrastructure that enables our fifty-six million customers to call, text, check email, or watch a video on their mobile device. Today we're so reliant on smartphones, and when there's a network outage it's understandable that customers become frustrated. So we're really conscious about threats to our network—whether it's from a construction crew accidentally cutting a fiber line or from weather events like storms, hurricanes, floods, or earthquakes.

What is the worst crisis or near-crisis you've experienced?

Before joining Sprint I spent seven years at Freddie Mac. I managed the public relations team and we had our fair share of crises from the government suddenly taking over control of the company, to foreclosures, to protests at company headquarters.

But the one crisis that stands out to me, and probably to most employees at that time, was waking up to the news that our CFO had committed suicide. It was completely unexpected and yet another major emotional shock to employees, who had already been through a lot. And to make matters worse, our critics tried to make the incident more of a conspiracy about "what did he know, and what was he hiding?"

What were the key steps you took to diffuse the situation?

My boss and I quickly drafted a public statement and he walked it down the hall to get approved by the CEO. We felt it was important not to use "corporate speak" and to express our sincere sorrow in plain English. That's critical in any crisis, but particularly one that involves a human tragedy. We talked about what kind of man and leader he was and how he will be most remembered for "his personal warmth, his sense of humor, and his quick wit." We posted the statement on our website and quickly sent it to reporters who covered us regularly. But given this was in the midst of the financial crisis, we had calls from all over the world, and from non-traditional outlets like Entertainment Tonight. I even did a radio interview with BBC, talking about the kind of person he was and what a tragedy it was for the company and his family. We also developed an internal communications plan that included a memorial event, and to respect his family's privacy, we developed protocol on who would have interaction with the family.

What are the organizational requirements to avoid surprises?

It's important to have designated crisis representatives from across the company. We have a person on Sprint's Corporate Communications team whose primary job is to manage crises, whenever they may occur. She has a backup, and he has a backup too. But she is part of a larger company-wide team and regularly works with crisis representatives from our Network division, corporate security, sales, marketing, legal, government affairs, IT, etc.

You may hear about a crisis occurring in a number of different ways—through social media, breaking news, or a phone call. But everyone needs to know who to escalate it to and that's why we have designated people. So whoever might first hear of a crisis, they know who to send it to for managing the issue.

Once you hear of a potential crisis, how do you begin to manage it?

Well, it's definitely a team effort, but I start by asking four simple questions at the onset of any crisis, no matter the issue or size of the organization:

1. What happened?
2. When did it happen?
3. What did you do once you found out it happened?
4. How can you assure the public that it won't happen again?

If you have decent answers to these basic questions, you'll survive the crisis. When you see a corporate or political crisis lasting longer than it should, usually there wasn't a solid answer to questions three and four.

After you have a sense of what happened and the scope of the problem, how do you communicate it internally and externally?

Tone is important, and a crisis is not a time for spin. Mike McCurry, President Clinton's former press secretary, advises corporate clients to think about the "C's" when communicating during a crisis:

- Clarity. Use understandable, plain English.
- Credibility. Be authentic and willing to address shortcomings.
- Compassion. Remember there's a person on the other side of this crisis.
- Commitment. Devote the time and resources to resolve issue.

KEY TAKEAWAYS

- *Every business should have a crisis management plan in place and review it annually.*

- *Designate a crisis management team and have them go through preparatory "fire drills."*

- *Before responding to a crisis, make sure you understand exactly what happened.*

Further reading:
Gary Vaynerchuk, *The Thank You Economy*

V. Silicon Rally

There's not much left to say about the totality with which digital technology has swept through every corner of marketing…except that it's just getting started. Think of where we were ten years ago when the big click-wheel 20GB iPods in our pockets were jaw-droppingly state of the art.

So I suppose all we can really do is hold on tight and brace for the next tidal wave of change, right?

Well, yes and no. We do need to do that—change is coming, it's coming fast, and there's no way to completely prepare for whatever lies ahead. But that's not all we can do. We can also heed the advice of the marketers who are leveraging marketing technologies the way we all should—wisely, efficiently, with foresight, and without succumbing to hype.

I'm talking about people like Rose Hamilton, who at Pet360 redefined the online user experience and in doing so ran circles around brick-and-mortar pet supply shops. Or John Costello, a seasoned veteran who combines deep experience with an ever-curious mindset and is guiding Dunkin' Donuts towards the future of mobile apps. Or Paul Greenberg, who's pulled off the enviable feat of boiling virality down to a repeatable science.

The theme I hope you notice across these marketers who are leading marketing's Silicon Rally is that they've taken the time and deliberate care to understand the technologies and tech-fueled tactics that have made them successful. They don't approach tech as some sort of plug-and-play, paint-by-numbers game

Cr
CRM

Md
Mobilizing
Digital

Im
Integrating
Mobile

Ee
Email
Efficacy

Rm
Real-Time
Marketing

Oo
Online
Optimization

We
Web
Experience

Gv
Going
Viral

where reaping its benefits requires little more than surfing the net all day and motor-mouthing the latest buzzwords and acronyms to anyone within earshot.

One quick and hopefully helpful aside about the element silicon, the purest .1% of which indeed makes possible the computer on which I'm typing this, the electronic device on which you're perhaps reading this, and all the topics covered in this section: Its name is derived from the Latin silex, which means "hard stone" or "flint." I like to remember this when the pace of technological change starts to make my head spin a little, as it reminds me there is something firm, solid, and constant underlying it all.

At its core, marketing is about communication, and from papyrus sheets to the printing press to the telegraph to the Android, technology is the great facilitator of communication. So when new tech gizmos wash over our transom, I find asking, "But will it truly help us communicate better?" is often a solid litmus test for whether it's going to have staying power.

And let's never forget that a communication tool is only as effective as the brains on the operating and receiving ends.

Anyway, let's switch our smartphones to silent for a few minutes and pay close attention to eight of the most tech-savvy minds in marketing.

Cr

CRM

Securing Brotherly Love, Win or Lose

"You simply do what's right for the fans. And it takes a lot of the complexity out of it."

Tim McDermott
Philadelphia 76ers

Being a CMO for a major pro sports team can be a roller-coaster ride. When the team is winning, you don't need to pull any marketing miracles out of your hat to keep the brand strong and growing. But when the team's fortunes change for the worse—and they inevitably will—it takes a consummate professional to keep the seats filled and the fans hopeful.

And in a city like Philadelphia, home of intensely passionate fans known for being very loud and clear when they're not happy with their beloved teams, the stakes are high for the teams' CMOs. So it's impressive, to say the least, that Tim McDermott has established himself at the front of the pack of sports marketing in Philly—first with his distinguished tenure as CMO of the Eagles, and now with the 76ers. I've been lucky enough to interview Tim in both roles. (He also served as CMO for the Washington Capitals professional hockey team, and during his tenure there the Caps sold out all forty-one home games in a season for the first time in franchise history.)

In this interview, Tim explains how—regardless of how the guys on the field or the court or the ice are performing—teams can keep relationships strong with their fans. The lessons are invaluable for all marketers, as they explain how and why to stay the course in spite of forces beyond our control.

How have data and CRM platforms figured into your work with the 76ers?

Data is a major part of our strategy. We're heavily invested in infrastructure, software, and human capital in order to re-engineer what we're doing on the data science side. We've rolled out Salesforce across the company, which also requires retooling our processes and our staffing efforts. We're trying to be much more a data-centric operation, using data to help us make more sophisticated and objective decisions. We're also building a data warehouse that will allow us to do a lot more sophisticated marketing.

So this is a big transformation. How is this impacting your role at the 76ers?

The last three years of my career have seen an amazing transformation from what it means to be a marketer. It's almost like you're a technology officer. You need to be able to speak the language of database marketing and understand what it is that we're building, how we build it, and what we do with it once it's built. If you look back a few years ago, it was easier to say, "Oh, that's the content group; that's the digital group; that's the Web group; that's the marketing group." Now "digital" strategy no longer operates in its own carved-out department.

Is marketing a sports team fundamentally different from marketing consumer packaged goods?

I think there are a lot of similarities between marketing a sports property and marketing for other companies. The reality is we're probably doing the same things that the marketers of other retail-oriented companies are doing. We've got "widgets" to sell in the form of tickets. And we go through the exercise of segmentation, targeting, and positioning our products and our brand the same way that other marketers do. We build brands. We engage in all the different forms of marketing and advertising as other companies do. So we're doing everything from market research to CRM implementations, to automated emails, to managing social digital campaigns, to direct marketing, to direct response. You name it and I think we do it.

But from a more strategic perspective, I think sports teams are really media companies. We aggregate millions of impressions from the people who come to our games, watch us on TV shows, websites, Facebook, Twitter, and all the different vehicles that are out there. At the end of the day, we can aggregate communities of people through all these channels. And as a result of that, I think you'll see us acting and executing in ways more like those of a media company.

Philadelphia sports fans are famously enthusiastic, to put it nicely. Talk to me about the role the fans play in building your brands.

If you are a sports executive or even if you're an owner of a sports team, I think you're really a steward of a brand. It's a public trust. And that's the way I tend to look at it. I think if you take that approach and you think of it as the fans being at the heart of team, then you'll always do the right thing. You simply do what's right for the fans. And it takes a lot of the complexity out of it. This approach makes it so that even in times that aren't so good on the field, or on the ice, or on the court, fans are still showing up.

Can you give me a specific example of how you engaged with your fans when you were with the Eagles?

With the Eagles, we created a 35-person advisory board of passionate season ticket holders, with membership running two years. It wasn't just a glorified focus group. The people who signed up to be part of this board signed up to be solutions providers. They told us what we were doing right and what we were doing wrong from the serious fan's perspective. The quid pro quo was, they also had to help us come up with solutions to the problem, not just tell us what we're doing wrong. We looked at them as an extension of our marketing department who would help us create solutions. It was truly a concept of listening, engaging, and developing trust with them.

KEY TAKEAWAYS

- *Effective CRM (Customer Relationship Management) programs start with a commitment to gathering data about your customers at every possible point of contact.*

- *Done correctly, CRM programs not only help the marketer communicate efficiently with customers but also create a better customer experience by delivering hyper-relevant messages.*

- *Your "digital" strategy should be an integral part of your overall strategy.*

Further reading:

Bryan and Jeffrey Eisenberg, *Waiting for Your Cat to Bark?: Persuading Customers When They Ignore Marketing*

Md
Mobilizing Digital

Mobilizing Macy's

"Be everywhere, do everything, and never forget to astonish the customer."

Martine Reardon
Macy's

The chance to talk to Macy's CMO Martine Reardon about marketing is a bit like shopping at the flagship Macy's store on Manhattan's West 34th Street. It's hard to know where to start! Martine's knowledge and expertise spans so many "departments," and the temptation to spend time browsing all of them—from leadership to brand building to customer experience to mix modeling and beyond—is strong.

But of course, she didn't have all day to chat with me. So I did my very best to stick to a "shopping list" of prime topics facing today's marketers—first and foremost, Web content with a focus on mobile. The Macy's Web presence is spectacular and constantly improving, and Martine is the creative driving force behind how it continues to evolve. The range of marketing activity alone is staggering, yet thanks to a few overarching principles, it's easy to see how Martine and her sizable team pull it all together and bring "The Magic of Macy's" to life.

Is there a phrase that sums up your approach to marketing?

We embrace a saying from Macy's very own Margaret Getchell (the first woman executive in retail), who said: "Be everywhere, do everything, and never forget to astonish the customer." It's a motto we live by here, and I think having a legacy of such pioneering executives is an inspiration to all of us. It has fostered an ambition and entrepreneurialism that is a part of our culture.

Considering that Macy's is a symbol of tradition, how important do you feel it is to take advantage of new trends and be early adopters of technologies such as Apple Pay and Shopkick?

Our top priority at Macy's is to serve the customer. With the customer at the center of every decision we make, it's essential for us to quickly and effectively address their needs. This is why you've seen Macy's at the forefront of testing new technologies and in some cases being early adopters of innovations that enhance our customers' shopping experiences. Whether it's more relevant, targeted marketing that cuts through the clutter and speaks to the needs and wants of that customer, or a technology that speeds up the check-out process, we will look to test and adopt strategies and innovations that provide customer value and support.

Of course, we're always testing newness in our omnichannel strategy and with technology—including our recent launch with Apple Pay, rolling out Shopkick nationally, launching Macy's My Wallet, enhancing our shopping apps, offering Macy's Image Search, expanding buy online/ pickup in store, and testing same-day delivery.

What have your experiences been with mobile marketing to date?

We've made sure that our mobile media strategy is grounded in a deep understanding of how our customers are engaging with their smartphone and tablet devices. Our customers at Macy's tend to be quite mobile-centric. To that end, we've invested in tactics such as mobile and tablet digital display, SMS, and mobile paid search.

We've also evaluated mobile usage penetration in cross-device channels like digital audio and social media, and use those insights to drive a mobile-first approach to those channels. In addition, we've recently relaunched our Macy's mobile app with significant improvements to the user experience and have launched a brand-new Macy's Image Search app that leverages visual recognition technology to populate search results. We're also continuing to explore the in-store beacons space. Looking ahead, we see a lot of white space in mobile analytics and attribution, and look forward to developments that will help us better understand the impact of mobile media investment to total omnichannel sales.

We also run mobile and tablet-based digital retargeting campaigns and are testing into cross-screen retargeting in Spring 2015. This is a powerful tactic that capitalizes on connecting with customers who've expressed intent to purchase with us. As well, we're launching a social shopping test in Q4 with Instagram, which will really help us better understand how to unlock the opportunity to drive sales through social media and potentially drive higher conversion directly on a mobile device.

What's working for you these days in social media? Did you try anything new this year that you can share?

We focus on a balanced approach between great publishing, meaningful engagement, and effective paid media. What's important is clearly defining what success metrics to apply, based on the social media tactic being evaluated. Targeted direct response campaigns serve quite a different purpose than top-funnel branded publishing, but when planned and executed holistically, provide real value for our brand.

We're always testing, learning, and iterating in the social media space. We're intrigued by the explosive growth of video on Facebook since the rollout of auto-play, and have run some campaigns over the last year using Facebook's video ad product. We continue to explore how best to leverage Twitter's natural affinity with TV, as a second-screen companion to broadcast and branded integrations. We're working hard to grow our footprint on YouTube through targeted pre-roll, original content, and content collaborations with creators. We recently ran a very fun UGC-based campaign on YouTube as part of our Back to School efforts.

We've also recently begun publishing on Wanelo, with the objective of connecting with their fast-growing and incredibly valuable audience base. And we continue to focus on our Pinterest publishing and paid media strategy. We think there is an enormous runway for us to utilize Pinterest not only as a means of showcasing great social publishing, but also as a visual search engine that allows us to facilitate product discovery and drive traffic to our eCommerce site.

KEY TAKEAWAYS

- *Having a mobile strategy starts with the realization that your customers are spending many hours every day on their mobile devices.*

- *Mobile is far more than a messaging platform. It is creating a number of ways to better service customers with things like bill pay and virtual dressing rooms.*

- *Ask yourself how mobile can enhance your customer's experience.*

Further reading:
Nir Eyal, *Hooked: How to Build Habit-Forming Products*

America Runs on Mobile

"Most great ideas flow from the consumer."

John Costello
Dunkin' Donuts

John Costello has one of marketing's most impressive resumes, with stints at Procter & Gamble, PepsiCo, The Home Depot, and other notable brands leading up to his current role as President, Global Marketing & Innovation at Dunkin' Brands. Dunkin' Donuts is a brand that's evolved successfully over the decades, while launching some of the most unforgettable marketing campaigns in America's collective memory, including the current "America Runs on Dunkin'" advertising campaign. With John now in charge of marketing, customer engagement, R&D, and consumer product efforts, the future looks bright for Dunkin' as mobile technology becomes a bigger presence in all our lives.

John's insights are invaluable for any marketer who knows that earning a share of precious space on "the small screen" of mobile devices must be a top priority. So grab a cup of America's favorite coffee and enjoy. (Be sure to also check out the interview before this one with Martine Reardon of Macy's for more killer mobile insights.)

How important is mobile marketing to Dunkin's overall marketing mix?

For a company like Dunkin' Donuts, mobile and marketing go hand-in-hand. The surge in mobile usage, coupled with the busy, on-the-go Dunkin' guest, creates a very compelling business case for us. By launching the Dunkin' Mobile App, DD Perks® Rewards Program, and offering mobile payments, we created an entirely new level of speed and convenience that further distinguishes our brand to current and new customers throughout the country.

Aside from the Dunkin' app, how are you leveraging mobile?

While the majority of our mobile efforts are focused on adding value for our consumers through the Dunkin' Mobile App, we do believe that it's critical to optimize for mobile across all of our digital touch points. With consumers increasingly reliant on their mobile devices for information, it's important that our website, online advertising, emails, social media communications, DD Perks Rewards Program, and more all be optimized for the mobile audience.

Each month, we also host a number of fun promotions and programs for our consumers on mobile-friendly social media platforms. We recently enhanced our involvement with ESPN's Monday Night Countdown using unique videos featuring famed NBA impersonator and social media sensation Brandon Armstrong (@BdotAdot5) celebrating excessive celebrations and the fun side of football culture. Additionally, Dunkin' Donuts was the first company to leverage ESPN's talent on Periscope. Fans are encouraged via posts on ESPN's and Dunkin' Donuts' social channels to tweet questions and messages related to each Monday Night Football game, using #DDFieldPass.

The goal of creating the content and sharing it across social media channels allows Dunkin' Donuts to engage with users who enjoy watching Monday Night Football while leveraging a mobile device to connect with others about the game.

We also partnered with Google's Waze navigation app to engage with people in mobile app environments. Dunkin' Donuts was one of the first brands to map our locations with Waze and we have used geo-targeted ads to target Waze users who are driving near Dunkin' Donuts restaurants. To capture the excitement for the start of football season and promote our new Tailgater Breakfast Sandwich, we recently enhanced our partnership with a fun, light-hearted campaign to bring the voice of New England Patriots player Rob Gronkowski to the Waze app.

Can you comment on the results you've seen from these initiatives?

Overall, we're very pleased with the response to our mobile initiatives. The success of these programs supports the importance of taking a 360-degree approach and thinking thoughtfully about the best platforms that will help us to engage with Dunkin' Donuts guests. The future of mobile for us is to continue putting Dunkin' in everyone's hands. We see a lot of potential for mobile to be an extension of the Dunkin' Donuts experience. The Dunkin' Mobile App has been very popular with our guests, with over 14 million downloads, and we see a strong opportunity with mobile having more than 3 million DD Perks® members since we launched the loyalty initiative nationally in early 2014.

Are you still finding TV to be effective at driving traffic for Dunkin' Donuts?

While traditional marketing remains very important for Dunkin', our investments in digital, social, mobile, and loyalty marketing are increasing even more rapidly.

What will determine the future balance of your marketing mix?

All of these investments are driven by five key principles: First, most great ideas flow from the consumer. Whether it's B2B or B2C, there's really no substitute for truly understanding your customers' pain points and how you can address them.

Second, building brand differentiation is the most important thing a marketer can focus on because it answers the fundamental question: Why should consumers choose your brand over all of their other choices?

Third, building a strong team both inside and outside of your organization is imperative. It's not just about the people who report to you, but also about your peers within the organization and the key agencies and technology partners with whom you work.

Fourth, tactics matter. While developing the right strategy is important, executing that strategy to the highest standards can really make a difference.

Fifth, agility. The environment in which we compete is changing more rapidly than ever before, so it's important to be agile and adapt your plans as needed.

The bottom line is that, while the way consumers learn about brands, consume information, and decide where to buy products has changed over the years, they are still looking for better solutions to their everyday challenges. All five of these principles flow from the core principle of understanding your consumers' unmet needs and meeting them better than anybody else.

KEY TAKEAWAYS

- *Integrating mobile is no longer an optional luxury but rather a required component of a satisfying customer experience.*

- *Well-designed mobile applications are driving purchase and increasing loyalty for brands like Dunkin' Donuts.*

- *Don't just rely on your internal team when it comes to implementing new technology like mobile apps.*

Further reading:
Ted Schadler, Josh Bernoff, and Julie Ask, *The Mobile Mind Shift: Engineer Your Business to Win in the Mobile Moment*

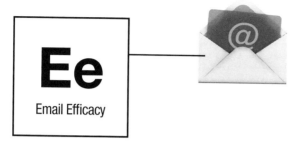

Ee

Email Efficacy

Email: Never Out of Style

"J.Crew is constantly working to improve the customer experience."

Shannon Smith
J.Crew

While social has opened amazing new possibilities for telling a brand story and connecting with customers, email has quietly held steady as the unglamorous workhorse of effectively engaging with an audience and driving sales online. Yes, we all get too many emails. But we still open and read the ones that catch our interest. And emails are a blank canvas on which marketers can communicate more or less freely, without being forced to fit their messaging inside a social network's decreed guidelines (like, for example, 140 characters).

As print media's woes continue to pile up, savvy marketers are realizing that an increased focus on email in the marketing mix is not only cost-effective but also a fantastic complement to the story they're weaving on social and elsewhere.

A data-driven marketer who has leveraged this fact very effectively is Shannon Smith, most of all when she was in charge of marketing for J.Crew. Shannon's focus on email was a "perfect fit" for the clothing mega-brand, and she generously shares the keys to its success here. We also chatted about related matters of customer engagement and retention that every marketer should understand.

Can you describe the initiative you led at J.Crew to use email in order to engage and sell to customers?

In 2013, I led J.Crew through the transition onto the Responsys email platform. (Responsys was subsequently acquired by Oracle and integrated into their Marketing Cloud.) They are a best-in-class service platform, which enabled J.Crew with a much more robust set of capabilities around customer segmentation and targeted marketing campaigns. Our email segmentation strategy became about capturing not only customer purchase history, but also website browse and email engagement behavior (opens, clicks, etc.). In addition, we launched a series of email triggers including Abandoned Cart and "Category Browse" campaigns that drove millions of incremental dollars in email revenue.

What were some of the benefits moving to that platform?

The capabilities it provided in bringing vast amounts of customer online behavior into our segmentation allowed us to significantly improve the productivity of our email campaigns through better segmentation of our customer base. We were able to incorporate products customers are interested in (indicated by browsing and email engagement) in addition to past purchases, which is incredibly powerful.

What were some changes you drove at J.Crew to improve the customer experience?

J.Crew is constantly working to improve the customer experience, from the design and fit of the clothes, to the services offered in stores, to the website functionality. My role in this endeavor was to constantly strive to deliver more relevant, personalized marketing communications to our customers, providing them with information about the products that would be of interest to them, whether it was our women's new arrivals, a new men's suiting line with a different fit, or great children's clothes. I worked towards this in our email marketing program, our catalog versioning, and our rewards program, the J.Crew credit card.

Can you discuss the evolution of the J.Crew brand while you worked there, and how you communicated that to customers?

The brand has shifted from a more traditional, basics-driven retailer (think roll-neck sweaters, barn jackets, khakis and button-downs) to a much more fashion-forward brand with runway shows during New York Fashion Week. This was largely driven by the design and merchant teams, with the evolution of the merchandise itself, and supported by the creative positioning of the marketing, including the site, catalog, and email.

It's not easy to change a brand's position in the eyes of the consumer, but J.Crew is fortunate in that most customers love the new styles. One thing that has been incredibly successful in shifting the brand's image is creative collaborations with high-end designers, from Comme des Garçon to Alden Shoe Company. The direct marketing team's role is to get the most relevant product in front of the customer, and communicate that the brand offers tremendous product breadth with a wide range of styles and price points.

Can you talk a bit about your experience with loyalty programs and what it takes to get them off the ground?

J.Crew's loyalty program is tied to the J.Crew credit card. But at Sephora, I managed the "Beauty Insider" program for four years, growing it from launch to an active customer base of over ten million members. In terms of getting it off the ground, it was an enormous company initiative involving everyone in the marketing, operations, store, and technical organizations. It had a tremendously successful launch and grew quickly, but loyalty programs require significant effort and funding to keep them fresh, top-of-mind, engaging, and meaningful.

At Sephora, I led the launch of the VIP premium tier and new types of program benefits, including new point-level rewards. The Beauty Insider program has been invaluable in that it enabled the company to build a customer database and personalize marketing communications to their enormous base of retail customers. However, I was constantly working with our analytics team to measure the ROI of the program holistically. It's not an easy thing to do.

I believe loyalty programs can have real value for companies, particularly when many retailers are selling the same products and competing for customers, like department stores. That said, I always caution a company considering a loyalty program to be very thoughtful and clear on the strategy for their program, how it aligns with their brand, and how they will derive value from it, because it's going to be a big investment.

KEY TAKEAWAYS

- *Email remains a potent weapon for most marketers.*

- *Sophisticated email systems that mine customer data can drive millions of dollars in incremental sales.*

- *Email success can be tied to relevance, timeliness, and a commitment to continuous testing.*

Further reading:
Peter Shankman, *Nice Companies Finish First: Why Cutthroat Management Is Over—and Collaboration Is In*

Catching Lightning in a Bottle

"As you would with a new acquaintance or friend in real life, find a common interest between you and the consumer and talk about that."

Adam Naide
Cox Communications

Marketing has always been a fast-paced business, and pouncing on a sudden opportunity can make a career. But before the advent of the Internet, such opportunities came along infrequently; by the time a marketing message reached the public, the moment was often forgotten.

Now, instead of having to buy ad space in a print publication and wait for it to run, or drop a bunch of direct mail off at the post office and cross your fingers hoping it will reach its destination, marketers can take to social media and get an ultra-timely and unforgettable message out to the entire world seconds after the event happens. And the results can be massive. This is Real-Time Marketing (RTM).

The iconic RTM example is still probably Oreo throwing together a "You Can Still Dunk in the Dark" mini-campaign within minutes of the power going out during the 2013 Super Bowl. The whole world was watching as Oreo—in a single unplanned stroke that cost a relative pittance—upstaged every mega-budgeted Super Bowl TV ad with a simple graphic that racked up 10,000 retweets in barely an hour.

It's not a fad. RTM is here to stay, and smart marketers in the social media space are now always on the lookout for the next viral explosion. One of the best is Adam Naide, Executive Director of Marketing for Social Media at Cox Communications. In this interview, Adam gives a pithy and honest look at what does and doesn't work when it comes to RTM.

What are some wins for Cox TV in the area of RTM?

First, the Breaking Bad final season. Our objective was to drive fan growth and increase engagement on @CoxTV during the final season of the show. There was a huge volume of social conversation, specifically on Twitter, around the final season of Breaking Bad. Our team developed a real-time campaign to cover each episode of the final season with live coverage, engaging custom content, Vine videos, and an RT-to-win contest. As a result, the campaign attracted 3,145 new followers, nearly doubling the follower base on Twitter. It also led to 5,757 retweets.

Second, National Donut Day. Our objective in this case was to capitalize on real-time opportunities as they presented themselves. In summary, custom creative was produced for Cox's Facebook page tying *The Simpsons* to National Donut Day. The post saw immediate lift on Facebook and was promoted to amplify impact. Seeing that #NationalDonutDay was trending on Twitter, the team quickly posted and promoted the creative on Twitter as well. As a result, the tweet saw 87 percent higher engagement than average tweets posted to @CoxTV and 67 percent greater cost efficiency than average promoted posts on the handle.

Can you give an example of a real-time program that didn't work as well as you hoped?

Sure. We had hoped to capitalize on social buzz around the MTV Video Music Awards to engage music fans on Twitter while growing the fan base. So @CoxTV live-tweeted the awards through an existing brand influencer "Sara" who had previously covered TV and entertainment for the brand. Unfortunately, Sara entered the live-tweeting event with a pre-existing personality that didn't jibe with the VMA audience. She wasn't a fan of the artists being featured and didn't participate in the conversion in a relatable way. In this case, the live-tweeting event garnered just 80 new followers and 1,024 retweets,

Why do you think brands fail so often to get RTM right?

Most failures stem from assuming the public perceives the brand in the same way that the brand perceives itself.

How do you avoid this?

Start with the current behavior of consumers and find ways to mimic, play off of, or join that activity. Don't force an unwanted idea or perception on consumers. Monitor what organically bubbles to the surface in your industry or trending hashtags that are relevant to the brand. As you would with a new acquaintance or friend in real life, find a common interest between you and the consumer and talk about that.

Let's review some of the logistical issues when dealing with RTM. Staffing?

Leveraging real-time opportunities requires full-time monitoring. Listening to social activity is the best way to find opportunities that bubble to the surface.

Client approval process?

To take advantage of real-time opportunities, a level of trust must exist between agency partners and the client. Planned opportunities are created by the agency and approved by the client, but many real-time opportunities must be created and promoted based on shared goals and strategies for the year, without client approval.

Things to avoid?

Brands should avoid forcing real-time content. Steer clear of touchy subjects and irrelevant holidays. For example, a baking brand should talk about Thanksgiving but should not talk about Veteran's Day.

Barriers to success?

Time and resources. Joining in on trending conversations requires the ability to identify the opportunity, ideate on a response, create content, gain approval, and post. This process can be complicated on weekends or after business hours.

Metrics?

Real-time marketing is really about exposure and sentiment. Metrics like reach, impressions, retweets, and earned positive buzz are all metrics that should be assessed.

KEY TAKEAWAYS

- *Relevancy: Do what makes sense for your brand, don't force it.*

- *Creativity: Stand out, in a good way.*

- *Process: Have a plan for the unexpected. Be ready to take on ad hoc opportunities.*

Further reading:
Brian Solis, *Engage: The Complete Guide for Brands and Businesses to Build, Cultivate, and Measure Success in the New Web*

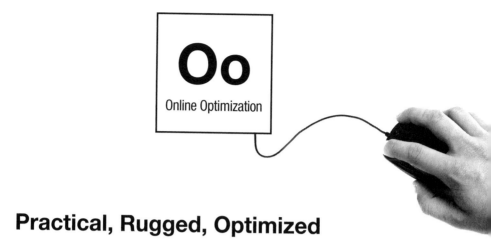

Oo

Online Optimization

Practical, Rugged, Optimized

"Too many changes at once makes it almost impossible to isolate performance."

Steve Fuller
L.L.Bean

Having issued its first mail order catalog in 1912, clothing company L.L.Bean knows a thing or two about customer acquisition and loyalty-building. Perhaps even more impressive than its longevity is how deftly L.L.Bean has navigated the changes to how marketing is done. Today it has a powerful online presence and vibrant eCommerce site along with its still-mighty catalog.

As a marketer, L.L.Bean's CMO Steve Fuller is a little like L.LBean clothes—prioritizing practicality and fundamental quality over flashiness and trend-hopping. This isn't to say he isn't forward-thinking, as you'll read shortly about his adoption of cutting-edge programmatic techniques. He's also refreshingly candid about where he and the company can still improve. Everyone can learn something of value from the way Steve keeps L.L.Bean's online presence optimized and customers engaged.

You have been at the forefront of eCommerce for a while. What have you been trying recently from a digital marketing standpoint that has worked particularly well?

In our case, it was better execution of the "basics." Our search programs—paid, natural, etc.—have been lacking in recent years and we definitely got those programs back on track in 2014. And after testing nearly every alternative available, it appears we might have finally beaten the in-house product recommendation engine that we built way back in 2005.

Did you try some things that didn't work as well as you'd hoped?

A few. We have a fairly robust analytics cloud in development. We like the overall direction of the project, but it's progressing slower than we would have hoped. L.L.Bean also moved to a new chat/social media tracking platform that has been a disappointment.

If you could wave a magic wand, what is the one thing you'd like to see fixed about digital marketing and why?

I'm not sure the right word is "fixed," but demand/investment attribution is still an undeveloped area. There are a lot of people doing interesting things, but the methodologies—and results—vary wildly. And while I understand the desire to protect proprietary research, the "black box" approach of many companies makes them a challenge to evaluate.

When bringing on new tech platforms what are some of the pitfalls to be avoided?

Expecting too much too soon. These are incredibly complex systems from both a production and analytics perspective. Implementation "sequencing" is also something to watch. Too many changes at once make it almost impossible to isolate performance.

How has programmatic marketing helped you reach your overall marketing objectives?

I want to be the first to say that we've got a long way to go with programmatic. We learn something each and every day. But we're especially pleased with its ability to help bring "scale" to those programs in an efficient way—both from a presentation and an analytics perspective.

What were some of the challenges of adopting programmatic and what advice would you give to another marketer who is just getting started?

The easiest thing to overlook is the amount of production work required to do it right. Ads need to be created, they need to be trafficked, etc.

The other advice is to find a good partner. We looked at a number of possible providers and ended up with MediaMath. Not only did we like their technology platform, but they were invaluable in helping us make the operational transition. Again, you've got a tremendous amount of detail and process to get right in order to leverage these new tools—MediaMath helped make that happen.

Programmatic media buying continues to gain share of overall digital spending. Are you finding this to be the case at L.L.Bean and, if so, what are the real advantages of programmatic buying?

Directionally, yes. Some of it depends on how you're defining "programmatic," but we've certainly moved a large portion of our digital spending into the category. And it's all about scale. Programmatic's ability to facilitate scale in targeting/personalization without major investments of human capital is often overlooked as a benefit.

The grand vision among programmatic advocates is that ultimately all media will become addressable, which in turn would create the opportunity to fully customize and optimize every type of communication. Is this an appealing vision to you as a marketer? Also, given the production requirements to effectively execute programmatic buying on digital, can you imagine doing this same level of customization with video channels?

Theoretically, it's awesome. I worry a little about the "shared experience" impact, but the ability to control investment and messaging across all channels redefines "marketing aspiration."

And my first reaction to your second sentence was "exactly." I can't even begin to imagine what it would be like to do true video customization/personalization for video. But then again, five years ago I couldn't have imagined that we'd be shooting our TV ads on digital SLRs, GoPros, and—in Apple's case—iPhones. When you think about the advancement in video over the past few years, it's truly amazing how quickly it's progressed.

Which leads to my last point—anything is possible.

KEY TAKEAWAYS

- *The online optimization process never ends.*
- *The advent of programmatic buying has made it possible to optimize multiple variables in real time.*

Further reading:
Craig Dempster and John Lee, *The Rise of the Platform Marketer: Performance Marketing with Google, Facebook, and Twitter, Plus the Latest High-Growth Digital Advertising Platforms*

We

Web Experience

Barking up the Right Online Tree

"We leverage technology and data every day to make quick enhancements that are in the best interest of our customers."

Rose Hamilton
Pet360

It's no longer news that eCommerce is a force to be reckoned with. As the Internet grows ever more important in how consumers make buying decisions and—more importantly—how they act on those decisions, our priorities as marketers need to change accordingly. For starters, it means shifting focus towards providing a seamless and engaging Web experience to prospective and returning customers alike. After all, it's very easy for them to close that browser tab.

How to do this is less obvious. But observing what Rose Hamilton has accomplished as EVP and CMO of Pet360.com furnishes excellent clues. At first glance, Pet360 may seem like an online pet supply shop…which it is, but it's also a lot more. Rose has crafted the site to be a one-stop destination for "pet parents" (a term any good pet owner should identify with) to find advice, community, and much more to help them better enjoy the presence of that special furry someone in their lives.

A CMO has a lot of choices in terms of where they invest their time. What have your top priorities been in the last couple of years?

As with any business, customer acquisition, retention, and loyalty are critical measures that require a strong and differentiated brand. To set ourselves apart from our competition, our focus has been on creating valuable and relevant experiences for pet parents. We know firsthand that pet parenting can be challenging and even a bit overwhelming at times. New obstacles can arise at every stage of a pet's life, and pet parents are in constant need of support.

Most will say their vet provides answers to their pet parenting challenges; however, a vet visit takes place on average once per year and only lasts around fifteen minutes. As a result, pet parents are looking to friends, family, and various online resources for answers to their questions. The problem is that not every pet has the same needs. A Golden Retriever puppy, for example, has very different needs than a senior Yorkshire Terrier. What works for some pets will not work for all.

Pet360 is a relatively young brand. Do you find you are more nimble than your larger competition?

Absolutely. As a digital brand, we don't have the distraction of brick and mortar operations. We leverage technology and data every day to make quick enhancements that are in the best interest of our customers.

How are you gaining competitive advantage?

We knew we would never win on price. Over the past two years, we have evolved from a pure play eCommerce business to a lifestyle brand focused on making pet parenting easier. Today, Pet360.com is the only experience (digital or offline) that truly improves pet parents' lives by offering expert information, an active community of pet parents, and a vast assortment of products all in a highly personalized manner. By bringing all three elements (community, content, and commerce) together with a layer of personalization, we're able to deliver a truly differentiated brand experience that builds engagement, trust, and ultimately advocacy, resulting in higher lifetime value and lower acquisition costs.

Pet lovers are famously passionate about their animals. How do you balance building emotional relationships with your customers and the need to drive transactions?

Emotional relationships come first and eventually lead to advocacy and trust longer term. Pet supplies can be a commodity, but the expert advice and connection to other pet parents set us apart. The Pet360 platform inspires engagement and emotional connection at every touch point along the pet parenting journey. By offering relevant solutions, we build trust, engagement, and frequency. As trust and emotional connection build, so will lifetime value and advocacy!

What role does social media play in what you do?

We prioritize building engagement over growing our popularity on social media. Social media enables us to engage with pet parents every day by answering questions, stimulating conversations, providing entertainment, gathering feedback, and connecting them to the people and resources they need most. Most importantly, social media is a way for us to connect 1:1 with pet parents in a very authentic way. It's an opportunity for us to continue to build and strengthen relationships with pet parents.

How about content marketing?

Content is at the core of our brand. We invest heavily in creating valuable content for pet parents that is delivered on our site, in social media, across traditional media, through our email communications, and by our various partners. Content marketing has been, and will continue to be, an area of investment and focus for Pet360. From a business model perspective, the efficiency and effectiveness of content marketing reduces the cost to acquire a customer and enables us to leverage paid channels in unique ways.

Since your customer relationship is primarily online, is it a challenge for you as CMO to stay close to your customers? If not, how are you doing it?

Actually, the digital space makes it easy for us to stay close to our customers. Every action they take online is measurable. We also monitor a variety of channels to keep a pulse on what our customers are saying, including our branded community, site behavior, surveys, call center reports, ratings and reviews, and social media. As a customer-centric brand, our customers guide our decisions at every turn. We're constantly reacting to consumer feedback and trends as we work to solve unmet pet parent needs.

KEY TAKEAWAYS

- *Exceptional Web experiences inspire engagement and make an emotional connection with the visitor.*

- *For online retailers, the trick is to blend content, community, and commerce with just the right level of personalization.*

- *Don't forget to build in feedback mechanisms and respond accordingly.*

Further reading:
Peter Shankman, *Zombie Loyalists: Using Great Service to Create Rabid Fans*

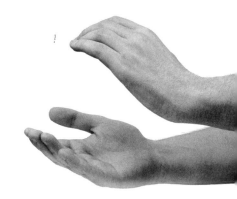

Secrets of a Viral Hitmaker

"Good ideas are wonderful, but they're a dime a dozen. It all comes down to execution"

Paul Greenberg
CollegeHumor Media

Stop me if you've heard this one: A rabbi, a priest, and a content marketer walk into a bar. The bartender asks: "Well gents, what'll it be?"

The rabbi glances around the crowded room lamenting, "I see you are serving some of my tribe here, would you mind sending them to temple on Friday night?"

The priest says, "Yes, and if you would send the lost sheep of my flock here to church on Sunday, that would be most kind."

Then the content marketer jumps onto the bar and shouts at the top of his lungs, "Drinks on me, everyone; our 'Ten Paths to Sobriety' video just went viral!"

Now that we've established that the comedy world dodged a bullet when I chose marketing as a career, please meet a young man who does know funny: Paul Greenberg, who at the time of this interview was CEO of CollegeHumor Media (owned by IAC). Paul's expertise goes beyond just getting laughs—he also knows, perhaps better than anyone else in the game, how to parlay quality Web content into the sort of profitable online traffic most marketers can only dream about.

Today, Paul is CEO of *Nylon* magazine. This snapshot of his successful tenure at CollegeHumor is timeless advice for any marketer who dreams of viral success online.

When did you join CollegeHumor, and how have things changed since you've been in charge?

I joined two and a half years ago. Since then, we've seen forty percent growth year over year in traffic. We're now the eighth largest YouTube channel with over 4.5 million subscribers, we have 15 million monthly unique visitors which again is way up over from where we were a couple of years ago, and we do 100 million video streams per month.

It sounds like CollegeHumor is a lot more than a website.

Definitely. We're a multi-platform, multimedia studio. We create an enormous amount of content and we publish it on our website, but also on YouTube, game consoles, and connected TVs. We're working on traditional long-form television shows and are close to deals with several major cable networks. We're also publishing books, videos, and have made one full-length movie, *Coffee Town*.

At what point do you realize you've got a viral hit on your hands?

Once it starts to get to the half-million views level, we start to really pay attention. And we don't just look at views. We're very social media-oriented and huge on data analysis—we want to know the ratio between likes/shares and views. Is something getting shared a lot but not watched a lot? Do we need to give it a little push somewhere? Is it getting watched a lot on our site but not shared very much? Is there something that doesn't make it go viral?

Do you have any way of predicting a video's viral success? And if you see early signs of a hit, do you do more to fuel the fire?

Yes, absolutely. Creatively, we have something called the "Sieve," which is our secret formula for viral videos. As you might imagine, we keep that very tightly protected, but as the evidence suggests, it works pretty well. How directly and thoroughly a video meets the "checkpoints" of the Sieve can be a good indicator of how it's going to do. Then when the numbers start coming in and they're good, we might say: "Alright, we've got to keep this on our homepage, or we need to make sure we post it again to Facebook," or something like that.

It sounds like rapid experimentation adjustments are important to your process.

Exactly. You can't be afraid to fail, you have to be willing to put yourself out there every day with something new. And they're not all going to be gems, but you get enough hits so that your audience starts to realize, "Wow, these guys have something interesting going on and I'll go along with them when something is not as great, but I know when I come back there's going to be something for me."

If you're putting out fifty videos per month, how many have to be big hits for you to be happy?

Two or three big hits, I would say. Which is not as easy as it sounds!

What are your thoughts on video length?

We try to keep it under two or two-and-a-half minutes. Anything longer and people really just glaze.

Is one type of video more likely to go viral than another?

Often the ones that go really viral are new sketches. Because it is a new idea, it gets introduced, people latch onto it, they love it, and they send it around.

Are series any different from a virality standpoint?

With a series you are less apt to get into the Zeitgeist really quickly, and so you build an audience over time. So in a series we'll often see episodes further down the chain do better than the original ones. Or better yet, we'll see people catching up via "binge-watching."

How about a few secrets to your success?

Never stop working, ever. Be as aggressive as possible, have a desire to win, and work your absolute hardest—because there is always somebody who is going to work harder than you. Good ideas are wonderful, but they're a dime a dozen. It all comes down to execution—doing it right and doing it well, consistently.

KEY TAKEAWAYS

- *Going viral is not an everyday result for even the most successful and talented content producers.*

- *Even if you create an amazing video, it may need the boost of paid media to push it "viral."*

- *Commit to creating original content on an ongoing basis and there's hope one just might catch on!*

Further reading:
Jonah Berger, *Contagious: Why Things Catch On*

VI. Noble Pursuits

Marketing is about commerce, and commerce is about money.

Our success or failure as marketers can be measured by several metrics, but at some point we all have to answer to whether or not the tangible effects of our marketing have justified the cumulative investment of time and resources. From this fact, one might superficially conclude that the "almighty dollar" has to come before all else in every marketing decision we make.

This begs the question: Are marketing campaigns and having a higher purpose inherently at odds with one another?

And perhaps also the question: Why do you get out of bed and dive headfirst into the trenches of marketing every morning?

Surely there's a financial incentive for what we do, but—despite what the public may be inclined to think at times—it's rarely the only incentive for the most successful marketers. Most of us who have lasted in this business got into it looking for not just money but also meaning. And then we learned it was a steep challenge to keep the bottom line strong while kindling the fire of our higher purpose, both on an individual campaign level and also on a career level.

There are times when it seems like there's an either-or choice of more profits or more meaningful communication, and then we're gripped by a sinking feeling that keeping our jobs might mean holding our collective noses and going for the quickest sale.

Sr
Marketing as Service

Ss
Social Customer Service

Pc
Pure Creativity

Cc
Customer Centricity

Bu
Building Community

Gg
Going Green

F
Foundations

Sd
Sustainable Design

Lb
Living the Brand

So
Social Purpose

So with a tip of the hat to the Noble Gases that occupy the rightward column of the chemical Periodic Table, I present marketing's Noble Pursuits. In the following conversations, you'll hear from marketers who have unflinchingly pursued higher purpose in their work…and unflinchingly delivered outstanding bottom-line results.

Perhaps more than any other section in this Periodic Table, I hope you'll use this one as a prompt for introspection. After reading these interviews, think about what your Noble Pursuit is. If you're in marketing for the long haul, it's so important that you stay connected to a higher purpose beyond mere fun and profit. Believe me, you will run out of gas sooner rather than later if you don't.

Don't get me wrong, Noble Pursuits don't have to be some politically-charged permutation of "saving the world." Certainly, many do pertain to social responsibility or being a good corporate citizen. But if it fits your business and personality better, yours can simply be a renewed and ultra-specific commitment to how you'll serve your customers better than anyone else has ever served them.

When you read why people like the CMO of Audi of America (Loren Angelo, whom you'll meet shortly) or KIND visionary Daniel Lubetzky attack their work every single day with the same zeal they did when they were starting out, you'll see a diversity of options for how you can infuse your marketing efforts with meaning and a commitment to service.

Your Noble Pursuit is the "why" that will sustain you throughout a long and fulfilling career in marketing. After reading this section, I hope you'll see it just a bit more clearly.

Well Done Is Better than Well Said

"We don't do things just because they're a trend; we do things because we think it's the right thing to do for our customer."

John Hayes
American Express

Soap box time. Of all the elements required to be a successful CMO, few are more overlooked than Marketing as Service. The basic idea is relatively easy to grasp: Rather than starting with what you want to say to your consumers, focus first on what you can do for them. Here's an example near and dear to my heart from when Renegade worked with HSBC: The BankCab. New Yorkers who were HSBC customers and were lucky enough to hail this classic Checker cab were treated to a free ride anywhere in the city from the most knowledgeable cabbie in the five boroughs. It made headlines, and more importantly it made "The World's Local Bank" more than just a slogan.

One company that practices Marketing as Service regularly and has done so for decades is American Express, which helps explain why AmEx has been my go-to source for content since I started blogging in 2006. Among my favorite examples is Small Business Saturday. The service in this case not only establishes a day that puts the spotlight on small businesses and rivals Black Friday and Cyber Monday, but also enables small businesses to be more competitive throughout the year with marketing toolkits that highlight their distinct advantages over their larger competitors.

And helping small businesses grow is hardly an altruistic endeavor for AmEx. Years ago, the company realized that when their customers grow, AmEx grows right along with them. Enlightened self-interest propelled them to provide highly useful content in the pre-Internet days, in the form of breakfasts, newsletters and magazines, and more recently in their carefully curated online OPEN Forum. Interestingly, this "do" turned out to be more than just a useful service to its customers; it also attracted prospects once AmEx decided to make all the content public.

Which brings me to my interview with John Hayes, the long-time CMO of American Express. Hayes, who started his career on the agency side, has presided over a successful stream of "Marketing as Service" programs from those mentioned above to Membership Rewards, CEO BootCamp, the Women's Business Initiative, and two relatively recent social media experiments called Link Like Love and Card Sync. The commonality? A relentless commitment to doing the right thing for the AmEx customer.

Has a service mentality always been front-and-center at American Express? How does being a great service company affect your marketing?

American Express has been around since 1850, and when we first started, we were a freight forwarding company, not a payments company. Then we slowly moved into the travel business and the traveler's check business. The company was 108 years old before the first American Express card appeared. Since the beginning, there has been a focus on being a great service company, whether that service was freight forwarding, opening up markets for people to travel and experience the world, offering a safer way to carry money with travelers checks, or offering something like the American Express card to simplify people's lives and make it more rewarding. All of those things come from a service culture, a company focused on service.

As I understand it, there is not yet a clear link between OPEN Forum (AmEx's content and networking platform for small business owners) and significant new revenue. Yet the program is very popular and widely seen as a success. How is this so?

I think there are some general trends that are very positive, but you're right. When you get to a granular level, it's difficult to say this program generated these many cards and this much spend for American Express.

We have a belief that if you serve people well, they'll become your customers; because everyone wants and deserves to be served well. We don't require people to be a cardholder to use OPEN Forum. We created the site because we knew that part of enabling the success of small businesses was helping them understand what other small businesses had already learned to help them be successful. That's why we created it, and that's why we made it an "open" network—so that small business owners could find others that would be of most value to them.

When you've contributed in a meaningful way to a small business's success and then say, "Hey, I've got some other services for you. I've got a card that could help you manage inventory better," they are quite open to it because they'll say, "Well, you guys have already been helping me grow my business, enabling my success," and that's the philosophy. Some programs we can measure on a granular level, and some we can't, but we're careful not to overvalue the things we can measure or undervalue the things we can't.

Given that everybody is creating content and other companies are targeting small businesses like you are, what are you doing to stay ahead?

What's really important is that we don't do things just because they're a trend; we do things because we think it's the right thing to do for our customers. In 1971, we started a publishing group called American Express Publishing. Wow, what a concept. Who was talking about content in 1971? But this company had the foresight to understand that in order to be a lifestyle services company for businesses and people, you need to talk to them about their life, not what they're going to use to pay for something.

The philosophy that got this company to create a publishing group in 1971 is no different than the way we think about our company today. If you're in the service business, every interaction with a prospect or a customer should be a service interaction. We provided those magazines as a lifestyle service and if you look at what we are doing with American Express UNSTAGED for example—bringing music to so many people around the world on a live-stream basis—the philosophy is the same. That is our way of serving customers, based on their life and passions. We should be helping our customers experience what it is they want to experience, and many of these experiences are open architecture because we also want prospects to know what it feels like to be a member.

Have you seen your role as a CMO evolve over the last ten years?

My role has evolved a lot. First, it's evolved from the standpoint of understanding what is happening in the world related to media. How are people consuming media? How are they absorbing new messages? Those things have changed fairly remarkably in the last decade. Part of my job is to make sure I understand how the world works today whether that's social media, digital, or traditional, and how it's changing. How are brands being established in the landscape today?

My role is also about identifying which elements of American Express will not change from its origins and which elements absolutely will, in terms of how we go to market. Trust, security, and service will not change. This company has existed for 165 years because it has reinvented itself many times, but always grounded in the enduring values of trust, security, and service.

What role is big data playing in your job today?

Data is a fundamental part of what we do today and it's a great opportunity because data can allow us to optimize on a much shorter cycle. We also see it as an opportunity to serve customers better and of course as a company known for trust and security, we believe in using it in a privacy-centric way. With data, I can anticipate your needs, I can help you with the things you want, I can begin to understand what you might need in the future, so data can be very useful in service and marketing. I won't talk about marketing without mentioning service, because I think there's a lot of marketing out there that is of no service to anyone and frankly doesn't have much impact. The things that are sustainable are the marketing elements that serve people well. So data becomes an enormous opportunity not only to find prospects and continue the dialogue with our customers, but also to understand them and offer things that are a real service to them. This enables us to begin the relationship on a service level and not just a sales level.

As the CMO, how much influence do you have on the entire customer experience?

I don't know of a company that is structured in a way where the CMO has control over all customer touch points and in reality it's not practical. That said, it is the responsibility of the CMO to influence customer value and measure that value over time. This is fundamental to building a strong brand and business.

KEY TAKEAWAYS

- *The idea behind Marketing as Service is simple and proven—do something for your target and they will thank you with their business.*

- *AmEx figured out a long time ago that if they help small businesses grow, AmEx will grow along with them.*

- *Think of Marketing as Service as making deposits into the "goodwill bank" of your customers that ultimately you can redeem for incremental sales, loyalty, and referrals.*

Further reading:

Benjamin Franklin, *The Autobiography of Ben Franklin*

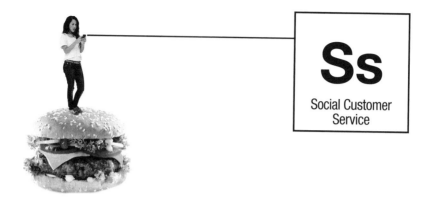

Ss

Social Customer
Service

The Twitterverse Is "Lovin' It"

"Every customer of McDonald's is important regardless of Klout, number of followers, or celebrity status."

Kim Musgrave
McDonald's

Somewhere out there, right now, as you read this, a marketer is hard at work trying to get more exposure on social media. And by "a marketer" I mean "a whole lot of marketers." The ability to consistently (and, being honest, rapidly) increase a brand's presence on social media has emerged as one of the most valuable skills in the industry.

But what do you do after you've got that huge following? If only the folks striving to get their brand's name to ring out louder on the social media airwaves could spend a few minutes in Kim Musgrave's chair... Until recently, Kim was the Social Media Team Leader at McDonald's, which means it was on her and her team to manage the one mention per second Mickey D's receives across its social media platforms. That's 3,600 per hour, 86,400 per day, every day.

Some of those mentions are praise, some are complaints. All of them need to be heard. So how did Kim ensure that the people reaching out to

McDonald's on social media get the attention they need to remain happy customers? Whether you have 500 or 5 million followers yourself, Kim's insights on interacting with your base are required reading if you want to win at social.

The Twitter handle @Reachout_McD is relatively new. Tell me a bit about the thinking behind this particular handle relative to @McDonalds and how it has worked thus far.

The @McDonalds Twitter handle was born in late 2009 as a way for our customers to follow us for the latest McDonald's news and promotions. As our follower count grew, so did the opportunity to give our customers a place to share feedback, ask a question, etc.

@ReachOut_McD Twitter tends to be mainly listening and responding versus creating original content. Just curious, why?

Our social service team responds to @McDonalds customer service issues via the @Reachout_McD dedicated handle. We wanted a place to celebrate our customers who have great experiences at McDonald's, so we retweet those as well.

There is a lot of chatter on Twitter about McDonald's every day. What kinds of challenges has this created from a listening standpoint?

McDonald's serves over twenty-eight million customers in the U.S. each day. In social media, McDonald's is currently mentioned every second! While tracking total volume/buzz is one metric, we really want to get to the "meat" of the conversations. Due to the fact that about 80 percent of our mentions are from Twitter, this context can be challenging with slang, sarcasm, and profanity. Is "Just killed this Big Mac" positive or negative? We are currently testing tools to get to the sentiment and emotion behind the mention.

Given all the noise, how do you decide what is worthy of a response? Or said differently, do you have different policies for how you deal with positive feedback from customers versus negative feedback?

Our cross-functional team focuses on @McDonalds for listening and engagement seven days a week. This team includes Customer Service (both at home office and call center), Communications, PR, and Agencies. As the volume of mentions has increased, we developed a "Playbook" with guidelines for response and a very simple Red, Yellow, Green light system.

Everyone talks about social listening but not every brand is doing it. How well do you think your team is listening, and are there any tools that are working particularly well for you?

McDonald's has been listening in social media since 2008 and the way we report to the business has evolved as we have communicated the value of social data. Sentiment is the most challenging, as I mentioned above, so having a tool that can capture the volume, then break down the context in an accurate way, continues to be an area of opportunity.

Can you provide an example of social listening that helped inform other business activities (marketing, product development, etc.)?

Improving the restaurant experience is one of the opportunities for McDonald's customer engagement in social. These engagement insights are combined with the traditional voice of customer insights to identify opportunities: How fast, accurate, and friendly is the service? Trending this over time (i.e., monthly) can provide opportunities for operations.

If a comment happens to come from a famous person, do you handle the response differently?

Every customer of McDonald's is important regardless of Klout, number of followers, or celebrity status. But we certainly do engage with celebrities when we can. McDonald's tweeted Al Roker because he missed his first day of work in thirty-nine years by sleeping in. We thought it would be fun to post about it regarding McCafé, and then they mentioned it on Good Morning America.

Let's talk about your social team structure. Do you have a separate group for brand social and service social?

We have a cross-functional team. Social customer service is my area, and I have a dedicated supervisor for Twitter customer service. We are currently working with a few of our call center agents to develop the social care process. Facebook is managed by an agency, but we stay very closely aligned and work on service processes.

How do you see service via social media evolving over the next 2 to 3 years? What kinds of things would you like to see improved?

I see the customer expecting brands to be very responsive (just like calling), but also authentic in social customer service—no auto replies. For brands with increasing mentions in social, having the best social tool for prioritization and routing will be a necessity.

KEY TAKEAWAYS

- *When approaching social media strategy, start first by asking how you can be of service to your customers rather than what you can say to them.*

- *Great social customer service is a 24/7 commitment to helping your customers whenever they need it.*

- *By carefully listening to issues customers express on social media, brands can identify a broad spectrum of opportunities for improvement.*

Further reading:
Jeanne Bliss, *"I Love You More Than My Dog": Five Decisions That Drive Extreme Customer Loyalty in Good Times and Bad*

Pc

Pure Creativity

Driving the Road Less Traveled

"A challenger spirit is crucial in everything we do."

Loren Angelo
Audi

Creativity is not optional for any marketing professional. But for premier brands such as luxury car maker Audi, it must be applied very judiciously or else years and even decades of progress can be undone by one "crazy-and-not-in-a-good-way" idea. (New Coke, anyone?). And with fast-paced digital media as the ascendant force in marketing, the opportunities to screw things up are more abundant than ever.

So it takes an EVP/CMO of Loren Angelo's caliber to ensure that creativity flows constantly for Audi of America, and also to ensure that only the best and most targeted new ideas reach Audi's audience. Loren's deep understanding of the relationship between form and function in marketing is just one ingredient in his astounding run of success at the brand, which includes forty-five consecutive monthly sales records and a 30 percent increase in brand opinion and consideration since 2006.

Creativity can emerge in a lot of different ways, from how you approach problems to creative marketing campaigns. How are you being creative in your current role?

Creativity is driven by staying authentic to your brand and your mission. I'm inspired by ideas where I can connect my brand with cultural moments that engage a conversation.

Some agency sages believe "it isn't creative unless it sells." Do you share that belief? If so, is there still a role for brand-building activities in your marketing mix that may not have an immediate or directly measurable impact on sales?

Building the Audi brand in America has been crucial to our current success of forty-five consecutive monthly sales records. Elevating brand opinion and consideration by over 30 percent since 2006 has come from an investment in repositioning Audi as the modern, progressive, luxury choice. When we bring smart, entertaining creative to market, demand rises and that drives sales.

Looking at the question above slightly differently, is there a case to be made for a brand like Audi that the medium can be the message? For example, does doing cutting edge marketing on, say, a mobile platform also say that Audi is a cutting edge brand that "gets it?"

Absolutely. Creativity comes in the message as well as the medium in which it's delivered. Building the brand with time-starved, affluent Americans requires us to bring unique ideas to a variety of channels. In addition to our unique thirty-second TV communications that tell culturally relevant stories versus using traditional automotive speak, Audi has been leading in digital connections as well. For example, this year Audi introduced several new entry-level luxury products to first-time luxury buyers of which a third were young Millennials. We used platforms such as Waze and TripAdvisor to link our Audi Q3 "Stray the Course" strategy to consumer behaviors on those channels and for the launch of the A3, we introduced a completely new voice and visual execution on Snapchat for Audi in the Super Bowl, which we carried through the entire season of Pretty Little Liars that drew 125,000 new followers in just nine months on that channel.

Does risk-taking factor into developing truly creative campaigns? If so, how do you mitigate that risk internally and or externally?

A challenger spirit is crucial in everything we do at Audi. Therefore, pushing our communication to be anything but traditional drives us internally and is why we seek out clever culturally-relevant storytelling.

What role does social media play in your marketing efforts? Are there any platforms that are working better for your brand than others?

We identified an opportunity to engage in a conversation with America through social media several years ago. It was the ideal platform to reinforce our provocative messages while establishing a clear voice for the brand. While our fan base has grown organically from our engaging content, we've established Audi in over ten social media channels. Each has its own engaging characteristics for that community, but we've found Instagram to be an increasingly enthusiastic and responsive channel that has grown exponentially because of the personalized, visual nature of the content.

How are you leveraging storytelling in your creative endeavors at Audi?

This is crucial to bringing a brand into the conversation with today's consumer. When we introduced TDI clean diesel in several of our new vehicles last year, we recognized that many of the misperceptions of diesel still existed, including that it was an old technology that was for slow, smoky, dirty old cars. Instead of just announcing that Audi had an all new line up of fuel efficient and environmentally friendly new TDI clean diesel solutions, we approached it with a story that exaggerated one of the misperceptions that high performance luxury sedans don't use diesel.

In this communication, an Audi A8 pulls into a fueling station where the driver begins to use the clean diesel pump when in slow motion the many bystanders attempt to stop her thinking she'd made a mistake. Towards the end, she simply responds "I know" illustrating she clearly knows what she is doing while signaling to another Audi A6 TDI clean diesel driver who gives her a confirming nod. It was a clever way of telling the story that Audi has many TDI clean diesel models and those in the know realize it's the smart solution for the future. The full campaign reinforced the range capabilities, and environmental benefits and dispelled many of the myths that brought the story to life in all consumer touchpoints.

KEY TAKEAWAYS

- *Pure creativity is rarely random—it is the result of a concerted commitment by a brand to connect with its target in a unique manner.*

- *Pure creativity necessitates taking calculated risks with not just your creative but also your media choices.*

- *Purely creative ideas are often built around a remarkably simple premise.*

Further reading:
Linda Kaplan Thaler and Robin Koval, *Bang!: Getting Your Message Heard in a Noisy World*

But Is it Good for the Customer?

"Get rid of funnels and think past the buying. If you don't have a good experience after you buy, you're not coming back for more."

Ani Matson
NEA Member Benefits

When Ani Matson took the reins as CMO of NEA (National Education Association) Member Benefits, the company was sending new customers over fifty separate pieces of communications offering a wide range of products and services. But Ani quickly saw that this was a prioritization of expediency over customer experience. After substantial study and consensus-building, Ani and her team were able to reduce the number of new member communications to just six touches.

The results? A 20 percent increase in participation and a significant spike in customer satisfaction ratings. Less was indeed more. Ani's move was risky, but by making the customer the center of the strategy from start to finish, she never doubted it was the right thing to do. While she's moved on from her position at NEA Member Benefits, the lessons in her accomplishments there—not just concerning why to put the customer first but also how—are evergreen.

Could you explain the business model of NEA Member Benefits and its relationship to NEA?

NEA Member Benefits is a for-profit entity owned by the NEA, the National Education Association, which represents public school teachers and other staff who work in public schools. NEA Member Benefits provides mostly financial services products and services to NEA members and their families. We talked to top providers, we ranked them, and then we offered the benefits to members.

NEA Member Benefits markets to three million members plus their families. It's certainly a very well defined target. How does that affect marketing?

You still need an intentional strategy. In fact, you have to be very precise because you are marketing to people who you want to have a relationship with for the length of their career and after they retire. It's not just about finding an audience for your product, it's about serving a defined group, with the best portfolio of products, in the most relevant way.

We can contact members via direct mail, which is the way we used to market for many years, but that doesn't always work because you can't just offer the same thing to three million people. So instead, as people go through their life stages, we try to provide relevant offers at specific times in their lives. At the end of the day, we are building offers and communications around a member's journey as they enter the profession and join the organization.

What are the keys to sending the right communications to the right customers?

Everything is set up and automated and triggered so that members can receive the appropriate information at the appropriate time based on their behavior, what they do, and what they tell us.

We've scored the whole membership file, and based on those scores, we decide which offers are most appropriate to market to whom. The key is to watch members and understand them deeply, understand their behavior, understand their needs, and understand their attributes, in order to be able to offer them the right thing. It's beautifully analytical. Like all of us, members have children, get married, go back to school, retire and as they go through those stages we have different offers customized for them.

Let's talk about a win that you've had where you were able to get the right product in front of the right person at the right time with the right message.

The one that I'm most proud of the team for doing is the reimagining of the content strategy and the way we deliver the content to the members. What we are trying to do is optimize the content at the right gaps of a member's journey. We have come up with a huge roadmap for delivering the right information to the right members.

But in terms of best results, so far the top results have come from the new member experience that we built. New members were cordoned off from receiving everything that other members would receive. Instead, we designed a different experience for them, basically welcoming them to the organization, showing them what's available to them, giving some freebies to them, and just inviting them to come and explore.

By not pushing, we were able to get better results than the way we had done it in the past. We touched them only six times last year and increased participation by 20 percent. In the past, we had touched their comparable cohort fifty times.

That's an incredible story. Did you have brand health metrics tracking so you know how people perceive you?

Yes. We were initially thinking of using Net Promoter Score, but then we came up with what we call a "Brand Index." It is similar to the Net

Promoter Score but it takes into consideration other factors we thought were important for our brand. Through a relationship with Harte Hanks, we have been running a longitudinal study and the "Brand Index" annually over the last seven years. This study has become a team energizer for us, because we present the results to the broader team of marketers and they see for themselves the impact their marketing has had on member perceptions of our brand and the parent NEA brand.

So, if you were to sit down with a fellow CMO, what sort of advice would you give them on these factors in order to get started?

Get rid of funnels and think past the buying. If you don't have a good experience after you buy, you're not coming back for more.

Look at the stages of the experience, the journey that any human being would go through when they have a need, and then as they look to fulfill their need. I would ask the question why, after every acquisition. What do they use it for? Where do they use it? And then I would start to build the experience around that.

KEY TAKEAWAYS

- *Customer centricity can not just be a marketing strategy, it must permeate the entire organization.*

- *Less can indeed be more. By reducing the number of communication touches from 50 to 6 and making these more targeted, both sales and brand perceptions improved.*

- *If you are only focused on closing the initial sale, then you're very unlikely to acquire customers for life.*

Further reading:
Don Peppers and Martha Rogers, *Return on Customer: Creating Maximum Value From Your Scarcest Resource*

Bu

Building Community

The Ultimate Fan Club

"If you work with the community and built trust...the community will support you."

Chip Rodgers
SAP

It's a dream of many, if not all, marketers to have their customers and fans come together in a self-sustaining community—these days, that usually means an online community—where they can discuss the products, help each other with support issues, and make friends.

It also remains a dream for most, and very few have succeeded on the level of the SAP Community Network led at the time of this interview by Chip Rodgers. In this interview, Chip candidly discusses the triumphs and challenges of growing and sustaining SAP's massive Community Network. As you'll see, it's an ongoing process and the nurturing never stops. In this interview, Chip shows why it's not as though once you hit a certain number of community members you can put your feet up on your desk and let the marketing take care of itself.

But with appropriate effort the rewards are great, and beyond just marketing, fostering community is a Noble Pursuit unto itself.

How big is the SAP Community Network?

We currently have about 2.5 million members, and it's a very active community. We get between a million and a million and a half unique visitors a month and about 3,000 to 4,000 posts a day in discussions and blogs and wiki pages.

Tell me about its membership breakdown.

It's about 50 percent customers and then probably another 30 percent partners and then we have a large group of employee members as well. There are also independent contractors, developers—just people who are interested in the SAP ecosystem. It's open to anyone that wants to join. There are a few core pieces of information that we ask for, like a unique email address.

In terms of content, are you constantly feeding this beast yourself, or is it somewhat self-sustaining with member-generated content?

I have two teams. The content team works with about 400 SAP experts to feed the community with a lot of our formal content: white papers, articles, solution briefs, eLearning, videos, etc. I have a team of about 12 working with a group of stakeholders who are SAP solution managers, or folks from support, or people in solution marketing that have all the actual information, the expertise, and are the ones actually building the content. I've also got a group of 6 that are managing the community-generated content, so that's our blogs and forums and wikis, and similarly they're working with a group of about 700 moderators in the community.

The scale of this community is kind of mind-boggling. Can you draw a direct line between your activities and your ROI?

More and more, we're able to show that there is a connection. We've gotten to the point where we're running a lot of webinars on different topic areas, different product areas. We've really cut back with list-buying and some of those traditional marketing costs to get people to come in and listen to a webinar, learn about a new product area, and then take the next step as a pipeline opportunity.

Was it tough in the beginning to get management behind the community?

We laid a lot of groundwork for social media within SAP. We were fortunate that we had a board member who thought it was the thing to do and defended it every time. When we first opened the communities with blogs and forums and wiki, some executives were nervously saying, "Why should we create a place just for people to complain?" But our feeling was that there are plenty of public places for people to criticize the company, why not create the place where we can be a part of the conversation? And fortunately, our board defended it.

How do you handle it when someone starts vehemently criticizing the brand within the community?

What we've found is if you work with the community and build trust, and you're open about how you engage and you answer questions and address issues that come up, the community will support you. It's not always SAP that has to defend [itself] when someone goes haywire. We see this all the time where somebody says something negative or even a little wacky in the community, and your knee-jerk reaction might be, "We have to answer that." And what ends up happening is a lot of other community members come in and say, "Well you might have a point here, but this is way over the line." The whole group comes together.

With 2.5 million community members, your activities are dwarfing anything SAP has going on Facebook or Twitter. Does this create any tension with your social team?

We actually work very well together and leverage each other's strengths on a nearly daily basis. But it's interesting that when we were first having discussions about communities joining marketing, our CMO was saying, "There's an opportunity to learn from what Community Network has done. We need to have more conversations and engage with our audience. We can't just create another email blast with a bunch of creative and offers." It's been a cultural change within the company.

Author's note: The remaining questions and answers are from a follow-up conversation I had with Chip right before this edition went to press.

Since we talked a couple of years ago, you've left SAP. Have you been involved in community building since and, if so, what lessons from your SAP days have you tried to apply?

Even with SAP things had changed since we first talked. One big change was that we de-emphasized number of members as a measure of community health. We shifted focus to measures of engagement: things like numbers of unique visitors per month, contributions to the community, numbers of blogs, questions, answers, comments, likes, and so on. Those are the metrics that really measure the health of a community.

Today I'm responsible for the Customer Experience marketing team at Ciena which includes social media and community, as well as all marketing events and executive briefing centers. Social media and community are so closely connected since they're both about transparency and enabling all the smart people in the organization to engage more directly and openly with customers, partners, developers, and others in the broader ecosystem. I'm definitely drawing on the experience and success we had at SAP to help grow our engagement and deepen those kinds of customer connections.

Given that Facebook has essentially become a pay-to-play network for marketers and LinkedIn groups have limited functionality, do you expect more B2B brands to invest in building and maintaining their own private communities?

Facebook has become much more challenging than it was in the early days for brands. LinkedIn does have some interesting capabilities like groups and Pulse, but you're right that it's still not a great place to "assemble a tribe" and bring folks together around key topics for your company. But I also think the question about whether to build a brand-based community depends on the company and the markets they serve. Some organizations' customers will be more receptive and more motivated to participate in a brand-related community. For example, technology companies have customers and partners that can be highly motivated to seek out and participate in an online community because they're always looking for answers to tough technical issues, trying to push the boundaries of what the technology can do, trying to learn tips and tricks from experts as well as wanting to build their reputation among their peers.

That may not be true for B2B organizations in other industries. For example, is there enough inherent motivation for customers of a food-service organization to come together in a branded community? You really have to look at what motivates customers to decide if it's worth the investment to build a separate community, or to work with existing communities or social channels like LinkedIn.

What are some of the pitfalls brands trying to build communities should try to avoid?

The classic advice that I believe will always be true is to make sure you have executive sponsorship and buy-in to what you're trying to achieve with a community. Community building takes investment, resources, focus, time, and patience to really get going. So you'll need to be in it for the long haul and that means having a good business case and an executive team that believes in the vision and ultimately the business benefits you'll achieve. Without those things, you might get started but never have the chance to really make it successful!

KEY TAKEAWAYS

- *SAP built a massive community of users that has nothing to do with Facebook and everything to do with helping its customers.*

- *You know you are on the right track when your community members take ownership of your brand and even rise to your defense.*

- *Communities, like gardens, require ongoing cultivation and fertilization.*

Further reading:

Dave Balter and John Butman, *Grapevine: The New Art of Word-of-Mouth Marketing*

Gg
Going Green

Green Is Good

"Find CSR programs and initiatives that aren't just good for the community, but are good for your business too. That makes it easy to justify the investment, and makes the efforts seem more genuine and sincere."

Tom Santora
Omni Hotels & Resorts

Cynics who insist that a deep, authentic focus on corporate social responsibility is incompatible with keeping a luxury hotel brand profitable and growing have obviously never met Tom Santora, CMO and Senior Vice President of Sales for Omni Hotels & Resorts.

At Omni, Tom has turned CSR—specifically, a focus on sustainable "green" initiatives—into big business, and the benefits are real for Omni's bottom line, its guests, and the planet.

This interview with Tom not only presents an assortment of great ideas for how a business can be more green, but also outlines one of the most effective big-picture approaches to CSR I've come across. Whether your company's CSR initiatives are environmentally-focused or not, listen to Tom.

How have you approached corporate social responsibility? Do you have a distinct set of metrics for CSR (versus product sales) that help rationalize these investments?

Sustainability is central to Omni Hotel & Resorts' entire business—from operations and procurement to architecture and construction. For example, our two newest builds, the Omni Nashville Hotel and Omni Dallas Hotel, are LEED Silver and LEED Gold certified, respectively. Our goal is for all future new builds to become LEED certified.

While this is a tremendous achievement for both Nashville and Dallas, earning Gold certification for the Omni Dallas was particularly notable. With 1,001 guest rooms and 110,000 square feet of meeting space, the Omni Dallas Hotel is the largest LEED Gold certified hotel outside of Las Vegas, and one of the only LEED Gold hotels in Texas. We are extremely proud to be able to say this.

Achieving LEED Gold status required careful planning and a disciplined approach to design and development. We worked with recycled and regionally-sourced materials and incorporated significant natural day lighting into our design. We also implemented a keycard-based guestroom energy management system and utilized a construction process to significantly reduce construction pollution and rolled out a number of water conservation initiatives. Omni Dallas Hotel's dining venue, Texas Spice, is even a certified Green Restaurant—two stars. Plus, the housekeeping associates collect unused soap to donate to the Global Soap Project.

We also are finding other ways to minimize our carbon footprint. We are increasing local and organic dining options by partnering with local farmers, growers, and seafood purveyors, as well as sourcing—and in some cases producing our own—environmentally preferred products. In addition, we are engaging our employees and guests in conservation efforts. For example, each Select Guest loyalty club member is invited to select "Eco-Friendly Services" in his other guest profile, indicating whether bed linens and towels should be changed only when requested. By giving our guests the option to re-use items that would normally be laundered in between uses, we can reduce water, chemical, and energy use.

Obviously, there are long-term operational cost benefits to building properties that consume fewer natural resources. This is one of our ways we rationalize our investments. But we also analyze guest feedback from Medallia to pinpoint how sustainability practices directly influence guest favorability and loyalty.

As CMO, what is your role related to CSR? Are there some initiatives that you think have been particularly effective?

As a smaller, privately held company, we are very nimble and communicate well across channels. As a result, I am usually involved in our CSR initiatives from the outset—particularly if they have the potential to benefit the guest experience and/or our brand reputation.

While our construction and development initiatives naturally fall outside the scope of my role as CMO, I often collaborate with that team to provide input on aspects of the design and development that will make Omni Hotels & Resorts more marketable to customers. For example, many large associations and groups seek venues or destinations that meet specific sustainability requirements. Naturally, our LEED Silver and Gold certified properties are extremely marketable to those groups. In fact, we have secured business solely because we have a LEED Gold certified hotel in Dallas.

How do you make sure that your CSR initiatives come across as a sincere commitment to doing good as opposed to being self-promotional?

We are fortunate in that our sustainability initiatives are not just good for our brand reputation; they make good business sense too. As I mentioned earlier, there are long-term operational cost benefits to building properties that consume fewer natural resources. We would utilize these practices whether or not they were marketable for our company.

These practices also deliver guest experiential benefits, making them even more appealing to our company. One of our core brand attributes is providing hotel properties that are unique and authentic to their local markets. By using building and design materials that are indigenous to the local region and providing culinary creations based on locally sourced ingredients, we can cater a true local experience. It's what makes us unique and it's what guests look forward to when staying with Omni.

What advice would you give to fellow CMOs who are just getting started on CSR programs?

My advice to other CMOs is to find CSR programs and initiatives that aren't just good for the community, but are good for your business too. That makes it easy to justify the investment, and makes the efforts seem more genuine and sincere.

KEY TAKEAWAYS

- *Going green requires careful planning, especially when it involves construction projects.*

- *Working with third-party certifiers like the USGBC (they set the LEED standards) will help make your green efforts more credible and therefore more marketable.*

- *Going green can be good for the community AND your business.*

Further reading:
Daniel W. Bena, *Sustain-Ability: How a Corporate Conscience Helps Business Sustain the Ability to Win*

F Foundations

Unleashing Goodwill

"We all know that today's consumers prefer to support businesses with a social conscience."

Bo Segers
PEDIGREE Foundation

As an unabashed dog lover and proud owner of a French bulldog, I've been a huge fan of PEDIGREE's "Dogs Rule" campaign since its outset. In fact, it was the subject of my first post on TheDrewBlog in February 2008. What I particularly admired about this campaign was that it went far deeper than advertising. For example, employees were encouraged to bring their dogs to work. If the building owners didn't like it, they actually moved operations to a more dog-friendly building. Salespeople were even allowed to bring their dogs to meetings with customers.

The *coup de grace,* at least for me, was setting up the PEDIGREE Pet Adoption Drive, a program that initially offered free pet food to individuals to encourage shelter adoptions. This program evolved into the Pedigree Foundation, which now inspires dog lovers to donate time and money to help find "loving and forever homes" for thousands of shelter dogs. Behind a lot of this goodness for the last three years has been Bo Segers, who became President of the foundation in 2015. Bo was kind enough to share some of his challenges and hard-earned wisdom in the interview that follows.

How much did you raise this year and where does that money go?

The foundation's revenues were $9,349,550 through the end of 2014. We will exceed $10 million this year. The majority of our money goes into our grant programs for distribution. We've also directed about $1.3 million to an endowment fund. We operate an office with a staff of one.

What role does the Pedigree brand play with the foundation today?

The current Board of Directors is comprised of MARS Petcare Associates, so we are aware of the brand's history of promoting shelter adoptions. We honor that history through our grant-making programs. We value the advice of members of the brand team and encourage their participation in our planning. Where there are opportunities to promote the foundation in brand media and marketing activities, the brand marketing team has proven to be a great partner.

As a private foundation, we are legally unable to directly promote the brand's products, but we strive to build a symbiotic relationship with the brand. This is especially important because the public generally perceives us as one entity.

PEDIGREE Adoption Drive events are executed today in almost every PEDIGREE global location, so we are hopeful to eventually mirror those activities and expand our grant-making activities internationally.

How do you get consumers involved with the foundation?

Like everyone else today, we have a website and we're active in social media. The brand creates promotions that benefit the foundation and communicates our message to the consumer. Additionally, we solicit promotional opportunities that are free or very low cost, just like any other nonprofit.

One of our best promotional activities is our grant-making itself. Our grantees appreciate the support we provide and they post about it to their own followers. The animal welfare community is small but powerful and we feel we have built a very credible identity through our grant awards.

What have been the biggest challenges at the foundation?

Resource development is the constant challenge we face: money and people. The number of requests we receive for support grows each year and our financial resources have not grown at nearly the same rate.

Since the brand is our largest donor, we have had to face the possibility that the demands of the business could impact the level of its annual financial commitment. So a few years ago, the board voted to create an endowment to ensure that the foundation could become less financially dependent on the brand. We would like to see an endowment of $40 million, but building a fund of that size doesn't happen overnight.

The foundation also requires engaged board members. Currently, all the members of our board are in leadership roles with the business and they are very busy people. In 2013, the board hired the first full-time director for the foundation. Activities that had been outsourced were brought back in-house and we revised our strategic plan to focus on our goals and assure that our actions were aligned. To achieve our goals we need to grow our board and we're currently considering a number of ways to do that.

What advice do you have for CMOs considering setting up foundations?

I would advise against setting up a foundation only as a marketing device. The PEDIGREE Foundation was created to support the philosophical ideals of the business: to make a better world for pets. That commitment to help homeless dogs and to promote adoption exists throughout the PEDIGREE brand and has matured over time to become a bedrock philosophy.

We all know that today's consumers prefer to support businesses with a social conscience. It is the same with today's workforce. We've found that the work of the PEDIGREE Foundation is a source of pride among current employees and is an outstanding recruiting tool.

What lessons can you share about building a brand-related foundation?

First and foremost, building a brand-related foundation takes more time and money than you ever plan for. So plan accordingly. I would advise having a solid financing plan in place for the first five years, so you can direct your energies to developing your program and making it meaningful.

Second, the people engaged in the endeavor (board members and volunteers) have to be passionate or you will never achieve your goals.

Lastly, don't underestimate the impact of what you're doing—both as a source of doing good in the world, but also in contributing to the recognition and regard for your brand.

KEY TAKEAWAYS

- *Setting up a foundation is a huge commitment of time and resources and should not be attempted as a mere marketing ploy.*

- *Ideally, the purpose of the foundation should be bigger than the brand and be able to attract both donations and volunteers from the outside.*

- *The benefits of doing good are huge: providing a source of pride for employees and generating enormous goodwill from customers.*

Further reading:
Linda Kaplan Thaler and Robin Koval, *The Power of Nice: How to Conquer the Business World with Kindness*

Sd

Sustainable Design

Designing a Better World

"We are also acutely aware of our responsibility to contribute to sustainable homes and workplaces, environments that promote a better world."

David Bright
Knoll

Before joining the board of New York City's Urban Green Council two years ago, my understanding of designing and building environmentally responsible products was comparable to your average kindergartner. Thankfully I've bulked up on the topic since then. It turns out sustainable design is a remarkably complex and constantly evolving art form. The choices are not always "green" or "not green" and instead require a sophisticated ability to weigh the options while rallying the industry to aim higher.

Few know and practice this better than David Bright, Senior Vice President of Communications at Knoll, a leader in the sustainable design movement for home and office furniture. As you will see in our interview below, it's not just a question of where the raw materials came from or how much energy it took to create and ship the product. Environmentally responsible brands must also consider the ongoing impact of the product on things like air quality AND be prepared for recycling once the product is worn out. Bright is a big proponent of third party certification, which as he puts it, "tells our customers that our commitment to sustainability is real."

For marketers considering or evaluating CSR initiatives, the key word here is "real." Today's sophisticated consumers can sniff out shallow or disingenuous CSR commitments an eco-mile away. Earnestness must run deep within the corporate DNA. As Bright explains, it "is a core principle, an integral part of a culture that has made Knoll an industry leader." Interestingly, in talking to companies like Knoll, the business case for CSR is less and less about "can we afford it?" and more and more "can we afford not to?" especially when the "we" includes employees, customers, shareholders and, yes, the world we all inhabit.

Unless you flipped straight to this chapter, you probably just read the interview with Tom Santora and how he's adjusted the operations of Omni Hotels and Resorts to greatly benefit the environment (as well as Omni's bottom line). Knoll is taking a different path to the same goal by zeroing in on design itself as the key to a greener future, and the results are very encouraging.

Can you provide an overview of Knoll's CSR priorities?

The kind of work we do means that our practices have a significant impact on the workplace, an arena where so many people spend their time. When we think about sustainability, we are not only framing our own corporate philosophy, but also making decisions that will shape the daily lives of our customers for decades. As a company, we consider environmental, economic, and social sustainability in all our design and management choices, from what kind of materials are used in our products to the well-being of our employees. But we are also acutely aware of our responsibility to contribute to sustainable homes and workplaces, environments that promote a better world.

Is there one recent program that you are particularly proud of?

Our commitment to sustainably sourced wood. We know that curbing deforestation is essential to stemming climate change. So for more than a decade, we have been developing supply chain practices that enable us to certify where our wood comes from and how it is harvested. Today, most of the wood we use is available with a Forest Stewardship Council (FSC) certified claim (C028824). FSC is the international standard-setting body for sustainable wood. Many of our competitors offer FSC wood as a more expensive option on many of their products. We don't give our customers a choice. If you buy standard Knoll Office products, you support sustainable forest practices.

Can you talk about the idea of sustainable design? Does this approach trickle down into marketing?

Sustainable design means considering the entire life of a product, from raw materials to the end of the product's life. We use powerful analytic tools (Life Cycle Assessments) to measure the environmental impact of each stage and identify opportunities for energy reduction and material reuse. And yes, the data we collect through this process is passed on to customers so that they can make informed decisions. We are moving toward a uniform "Environmental Product Declaration," a sort of nutritional information label for durable goods. This transparency is valuable to our customers.

How important is third-party certification?

Third-party certification is essential. It tells our customers that our commitment to sustainability is real. In addition to the FSC wood certification, Knoll products are also monitored by GREENGUARD for their impact on indoor air quality and by a range of industry-wide certification programs for sustainability. We maintain environmental databases for each of our products, which help clients build LEED-certified workspaces. Knoll does most of its own manufacturing, but when we outsource part of the process, we make sure our partners' facilities meet the same requirements. The positive pressure that these programs put on our entire supply chain means real industry-wide progress towards sustainable practices.

How do you measure the impact of Knoll's CSR initiatives?

We can measure some of our impacts, and these metrics are important both for internal planning and for marketing. For example, our manufacturing facility in Pennsylvania is now landfill free. And our recycling programs for products that have reached the end of their usable life divert many hundred of tons of waste from landfills every year. These are significant and quantifiable changes that we are proud to report. But I think a lot of the impacts from our sustainable practices are intangible. They will be felt over many years in the homes and offices of our customers, in the communities where we work, in the forests we have left intact.

Is CSR a source of competitive advantage for Knoll?

Knoll's commitment to environmental, social, and economic sustainability is a core principle, an integral part of a culture that has made Knoll an industry leader. We are motivated to build furniture that is always beautifully and sustainably designed, and our customers and employees believe in these products.

KEY TAKEAWAYS

- *Sustainable design requires powerful analytics tools that can look at the environmental impact of a product through its entire lifecycle.*

- *As with other environmental efforts, third-party certification is extremely helpful as validation that you're doing the right things.*

- *The impact of sustainable design on sales may be tough to quantify but its impact on the environment won't be.*

Further reading:
Jim Stengel, *Grow: How Ideals Power Growth and Profit at the World's Greatest Companies*

Lb

Living the Brand

Selling Your "Why"

"I sometimes have to remind people internally that we don't need to just rely on our own perspectives. If in doubt ask the kids."

Cammie Dunaway
KidZania

How deeply is your company's purpose woven into the brand identity and marketing communications your customers see? Be honest. If it's just an afterthought—or not there at all—then there could be rough seas ahead, as purpose-driven companies are seeing great results from infusing a strong sense of "why" into their marketing. And this is especially true if your customers are kids, as it's the ultimate in cynicism to present one brand persona to your trusting, impressionable audience and then be someone else entirely once the transaction is complete.

The right way to do it is embodied by Cammie Dunaway's work at KidZania. KidZania is a novel idea, to say the very least: It's a family entertainment center the size of a soccer field where kids try their hands at jobs and careers ranging from factory worker to dentist to chef and beyond, and earn simulated money called "KidZos" which they can use within KidZania as they choose. KidZania's explosive growth—sixteen locations worldwide with nine more under development—means they need someone who really understands kids (and parents) in charge of communicating the brand's purpose.

Enter Cammie, formerly Head of Marketing at a company that knows a thing or two about kid-centric marketing: Nintendo. Now her task is to tell the world about a place where kids can start practicing essential life skills...and have the time of their lives in the process. Here's a peek at how she's doing it.

You were the head of marketing at Yahoo! and Nintendo before joining KidZania in 2010. What are the most notable differences between marketing a giant corporation and marketing a smaller, more experimental venture?

Whether the company is large or small, the role of marketing is to deliver profitable growth by understanding your consumers and delighting them with your product or service. At Y! we provided content and services that made our users lives easier. At Nintendo we made it possible for everyone from gamers to grandmas to enjoy video games. At KidZania we are empowering kids and training them for future success. Small companies tend to move more quickly and limited resources make you sweat each decision a little more, but the challenges of being relevant to consumers and accountable for financial results are really the same.

KidZania has plans to expand into the United States in the next few years. How has having such ambitious growth plans impacted your role as CMO?

The expansion of KidZania is truly exciting. When I started we had seven locations. Currently we have nineteen open and seven additional under development. The diversity of cultures and norms from Mumbai to Sao Paulo to Seoul creates some unique marketing challenges. Fortunately we see that parents everywhere want to equip their children for future success and kids everywhere love learning through role-play. Being able to travel around the world as CMO has given me lots of great ideas for what we can do in the U.S. I want to take the best practices from all of our KidZanias and create an amazing experience here.

Can you talk a little bit about KidZania branding and how that extends to employee titles and roles? While you're at it, feel free to talk about your efforts to get the entire company engaged.

Story is at the heart of everything we do. We believe that KidZania exists because kids were frustrated with how adults were running the world and decided to create their own city to practice for the day they will take over from us and improve things. We bring this story to life in all aspects of our business from our titles (I am a Minister of Communication and a Governor, not a CMO and President!) We have a national anthem, monuments, our own special language and holidays. Infusing this into our culture starts with hiring practices—we have to hire people who really like kids! Then we constantly reinforce the culture through training and our daily practices. Everyone from the CEO down spends time in the facilities working with the kids. If employees are having fun and constantly learning, then they will be fulfilling our mission to empower kids.

How have you been able to impact the customer experience in your current role?

As a CMO you really need to find a way to bring the voice of your customer into the conversation. I sometimes have to remind people internally that we don't need to just rely on our own perspectives. If in doubt ask the kids. We have a kid's "CongreZZ" in each KidZania. It is essentially a group of children chosen annually that help us stay current and provide feedback on our experience. As long as I am channeling them, I am usually able to move us in the right direction.

Loyalty programs can be tough to get off the ground. If you have one in place, can you describe the program and talk about the costs/benefits of the program?

Our loyalty program, called "B·KidZanian," is one of our most powerful marketing tools. Our CEO recognized that the investment, which was quite significant for a company of our size, would provide benefits both in more deeply engaging our kids and in developing an efficient new marketing channel. In our program, kids become Citizens of KidZania and receive a passport and stamps for the different activities that they do. The more often they visit and the more they participate, the more privileges they receive. Parents opt into the program and receive very personal communication about their children's activities and offers geared to their unique interests. We have been able to demonstrate a measurable lift in visits and spending among our members and, most important, kids love the program.

KEY TAKEAWAYS

- *Living the brand means bringing your brand story to life across all aspects of your business, not just your communications.*

- *Great marketers find ways to bring the voice of the customer into the decision-making process.*

- *Loyalty programs can and should extend the brand story while delivering meaningful benefits to the customer.*

Further reading:

Tony Hsieh, *Delivering Happiness: A Path to Profits, Passion, and Purpose*

So

Social Purpose

Killing It with Kindness

"There's a trend for society to appreciate the power of businesses incorporating social purpose into their mission...when it's sincere."

Daniel Lubetzky
KIND

The front-runner for my favorite "founder memoir" business book of the twenty-tens decade is *Do The KIND Thing* by KIND founder Daniel Lubetzky. As you might have read in interviews earlier in this section, I'm a bit of a sucker for brands that do well by doing good. But even if you're not, Daniel's book is gripping, and also essential. Why? Purpose branding—where a powerful sense of mission is baked into the entire marketing strategy—was not just a flash in the pan. If anything it's becoming more important, and brands that reject it outright are working under an increasing disadvantage.

At KIND, Daniel is a purpose branding virtuoso, and I was really excited to sit down with him to chat about the book, the brand, the mistakes he made, and how he overcame them. The big question remains: Does a brand's purpose have to be a social, "save the world" purpose to reap the benefits of purpose branding? Maybe, maybe not. At any rate, with each passing day the future of business looks more like what Daniel is pioneering and it would behoove us all to listen closely to him.

You're a busy guy, to say the least. What compelled you to make the time to write the book?

A few things. One is that I've been the recipient of a ton of guidance and advice from people over the years. And I felt I needed to do the same things for others. The book also shares very honestly a lot of my mistakes and hopefully will help others avoid them.

The second one was that I very sincerely aspire for KIND to do something very different from what other companies have done—to really push the frontiers, to transform the company into a movement and a state of mind, a community that people connect to. And by no means do I think we are there. But to get closer to this aspiration, we have to share our vision with others and stake a claim to what we are and what we're living to accomplish, to get a community to help us build the movement and take ownership over it. Writing a book was the first step in sharing more of our philosophy, a little bit of where we're coming from, what we're aiming to do so that people can hopefully join us in pursuing our vision.

Any other reasons?

I also wanted to write a book because, frankly, I'm very aware of my own mortality because my father was a Holocaust survivor and I just think about those issues perhaps more often than many others. I have four children and I just wanted to document my values and my way of life for them. And I also wanted to share these ideas with the KIND team, which is especially important as we grow. So there was a lot of motivation.

Speaking as an entrepreneur who made more than his fair share of mistakes, I love how honest you are about yours.

It shows a certain sincerity and ability to look at yourself with a degree of circumspection. It also makes your success that much more impressive.

You spend a fair amount of time in the book talking about purpose. Do you think every company needs a purpose, and does that purpose necessarily need to be tied to social good?

I think every company that is trying to succeed has to have a purpose, because it's another way of saying that it has some sort of reason to succeed. As far as a social purpose, I don't think every company has to have it, though I think companies that have it feel fulfilled and motivated more consistently. But it can be dangerous to inauthentically incorporate a social purpose. It's not the same if the people that are driving the business don't wake up in the morning and feel the purpose is important to them. Consumers will be able to tell if a purpose is not authentic and it will probably backfire.

Does having a purpose help you as the leader?

I personally derive meaning from having more than a financial purpose and doing our small part to make this world a little better. And I do think there's a trend for society to appreciate the power of businesses incorporating social purpose into their mission…when it's sincere. But I don't think it's a requirement and I think it's very dangerous to force it into something where it doesn't fit.

How else does having a purpose help?

I also think the exercise of talking to people about their core principles and asking about what's important to them can help them pursue a bigger vision. But it has to really, really connect with their efforts, with their spirit, with their DNA, with who they are, with what they stand for and frankly with the brand heritage.

What about brands that don't have a social purpose?

I think there are incredible brands like Snickers whose purpose might just be to satisfy a hungry craving. And they don't need to pretend to be something that they're not, and they play a role as a fun and delicious experience of a satisfying candy bar. I think there are many other great brands that they do what they promise to do and are very successful without a social purpose.

KEY TAKEAWAYS

- *Brands with a strong social purpose still need to perform on the category prerequisites like taste and ingredient quality.*

- *Make sure your social purpose is authentic and not just a gossamer claim that consumers will see right through.*

- *Having a social purpose will make it easier to recruit and retain a highly motivated and like-minded staff.*

Further reading:
Daniel Lubetzky, *Do the KIND Thing: Think Boundlessly, Work Purposefully, Live Passionately*

VII. Inert Fundamentals

As we come to the end of the Periodic Table, I'd like to look back to the beginning. We started on the Basic Elements, ten fundamental concepts every marketer with aspirations of CMO-level greatness ought to master.

I want to conclude with ten more fundamentals, but these ones are different from the first ten in an important way. These are the Inert Fundamentals.

In chemistry, an inert gas is one that is mostly or completely non-reactive with other elements and substances. Under most typical circumstances, inert gases are "self-contained," which is to say they perform whatever function they perform on their own, instead of in tandem with some other element.

The Inert Fundamentals on this Periodic Table have a similar self-contained nature. They are the fundamentals that exist inside the CMO's brain (and spirit, if you believe in that sort of thing), rather than the externally-focused, highly-reactive ones that kicked off this book. As discussed by the ten marketers I had the privilege of interviewing for this section, they don't require much if any participation from the rest of the company or even the rest of the team.

These Inert Fundamentals are mindsets, not tactics. They are disciplines, not nuts-and-bolts. And they are personal qualities that have a strong tendency to positively spill over into our lives outside the office.

To return to inert gases for a moment, one of their common commercial uses is to protect perishable goods from oxidative reactions that might spoil them.

Sc
Showing Courage

Pb
Personal Branding

Li
Listening

L
Learning

Ev
Evolving

Em
Empathizing

N
Networking

Pn
Power Networking

Sp
Sharing Passion

Ai
Always Innovating

For example, all that "airspace" in a bag of potato chips? Believe it or not, it's not there to make the bag look bigger. It's a protective layer of inert gas—usually nitrogen—that blocks oxygen from degrading the chips and ensures they're fresh when you crunch into them.

When you master the Inert Fundamentals of marketing, you will be similarly protected against many external threats...ugly things like self-doubt, creative stagnation, and even office politics. Marketing can feel like a battlefield at times. Your Inert Fundamentals are your "armor," and it's up to you to keep it strong as iron.

On that note, we'll kick off with Sir Terry Leahy, a knight who may not literally ride to the office on a mighty steed, but wields courage worthy of Arthur's Round Table. Later, my former colleague Trip Hunter offers a clinic on what it means to truly listen, and Roberto Medrano gives the lowdown on what it means to constantly evolve as a CMO. Closing things out is an interview I'm very proud to present with GE CMO Beth Comstock, focusing on the all-important subject of innovation.

The Inert Fundamentals are the foundation of every successful chemical reaction we marketing scientists mix up. If they're not understood and practiced every day, little else is going to work. Please take your time with these insights, absorb them well, and let them become the foundation of your future success.

Sc

Showing Courage

CMOs of the Roundtable

"If this had gone wrong, as many predicted it would, I would have been finished."

Sir Terry Leahy
Tesco

Hear ye, hear ye! A lot of marketing pros will happily talk your ear off about the role courage plays in their work, and some of them might even tell you something worthwhile. But I'd rather listen first to what an honest-to-goodness knight of the realm has to say on the topic of courage, and I had the rare chance to do just that when I interviewed Sir Terry Leahy after his keynote address at the IBM Smarter Commerce Global Summit.

Sir Terry's courage was apparent from the start of his career at the British grocery titan Tesco, and it eventually propelled him out of the CMO seat and made him the clear choice to captain the mighty ship as CEO for fourteen years. We discussed this promotion in our chat, unearthing insights that are "Excalibur" for any marketer with executive ambitions. We also delved into big data, as well as when and when not to ethically borrow ideas from your competition.

A lot of companies seem to lack the courage to make big bets, and do things tentatively instead. Talk to me about the importance of courage and big bets, and the risks of such an approach.

Courage is an unusual word in the context of business. But, I think it's at the heart of business. And in fact, I think entrepreneurs would understand that. They place the biggest bet of all—their livelihood—when they start a business. But in an organization it still applies. Many people are fearful of upsetting their boss and affecting their promotion prospects, when the truth is that you've got to be prepared to risk everything.

What's an example of a big bet you made in your career?

One was the launch of the Club Card, which gave us important information about our customers. In order to do it, we had to incentivize customers to use it. That was going to cost us a quarter of our entire profits at the time. If this had gone wrong, as many predicted it would, I would have been finished.

If you were starting out now and strategizing how to land a CMO job ten to fifteen years in the future, what would you be focused on?

Well, I think it's a really exciting time now because back when the Club Card started, Tesco was one of the first in the world using data, as soon as computers were powerful enough. Now the opportunity to access data from social networks, from shopping data, from operations, and from so many other things, it's without limit. And, yet, organizations don't fully use that data. They don't bring it in and use it to inform the way products are developed, to drive the direction of the business. So I think that still is the opportunity: How do we make business decisions on the basis of knowledge—knowledge of the world around us?

You, a CMO, became CEO of a major company in an increasingly big data-driven business world—where CTOs often have the inside track to the top spot. How did you achieve this, and what could other marketers who aspire to be CEOs one day learn from your experience?

It is unusual. I was able to use Club Card and some other innovations to be the voice of the customer in the business. So I was able to give leadership for the company from the marketing position. And that, therefore, was a small step into the CEO office.

I think other CMOs can do that. I think that they can step forward and lead the business from the marketing position, particularly if they harness the customer. The customer is the biggest power base within an organization. And if you use it in the right way, it's hard for a colleague from Finance or Operations to challenge the voice of the customer. If you have the customer on your side, you're the most powerful person in the organization.

Does all the big data out there today make it harder to achieve simplicity, or does it make it easier?

Well it potentially makes it harder. There's a real danger that an organization can be flooded by data. And information can get in the way of actually accessing the things that really matter for the consumer and what will really drive your organization forward, if you make decisions on those things. Our data is so complex now. So powerful. It's even a danger that it can become detached from most ordinary people. And that can be very harmful for an organization. You want data to be more accessible and to be placed right at the heart of the organization. Right where the decisions are made.

When some companies see what their competition is doing, they try to replicate it. How does one strike the balance between ethically borrowing ideas from competitors while remaining true to oneself?

In the first ten years of my career, essentially I copied the competition because our competitors in my industry were outstanding firms—the best in the country and arguably the best in the world at what they did. So, I didn't have to look far for ideas. I just copied them.

But what I found as we got closer and closer to this benchmark was that we could never overtake them. Because if you're just like the original, people will always choose the original. And it was only when I stopped copying the competition and started following our own customers and letting them be my lead that we overtook them...within a year.

It was an amazing thing that I learned. From that day forward I respected and learned everything I could from the competition. But I never followed competition. All the focus was on the customer, which made what we were doing much more original, and more importantly, more authentic. Customers spotted that we were doing it first and doing it for them—we weren't doing it because some competitor did it first.

KEY TAKEAWAYS

- *Entrepreneurs aren't the only ones that need to be courageous. Senior marketers that aspire to be CEOs need to show a willingness to take calculated risks.*

- *If the risk you are considering is of benefit to your customers, then it is probably a good idea.*

- *Don't let access to mountains of data separate you from the ongoing need to talk to your customers.*

Further reading:

Terry Leahy, *Management in Ten Words: Practical Advice from the Man Who Created One of the World's Largest Retailers*

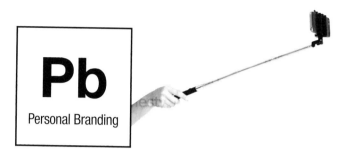

Pb

Personal Branding

Let's Get Personal

"A personal brand is in the way that you carry yourself as an individual in every walk of life."

Maria Winans
IBM

As one of two Y-chromosome bearers (i.e., men) in attendance for the Women's Luncheon at IBM's Amplify Conference in San Diego, I felt just a little conspicuous approaching Maria Winans for an interview after her panel discussion on personal branding. But I knew I had to hear more from this remarkable executive, who had maintained her individuality over a 25-year career at one of the world's largest businesses.

Maria, whose title is CMO, IBM Commerce, Mobile and Social, is a believer in the power of "and." By that I mean she is a business executive and a mother; a friend and a trainer; an artist and a boxing student; a first-generation American and a Latina...and all this merely scratches the surface of her indelible identity.

Lucky for us, she is also incredibly generous when it comes to sharing her keys to personal branding. In short, it's all about substance. Reputation, as she points out, cannot be purchased. It must be earned.

And a willingness to abandon fear of failure and reject well-traveled roads are priceless assets. Read on to get the details on how to start building your personal brand so that one day it may shine as brightly as the one proudly worn by this truly "Renegade" CMO.

Talk to me about your personal brand.

I take great pride in what I do, how I lead a team, and what I stand for. I grew up in an environment of tremendous respect for my parents, for actions they took in bringing us to the U.S., for encouraging personal growth for my siblings and myself. So I came from a very strong culture of achievement and the understanding that diversity is something that you should embrace, cultivate, and cherish as a gift. So my whole philosophy when it came to building my career at IBM very early on was that I wanted to establish goals, I wanted to be successful, I wanted to grow my career, and I knew that there were different stages of that growth path.

How did this play out early in your career?

I came into IBM with my eyes wide open. I didn't know if I was going to head into marketing or sales or strategy or finance. And so very early on I told myself I needed to find my passions and learn as much as possible. But I also had a vision and a goal. I wanted to establish myself as a professional, I wanted to lead from the front, I wanted to become an executive, and I wanted to be a Vice President by the time I turned forty. I had very established goals, and with that I set forward on really understanding what it was going to take for me to continue to grow in my career.

So how did you differentiate yourself?

I looked for opportunities that were about new initiatives and were about creating new businesses. I started to develop a skill set as an innovator, somebody who took risks and looked for opportunities that were different and required finding new teams and developing new skills. I cultivated that, and with that, created an environment for people to see that through my actions, that collaboration was a top priority, bright ideas were welcomed, innovation was the priority, and no idea was a bad idea.

Did your personal brand evolve?

I think a personal brand is in the way that you carry yourself as an individual in every walk of life; in your business and in your personal life. And at the same time, I'm learning every day. I don't think a personal brand is something that you create and then never changes. I think it evolves—if your career evolves, it evolves in the type of jobs. But I think the core of who you are, your character, stays true within that. I am avid believer in the need to never stop learning. And I think when you look at strongest leaders in business, you see most are lifelong students. They remain curious, and aren't afraid to tackle new initiatives and seek new paths forward.

Many women seek your advice about personal branding. What's the first thing you tell them?

In life you can buy anything except your reputation. Your reputation has to be earned. And so protect it, live it. For example, just because your title says CMO, just because you lead a very large team, you still need to earn your leadership every day. And this is what I reinforce to people that I mentor, especially in the business, your reputation is something you earn, something you work hard for and you stay true to.

And the second?

I always get asked about risk-taking because I'm a risk-taker. I love innovation, I love trying new things and putting projects with people and saying to the team, "Let's go try it—the worst thing that can happen if it fails is that we learn from it and we move forward." My biggest fear is regret. I fear looking back and saying 'If we only had taken that chance.'

A lot of people fear risk-taking, especially women…[many are] afraid to take those chances and feel everything has to be perfect with T's crossed and I's dotted. My message is that risk-taking actually makes work and careers even more exciting.

Do you think there's a point when it comes to personal branding that an individual can go too far in self-promotion? How do you avoid crossing that line?

There's always that self-promotional risk that you're talking about yourself too much. We've all seen people that are self-promoters; it's all about them, you know, their photo on everything. But I think that sometimes, we as women hold ourselves back. Sometimes we're afraid as women that maybe we're too visible, maybe we're too self-promoting, we're talking too much, we're showing too much aggressiveness. So I encourage women to be vocal, to be ambitious, to show what they know and who they are, to promote themselves through their work and with that their personal brands.

KEY TAKEAWAYS

- *Personal brands are built up over time by one's actions at work and at play.*

- *Own your reputation by setting goals and living up to them.*

- *If you are naturally risk-adverse AND in a marketing role, challenge yourself to try new things.*

Further reading:
Peter Montoya, *The Brand Called You: The Ultimate Brand-Building and Business Development Handbook to Transform Anyone into an Indispensable Personal Brand*

Listening

Listening Is More than Waiting to Speak

"Listening is like searching for a gold nugget on the bank of a river. Somewhere among all of the worthless pebbles is the nugget you are searching for."

Trip Hunter
Fusion-io

Bias alert: Before he headed west to oversee Corporate Marketing for data innovator Fusion-io, the brilliant Trip Hunter sharpened his chops working with yours truly at Renegade. So needless to say, I'm a fan. But Trip's success at Fusion-io is hardly a subjective assessment—to put it bluntly, he kicked butt over there.

There are a lot of things the man does really well, but the one that always jumped out at me first and foremost was his ability to listen—whether it was to a boss, colleague, assistant, current client, or prospective client. And in my view, that listening ability has been the linchpin of the great things he accomplished at Fusion-io. (Last year he parted ways with the company to launch his boutique marketing firm, Neuron Strategies). I'm glad you're here to listen in as we discuss how he leverages new media to "hear" the things other marketers might not, and turn that information into decisive and impactful actions.

Can you give an example of how you "listened" at Fusion-io?

When Fusion-io turned its attention to growing market share in Europe, we had no awareness among the developer community, which represented a key audience for us. So we conducted interviews, held pizza nights, and became a part of local SQL user groups to hear about the top challenges they faced. A huge one was the bad code that was inherent in their environment and no good way to get it out.

So we created the Crappy Code Games. The objective of the Crappy Code Games was to encourage the best SQL developers in England to write code so badly that they could adversely affect the performance of a Fusion-io card. We launched the idea through social media and a golden toilet. On certain days throughout the week, we tweeted the location of a large golden toilet hidden in random pubs throughout the city. The first SQL developer who found the toilet and tweeted "SQL by the SEA" won a pass to the largest SQL developer conference in England. We would also host a happy hour for everyone who showed up.

These events were designed to promote the larger Crappy Code Games, held in five European cities, where developers gathered to write the worst code they could dream up. The Fusion-io cards were so fast, they literally flushed crappy code down the toilet. We generated a tremendous amount of buzz and press around the performance of our cards, and an incredible amount of good will among skeptical developers.

Since there is so much noise out there especially in the developer space, how did you identify the conversations that mattered?

We actively supported the communities we engaged with. We helped them achieve their goals, and listened to their challenges, so when we missed, there was an understanding of what we were trying to do for them, versus just trying to sell them something. This gave us a little leeway to make a mistake or two.

Do you think listening is a skill that can be developed and improved upon?

I credit my first wife with teaching me to listen better because she never stopped talking, but that's another story.

The challenge to listening well is knowing what you are listening for. There is a quote that says, "Listening is the secret to discovering a great story." This is absolutely true and telling compelling stories is our business, but in order to get the great story, you have to become knowledgeable about what is important so you can ask the right questions. Listening is like searching for a gold nugget on the bank of a river. Somewhere among all of the worthless pebbles is the nugget you are searching for. You just have to pay attention, and be patient.

The only other advice I would add is that I soon realized that most people know a lot more than I do, so if I am talking, I am not learning anything.

I think a lot of people get their ego caught up in what they do, and try and prove how smart they are by talking all the time. Marketing people are interpreters. We translate other people's experiences and stories into experiences that a broad audience can understand. So put your ego away and stop trying to be the smartest, funniest, most interesting person in the room. Because it's not about you.

Most companies struggle to develop engaging content and get their customers to pitch in. How have you been able to accomplish this?

Growing engagement with our customers was a constant effort, and we often felt as though we were not as far along as we would have liked to be. That said, we were so new that a broad understanding of our technology didn't exist yet. People wanted to know more, so getting them involved wasn't as hard as it might be for others.

We treat them like the intelligent, opinionated, passionate human beings they are. B2B companies' customers are still consumers and human beings. We may not have the massive number of followers that consumer brands do, but our fans are just as loyal and passionate.

What did you hope to learn through audits of your social channels?

A lot of things, especially where we stood relative to our competitors. At one point we saw that even though we were much tinier than our largest competitor, we were gaining followers as a percentage of overall audience faster than they were. And in the area of measurement that really matters—shares—we were also ahead. People clicked on our links and shared our content on Twitter more than they did with our largest competitor, which was very promising.

We also wanted to find out what we needed to do better. B2C companies are known for creating very engaging content on channels such as Facebook and Twitter. We always were eager to learn a lot from them and how some types of B2C efforts can translate across to B2B.

KEY TAKEAWAYS

- *Listening is an underestimated skill that separates the good from the great marketer.*

- *When you show your customers that you are listening to them, they are far more forgiving if you trip up along the way.*

- *Given all the noise in the marketplace, knowing what to listen for takes ongoing practice.*

Further reading:
John C. Maxwell, *Good Leaders Ask Great Questions*

Learning

Building Blocks

"You can't effectively market something until you have a solid idea of what it's going to be, how you want it to be perceived, and what the business goals are."

Kate Chinn
Tishman Speyer

When Tishman Speyer—one of the biggest players in the very big game of New York City commercial real estate—decided it was time to relaunch the famous Rainbow Room restaurant atop "30 Rock" (30 Rockefeller Plaza), it meant Senior Director of Marketing Kate Chinn and her team were going to have to master a few new disciplines. Naming? Experience design? Uniform selection? Operations? These hadn't been among Kate's responsibilities on previous projects, and lesser marketers may have panicked.

But as you'll see momentarily, Kate's rise as a marketing professional has always been rooted in her commitment to learning new things and stepping outside her comfort zone. So driving the successful reinvention of one of New York's most venerable dining institutions just meant doing more of what she did best. And with the new Rainbow Room—plus its attached bar—SixtyFive—thriving, Kate's commitment to lifelong learning is clearly paying off.

The science of marketing continues to evolve rapidly. How do you keep yourself up-to-date?

That is so true. The digital world is evolving so fast it feels almost impossible to keep up with it. We make sure someone from our team is attending all the marketing summits and conferences that luckily, usually, come to NYC to ensure we are on track with the latest and best digital marketing opportunities. I think you also just have to pay close attention to your competitors, and take note of any advertisers that find a way to move you, as an individual and not necessarily as a marketer.

What have you learned lately that you've been able to apply?

At Top of the Rock, we have learned that targeted social media ads convert for us, big time. At Rainbow Room, we have learned that good PR is more important than anything paid we could possibly dream up.

Are there brands that you look to for inspiration?

I am always paying attention to everything I see around me. Recently, a Whole Foods opened up in my Brooklyn neighborhood. They had an agency create a targeted campaign specifically for this Brooklyn audience. The look and feel was perfect, and separate from the national Whole Foods brand. The advertising placements were brilliant—subways, turnstiles, bus shelters, etc. I was inspired, both to be a better marketer and also to go spend all my money at Whole Foods!

What were the challenges of the relaunch of the Rainbow Room?

With this relaunch in particular, there were very high expectations, especially since the Rainbow Room is such a famous, historic, and iconic venue. For the last two years, the marketing team has closely worked with the operations/management team to define the business goals in order to correctly position each segment of the new Rainbow Room in the marketplace. You can't effectively market something until you have a solid idea of what it's going to be, how you want it to be perceived, and what the business goals are.

What made this even more challenging was the fact that it wasn't just the Rainbow Room, it was the Rainbow Room as an event venue, the Rainbow Room as a Sunday brunch location, and the Rainbow Room as a destination for Monday night dinner and entertainment. At the same time, we launched SixtyFive, the brand new bar and cocktail lounge, with its own identity and marketing needs. Finally, there is an executive dining club that is by invitation only, which also required us to develop a look and feel, menu covers, invitations, etc. With new businesses, you find yourself doing anything and everything that needs to happen in order to get that business open, regardless of whether or not it is actually "marketing." My team was involved in everything from logo design to uniform selection to actually naming the bar "SixtyFive Bar & Cocktail Lounge."

Can you talk specifically about your channel strategy?

It was a different strategy for each of the businesses. For the events business, we began advertising a year out because we know that many weddings book over a year in advance, and we wanted people to know that the Rainbow Room was coming back. Once we set that opening date of October 5th, we pulled the trigger on advertising in some of the larger and more upscale bridal publications in particular.

Our biggest challenge was that we had absolutely no photography assets. We created a beautiful brochure out of complete air. Our ads were very vague, but at least contained the Rainbow Room logo and we had to have something for the sales team, so it forced us to be very creative!

Sunday brunch is a beautiful, elaborate set up with a round buffet table set up on the dance floor and every kind of food you can imagine from around the globe. It was so impressive that we decided we really couldn't pay to market that until we had a photo of the actual brunch. Monday night dinner and entertainment also came later and are still developing as we continue to evolve our entertainment strategy. The first performance we had was The Roots. We managed to flip a *New York Times* full page out right before opening that made a big splash.

Is that kind of word of mouth sustainable?

Speaking specifically to SixtyFive, this has been my first time doing any sort of marketing surrounding a bar and we planned to do an initial push with PR. We have found that with Top of the Rock, word of mouth is so important and keeps people coming back. In fact, according to some audience research we conducted, over 50 percent claim that "word of mouth" was their main reason for visiting. I have to believe the same thing would be true for a premier cocktail bar at Rockefeller Center. So I think it's a continual effort—and really relies on a great guest experience much more so than anything paid.

KEY TAKEAWAYS

- *Look to the successes outside of your category for inspiration.*

- *Don't forget to get out of your office and see what's going on in the "real world."*

- *When you stop learning it's time to get out of the marketing game.*

Further reading:
Donald T. Philips, *Lincoln on Leadership: Executive Strategies for Tough Times*

Evolving

Natural Selection

"I felt the need to communicate Akana's point of view as an industry thought leader besides just sending press releases or asking the press to take a point of view."

Roberto Medrano
Akana

Akana CMO Roberto Medrano didn't seem like the type who would become an effective blogger for a California-based company. For one, English wasn't his first language. Even in his native language, Spanish, writing was never a great strength of his. Oh, and there was also the whole "massive day-to-day responsibilities of the CMO" thing. But Roberto got to where he is today by constantly evolving, and he saw the value he could add to his career and his company if he committed to blogging and stuck to it.

Today, his blogging at http://blog.Akana.com demonstrates that Akana is a thought leader in the software industry, raising key issues and spotting opportunities before many if not all their competitors. Roberto's writing also helps coalesce internal points of view on where the company and the industry is headed, and more recently has been looked to by the press as a source of content for their own stories. All because Roberto was determined to get outside his comfort zone and evolve.

Evolving is like "Learning 2.0," and a CMO who fails to evolve gets left behind in the primordial soup. And evolving is a bigger-picture consideration than merely picking up new skills. Whether evolution for you means taking the plunge into blogging, public speaking, learning to write basic code, or whatever will get you to the next level, it has to be a daily practice.

How long have you been blogging and what motivated you to get started?

I started blogging about three years ago. I felt the need to communicate Akana's point of view as an industry thought leader besides just sending press releases or asking the press to take a point of view. And there are less press reporters now. That motivated us to say, "How do we do that?" And we also saw that other companies were using blogs effectively. So then we said, "Okay. We've got to do our own" and I was the guy who started writing them.

How did you decide what to write about?

Whatever we thought would be relevant to our target. We wanted to provide insights about security, mobile, cloud, application lifecycle development, and some related business with the use of APIs. Now in the digital world everything is connected through APIs. We covered the technical aspects of building APIs and building applications. Or for companies looking to use the cloud, we covered what applications have to be able to be cloud-ready. We just wanted to make it easy for our customers and prospects to find relevant content, whether it was high-level or more detailed technology use.

A lot of senior marketers tell me they don't have time to write or don't like doing it, and these are folks for whom English is a first language. Was it particularly hard for you to get started given that Spanish is your native tongue?

I never really believed that I was a writer, but I've always had ideas to communicate. So I started thinking of how to communicate those to a broader audience in writing. At first, I felt very uncomfortable blogging, and I had to get some help from people who were actual writers and proofreaders to review some of the posts before they went live.

Did it get easier?

I have become more comfortable over the last three years as more and more posts went up. I do a lot more of the editing myself, but still pass the posts by others for comments or edits. The editing has been less and less in terms of style and more about the details of the points that need to be communicated.

Have there been results that surprised you?

Well, I didn't expect that some press would read my posts and refer to them in their articles. That was not on my radar. Now I see more and more reporters referring to my posts, which is kind of interesting especially since we have never promoted the blog to press. Recently, a reporter asked, "Do you have a blog?" and told me they would wait for my post on a particular topic, and then quoted from it a day after it ran. That's definitely a new thing for me, and it's reassuring since it means the press believes there's something of value in my posts.

The other thing that's happened to me is that I get recognized at conferences! I'll be walking around and then some people just come up to me to talk about something that I published. I don't know these people, but they just see my picture and they recognize me. They want to talk to me about the blogs. So far, I've never had anyone come up to me to argue or be negative in a meeting like this, which is a relief!

Are there other benefits of having a disciplined regular blogging program?

Yes, because people subscribe to the blog and read it regularly, they have a deeper connection with us. And they want to connect to see what we're thinking about. In many cases, even when they're considering a product, they go to the blog and try to see what posts are related to what they're thinking about buying or doing.

What would you say are the top benefits of consistent blogging?

The more content you create, the more ideas you have in the marketplace, and the more there is for people to find and read. The organic search benefits are huge. If people are looking for certain topics like APIs, SOA, and "enterprise service bus," our blog comes up at the top. And if the content is good enough, people will subscribe and continue to share your content and your voice. That will establish you and your company as legitimate thought leaders.

KEY TAKEAWAYS

- *The marketing landscape is constantly evolving. Effective marketers adapt to and participate in these changes.*

- *Current and aspiring CMOs should blog. It helps them learn, lead, and build organizational consensus.*

- *To blog is to understand!*

Further reading:
Bob Gilbreath, *The Next Evolution of Marketing: Connect with Your Customers by Marketing with Meaning*

Empathizing

The Heart of the Matter

"It made me a better person because I could have that empathy, whether I apply it towards everyday life or apply it to my job."

Alicia Jansen
MD Anderson

In our service-dominated economy, the standards of excellence continue to rise, impacting every industry from restaurant to retail and entertainment to travel. As consumers, we all appreciate great service and as social media-savvy sharers, we are collectively quick to point out when the standards slip below our expectations. Yet as marketers, we all too often forget the notion of service, preferring instead to focus on which message on what medium will drive the most leads.

For the healthcare industry, establishing a reputation for superior customer service is still very much a work in progress. Which is why I found my conversation with Alicia Jansen, CMO at MD Anderson, a leading cancer center based in Texas, especially enlightening (not to mention encouraging). Alicia was so appreciative of the service her mother-in-law received at MD Anderson that she applied for a marketing role at the company and landed it! Eleven years later, Alicia brings her heartfelt empathy for patients to every aspect of MD Anderson's marketing activities.

You've been at MD Anderson for eleven years, but before that you were working at Compaq. Selling computers and selling cancer treatment are pretty different things. Were you able to take any of the things that you learned at Compaq and apply them to what you've been doing at MD Anderson?

Yes, I have. I believe that marketing is a type of job that you can apply to so many different industries. In my opinion, there are a couple of characteristics that you have to have in order to really enjoy it; one of them is that you have to be curious. You have to be able to raise your hand and say, "Let me learn as much as I possibly can about this business, because in order for me to be able to market it and tell other people about it, I need to know it." You can do that in any industry. I did that with computers and software and found it very intriguing, and I find the same thing at MD Anderson. One thing about MD Anderson that I find very satisfying as a marketer is that we are doing something to help other people go through this cancer journey, and that's very satisfying at a personal level.

I think marketers also have to be able to tell a story. They have to be able to learn what the business is about and understand who the audience is that you're talking to so you can translate that to something that they can understand and that will move them in some way; whether it's to move them to buy something, move them to talk about it, or move them to donate. I think good marketers have the ability to tell a good story and to get others to tell the story as well, and that applies to any industry.

When you are selling cancer care, the degree of empathy and the sensitivity required is quite a bit different than when you are selling computers or software. How does that factor into the story you tell at MD Anderson?

My story of working at MD Anderson probably influences the way I do my job. Many people who work for MD Anderson have similar stories. My mother-in-law was diagnosed with cancer in 2000 and I was the primary caregiver. I was at MD Anderson every day. I witnessed her journey and I was able to see what it is like to fight this disease. It made me a better person because I could have that empathy, whether I apply it towards everyday life or apply it to my job. It influenced me so much that when I heard a job opening was available at MD Anderson in the marketing department, I raised my hand, was hired, and eventually took over the department.

That initial experience of being with my mother-in-law through her cancer journey taught me the lessons of why people go through this and what I can do to make the journey better, what I can say, what programs I can initiate, what are the things that I can help MD Anderson do better in order to make it easier on our patients and their families. I realized that this is where I need to be and that's why I took the job. I find working here very inspiring because of the customers that I work with every day.

How have you been able to impact the customer experience in your current role?

The patient experience to me is a passion because I experienced it with my mother-in-law and it is something that I am extremely excited about helping MD Anderson do better. A couple of years ago we started doing market research by talking to patients and their families while they were going through treatment here. We also spoke with members of the community to understand their needs and their expectations and how they would behave if they were faced with this decision to treat cancer. I took that information back to our leadership and said, "We have a lot of patients here who feel that we do a fantastic job, but when you peel back the onion there are a couple of things that keep surfacing, and I'm seeing a few trends of some things that we could be doing better."

I truly believe that in order to be appreciated and have a seat at the table you have to be more than an order taker. You have to offer more than the latest ad or brochure or update to the website. You have to show that you're bringing valuable information to the table that will enhance the decision-making process and help executives and yourself be able to make better decisions in order to satisfy the customer, exceed their expectations, and run the business better. Marketers today have to gather knowledge, and this goes back to being curious, knowing the business, and bringing information to the table that's going to help the business.

KEY TAKEAWAYS

- *Empathizing with your customers will enable you to improve their experience.*

- *Empathy needs to be more than skin deep. Qualitative and quantitative research can help you see below the surface.*

- *Senior marketers need to understand the entire customer journey and, if need be, work within the organization to fix shortcomings.*

Further reading:
Stephen Covey, *The 7 Habits of Highly Effective People: Powerful Lessons in Personal Change*

N

Networking

Wide-Angle Relationships

"When you're not around marketing peers your confidence tends to drop, as others seem clueless and negative about the new ideas you have."

Matt Sweetwood
Unique Photo

Camera users, what do you think: Has "Smartphone Killed the DSLR" the way "Video Killed the Radio Star" at the dawn of MTV? The numbers are not terribly encouraging for the traditional camera industry, with annual declines as high as 40 percent in recent years and image quality from iPhone and Android devices getting better and better.

But for smart marketers like Matt Sweetwood, President of camera superstore Unique Photo, the sky is not yet falling. Through creative storytelling and massive investment in customer service and customer education, Matt has kept Unique Photo's sales healthy and its niche in the world of photography secure for the time being. As you'll see in our interview (and hopefully take to heart in your own work), a strong peer network is essential to weathering rough marketing seas.

Matt is a perfect example of what happens when you stop worrying about what you can't control and devote your full talents to what you can control.

P.S. I don't know about you, but I don't see MTV playing too many music videos these days. Meanwhile, old and new forms of radio are holding steady…just saying, keep at it, Matt!

How important is having a strong peer network to your ability to do your job well?

Very. I use the ultimate peer network, The CMO Club, as an example. There have been numerous times when someone has simply said something at a CMO Club meeting that has spurred a new program or idea. As a business owner it is so very easy to "stay at home" and not get to see what others are doing or thinking.

For me personally, as the only marketer in my business, having a strong peer network reminds me there are others out there who think like me and that gives me the extra confidence to implement new ideas. When you're not around marketing peers your confidence tends to drop, as others seem clueless and negative about the new ideas you have.

One of the things I've observed about networking is that "the more you give, the more you get" but the quid pro quo is rarely direct nor immediate. What kinds of things do you do on the "giving" side and do you ever keep a mental balance sheet?

I don't really keep accounting of the things I give. Networking is not something you do, it's a way of life. I wish all of my connections a happy birthday and I always offer advice (personal, photographic, parenting, marketing, etc.) when I can. I can't usually quantify the value of this but my network and reach grow daily.

I heard someone recently say they'd rather have one deep conversation at a networking event than ten superficial ones. Do you agree with that approach and, if so, why?

That gets an answer of "not necessarily." Sometimes you get caught up in a conversation because you find the person attractive or interesting in whatever way that may be. But that may never lead to anything useful. It is important to touch many people at a networking event because sometimes the simple exchange of a business card can lead to much more down the road than the person who you gabbed with for forty-five minutes. I try to touch as many people as possible at networking events. And I can say I have rarely walked away without something good.

Sustaining a large network is time-consuming. How do you keep up with your network?

Work tirelessly and be OCD organized. How badly do you want to be successful?

Some people try to keep their personal networks and their business networks separate. Do you?

A favorite topic of mine. I find that my networking is most successful when I present my overall personal brand to both personal and business contacts. And that includes all the networks and businesses I am involved with. For example, I may be at a photography event, but letting people know that I am a single dad of five or am writing a book on parenting leads to more memorable and useful interactions. In today's connected world I believe all networks ultimately are connected in some way. People from my work networks have interacted with me on personal issues and vice versa.

How are you staying on top of all the new digital marketing techniques and opportunities?

Practice what you preach. I network frequently, I am very open to being solicited from digital marketing vendors as you learn when they present even if you don't buy. I belong to The CMO Club and I have paralleled the company brand with my personal brand as I engage in digital techniques to build my own brand (which I consider somewhat successful). Basically, I am always out there looking and learning. To stay on top, you have to view knowledge like food. You need at least three meals every day.

What tool has been the single greatest improvement to digital marketing for your personal brand over the last year?

For my personal brand, it has been Facebook. I've leveraged my Facebook page to establish me as the most recognized figure in the photography business. That brings enormous benefits to me from vendors, consultants, customers, and media who regularly follow me.

What role does social media play in your marketing efforts?

It is a fundamental component of my personal and company brand. In 2014, Unique Photo reduced traditional advertising by 75 percent and increased our social media spend by three times. That trend continued in 2015.

KEY TAKEAWAYS

- *Every marketer can benefit from a peer network as a source of new ideas.*

- *Networking is as much about giving as getting and the more you give the more you get.*

- *Sustaining a large network is time-consuming yet invaluable.*

Further reading:
Harvey Mackay, *Dig Your Well Before You're Thirsty: The Only Networking Book You'll Ever Need*

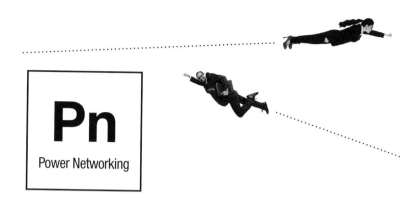

Pn

Power Networking

Upgrading Your Network

"If you put more energy into relationships, you can have a lot more productivity, success, and happiness."

Porter Gale
Globality

If you've had the good fortune to fly on Virgin America, I'm going to presume you "get it"…You get how Virgin offers a fundamentally different flying experience than pretty much any other domestic airline. It's hip, it's comfortable, they have purple mood lighting for Pete's sake!

A key figure in helping Sir Richard Branson get his scrappy start-up off the ground was now-departed VP of Marketing Porter Gale. During her four years handling Virgin America's marketing, she distinguished the brand with the original out-of-the-box seatbelt safety video, the no-hassle no-headache reservation system, and myriad points in between.

Since leaving Virgin, Porter has established herself as an in-demand marketing advisor to cutting-edge online and offline companies including Dollarshaveclub.com, WePay.com, and The Mina Group. Oh, and she's also produced or directed documentaries that have aired on Lifetime, PBS, Channel 4/England, and in film festivals around the globe. Porter's film work has been honored by the Directors Guild of America, The Academy of Motion Picture Arts and Sciences, and Filmmaker Magazine.

I got to interview Porter during her whirlwind promotional tour for her book *Your Network Is Your Net Worth*. Porter has always deeply understood the fact that great ideas aren't enough—a successful creative needs to pursue and solidify the relationships that will make those ideas reality. She divulged some of her power networking skills to me in this interview, and we also got to riff on how big data is changing the airline industry.

Give me the rundown on your book.

It's all about the power of connections and networks and it talks about how important our relationships are but there is also a lot of digital media strategy and conversation about how the world is changing because of social. So it's a fascinating book with lots of great interviews, and my mom loved it and I hope that you will.

Where is all this networking happening?

Networking can be inside the organization with just the employees and how they're connecting and collaborating, and it can be with your customers too. What I really wanted people to understand is that if you put more energy into relationships, you can have a lot more productivity, more success, and more happiness. And that's true both personally and professionally.

You mention it's no longer "six degrees of separation," or "of Kevin Bacon," it's four degrees. Where did those other two go?

That is actually a fact. I worked with PeopleBrowsr and they analyzed Twitter data from 2007 to the present and they figured out the number of degrees of separation between people. The analysis concluded that the old saying "six degrees of Kevin Bacon" is now four.

Got it. So what are implications of fewer degrees of separation?

What this means is that every single connection is more important than before. Because we're more closely linked, we also have larger circles of empathy. This means that we're connected to more people, our thoughts and our feelings are impacting more people, there are emotions that are spreading through social networks, and so the way that we connect and talk to each other and influence decisions has completely changed.

I like to think of it as the world getting smaller and smaller. So a connection that could change your life may very well be just one person away.

Let's talk about this network and the role that big data plays in all of this.

Data is completely changing the game. Let's take the example of an airline. We might know your seat preferences, your drink preferences, and what routes you like to fly. There are all sorts of opportunities for personalization. That personalization improves your potential for networking, because networking is really based on having authentic relationships that are connected and based on shared values and passions.

Is there an opportunity for small businesses to use big data?

I think there are some really great advantages for a small business. One, you won't get into analysis paralysis because you don't have the time and the resources. My advice for the small business would be to pick three core metrics that you want to focus on, then find an analytics platform that is affordable to you. It could be something as simple as Google Analytics, but make sure that you are checking your data and figuring out the important variables. Maybe your conversion rate is really important, or maybe it was the cost per acquisition. Whatever it is, figure out the metrics, track it, and make sure that you are staying connected and true to your customers.

KEY TAKEAWAYS

- *Power networking recognizes that social media has collapsed the degrees of separation between individuals making it easier to have more mutually beneficial relationships.*

- *Treat every connection like you would your best customer and you will soon become a power networker.*

- *The key to power networking is personalization, whether you're a brand or an individual.*

Further reading:

Porter Gale, *Your Network Is Your Net Worth: Unlock the Hidden Power of Connections for Wealth, Success, and Happiness in the Digital Age*

Marketing's Rocket Fuel

"It just hit me that these people cared and I wanted to engage with them."

John Yembrick
NASA

Go to enough social media conferences and you can't help but become jaded. So many of the cases presented are fluff and the few true success stories are told over and over. That was certainly the case for me until I saw John Yembrick, NASA's Social Media Manager, speak earlier this year at the Social Media Shake-up. John definitely "shook me up" with his honesty, innumerable examples of social media ingenuity, and, most of all, with his passion for both his product and channel of choice.

John's passion for all things NASA and social media are truly contagious and reminded me how essential this element is to the success of marketers, both as individuals and as brands. With passion you are graciously sharing your ideas, products, or services. Without, you are selling, often with a lack of conviction that is readily apparent. Passion makes work less work-like and turns subordinates into comrades in arms.

Passion is transformative, as you will see in our interview below. Combined with talents like the ability to spot trends in the making and cleverly translate these into engaging content, passion has helped NASA become a true force in the social media landscape.

NASA is one of a handful of brands that have a Klout score of 99, a number that reflects both the size of their footprint (11 million on Twitter, 11 million on Facebook, and over 4 million on Instagram) and the degree of ongoing fan engagement. Here's why:

Your passion for space and astronomy is palpable. Where did that come from?

I've always personally had a huge passion for space and I followed NASA closely before I ever worked for NASA. Honestly, I never understood why everyone doesn't share my enthusiasm. I'm not so naïve as to think that everyone will, but that doesn't stop me from trying. I feel like if you put content in front of people and show them why it is relevant to their lives and how cool it is, they will get excited. Yesterday I was showing someone I just met this photo of Pluto, and their eyes lit up and they were excited to learn about something that humanity has never seen before. And that happens all of the time at NASA.

How does this passion impact your ability to do your job?

One of the reasons why I think that our content, especially on the flagship NASA account, plays so well on social media is because both my associate Jason Townsend and I are passionate about this content and we think it matters. If you are working on a brand and don't care about the product, it's very difficult to really communicate it to the best of your ability. Mine stems from childhood, just loving space, playing with toy spaceships and looking up at the stars. I love them. I am one of those people who looks up at the nighttime sky wondering what I'm seeing, wondering what's out there. And I love the fact that NASA is helping to answer those questions.

You mentioned in your speech that the press didn't always tell the stories NASA wanted told in the pre-social media days. Can you elaborate on that?

Sure. In the pre-social days, the press was the filter. They might care about a spacewalk, a launch, or when something went wrong, but they didn't care about 99 percent of the other things NASA was doing. Social media changed that, although back in 2008 I was a skeptic like everyone else. But I had a "Eureka!" moment when there was some downtime during a spacewalk on a space shuttle mission. I decided to look at Twitter and to my surprise, a robust conversation was happening around my recent tweet—and I wasn't even participating in it. People were saying, "Oh my gosh, I can't leave my computer, I'm on the edge of my seat, this is a coolest thing I've ever seen and I don't want to go back to work." It was in the middle of the workday and I wanted NASA to be part of the conversation, so I joined in and started answering questions.

And that was the moment. I just didn't care about anything else. I thought this was the most important thing I should be doing even though I was only interacting with a few thousand people. It just hit me that these people cared and I wanted to engage with them. I wanted to make them happy with the content I was putting out. I thought, "Wow, you never get this kind of enthusiasm from the news media." I could actually see real people caring about the work I was doing. And that was a really life-changing moment for me.

Do you think your passion is contagious?

I am passionate about the brand. I think this brand matters more than anything else in the world and in regard to advancing humanity forward. But I'm certainly not alone here. During the government shutdown a couple of years back we were not allowed to post anything on social media. But the great NASA social community we had built posted things while we couldn't. That is one of things I'm most proud of. It just shows that we nurtured these ambassadors out there and they welcomed the opportunity to support our mission.

You all seem to be the masters of real-time marketing, particularly with big events like the Oscars.

I would say one of our most surprising successes really was with the movie *Gravity* at the Oscars. It was up for a bunch of Oscars that night and we were watching it. Throughout the whole Oscar program and especially when *Gravity* would win something, we would post real images from space with various relevant hashtags. These beautiful images looked like photos from the fictional movie like a spacewalk or the International Space Station but ours were the real thing. Our content ended up being one of the top trending topics during the Oscars—it was a hugely successful campaign.

When you look at your career trajectory, can you talk about the elements that have propelled your success?

I'm a little humbled by what you call career success. But I will tell you that throughout my career, I have always been willing to try new things, I've relocated several times, and when opportunities arose I embraced them. Also, I have always been willing to take chances, whether working for a space operation or at a field center, and then I jumped headfirst into social media.

KEY TAKEAWAYS

- *If you have genuine passion for your product/service, you will enjoy your job more and do it better.*

- *Passion is contagious both internally and externally.*

- *Passion is one of the real secrets to success on social media.*

Further reading:
Kate Newlin, *Passion Brands: Why Some Brands Are Just Gotta Have, Drive All Night for and Tell All your Friends About*

Ai

Always Innovating

Marketing's Holy Grail

"Innovation can't just be about fun ideas or wonky theories."

Beth Comstock
GE

It's convenient to think of companies like planets: The bigger they get, the stronger and more irresistible their gravitational pull. In this case, the gravitational pull is presumed to be a source of inertia—a force that resists novel thinking and innovation, stifling it under endless red tape and naysaying.

In such a universe, GE—the corporate equivalent of Jupiter if not the Sun itself—should have an overwhelming gravitational pull that crushes new and exciting ideas, right?

Not on Beth Comstock's watch. With Beth in charge as both CMO and President & CEO, GE Business Innovations, GE remains at the forefront of digital innovations, running circles around smaller and presumably more nimble competitors. Beth's outstanding work proves no marketer can blame a lack of innovation on company size.

For several years now, GE has been ahead of the curve when it comes to experimenting with new channels. What is the strategy behind all of this experimentation? Is the medium essentially the message?

GE's a leading technology company so we believe it important to be aligned with leading edge technology channels. Our audiences expect GE to be where they are—they aren't going to always come looking for us. We like to experiment as a way of learning, but our efforts have to align with our goal of connecting with our target audiences, which are largely industrial technologists and enthusiasts. And we've adapted our strategy around being micro-relevant—meaning targeting the right audience in the right way. It doesn't have to be a big audience, just the right one.

As the CMO, is it a mandate of yours that GE explore all the newest, coolest channels? If so, how are you finding them?

We have an awesome media team that identifies themselves as digital explorers. We also take risks with new ideas and small companies as a way to learn and as a way to augment more traditional plays. I'm a big believer in carving out a percentage of your budget to develop new models.

Naysayers struggle to understand how a photo contest on Instagram or a promotion on Pinterest can help you sell GE products like aircraft engines. What do you say to those folks?

A jet engine is a complicated sale. Many people influence the purchase decision. And since GE is a company that traverses multiple industries, pretty quickly you're targeting decision makers across a wide range of the economy and functional roles of business, which is why we believe in the importance of building a vibrant umbrella brand. In addition to those who buy our products, we target enthusiasts, recruits, and GE retail shar-eowners who want to experience GE in various dimensions. Industrial technology is exciting, yes, even fun…and some of these outlets allow us the opportunity to open up and express ourselves in new ways. People want to see that you are approachable.

GE is primarily a B2B company, yet you seem to act a lot more like a B2C company in terms of creating emotionally-rich consumer-friendly communications. Any thoughts on why that is?

Since when does B2B have to be boring? Businesspeople are people too. We are emotional beings, we don't just rely on logic when it comes to business decisions. Good marketing is about making a connection and delivering perceived value. Period. In some ways, business marketers have an advantage in that they are closer to their customers and in theory should be more responsive and intuitive.

Marketing seems to be getting increasingly complex in terms of ways to spend and ways to monitor. Has it gotten more complex for you and, if so, how are you dealing with that complexity?

Yes, it is more complex—we have a multitude of outlets and a range of content types to consider. You need good partners, room for experimentation, and a good dose of curiosity. Trust me, it's not about the size of your budget, it's about the ability to use complexity to amplify your efforts, not stifle them.

What does "innovation" mean to you as GE's CMO?

Innovation can't just be about fun ideas or wonky theories. Innovation means new methods that yield results. The challenge is often that time, trial and error are required to get to scale. I'm a big believer in pilot projects to create proof points and staged development to make sure you get results. Innovation without process is chaos. Trendspotting without translation leaves you empty.

Besides your efforts on Pinterest and Instagram, can you speak about another recent innovative program that you are particularly proud of?

I'm especially proud of the work we are doing to help define what the industrial Internet can mean to business productivity. It's a new category for business, not just GE. We've put a lot of science and analysis into connecting with our customers and new tech partners in this area. We're doing much more in open innovation—meaning using digital communities to drive new methods at GE. A recent example is a data science challenge with Kaggle that is shaving off minutes and fuel from flight landings—something once thought unattainable. And we're having fun with Vine, having had a successful #SixSecondScience effort this summer that shows how science can be fun and connects with tech enthusiasts.

I couldn't help but notice you were an undergraduate biology major, which is not exactly the typical path of a future marketer. Did you imagine yourself being a marketer when you were studying biology?

Not at all. I was torn between anthropology, psychology, and biology and I picked biology because I thought I wanted to go to medical school. But it turns out that biology is actually a great background for marketing. Something that biology and marketing have in common is that they both deal with the interconnectivity of each individual living thing to a broader system and that's the world we live in. We are all connected. We can't innovate without partnership. I think my study of ecology and my study of systems has trained me to think in a more systematic way and view the world—and certainly the business world— more systematically.

I know you've talked about spending upwards of 25 percent of your time in Silicon Valley talking to your GE team out there. That's a lot of time relative to all the things that you have to do. How do you rationalize that investment relative to other ways of spending your time?

Silicon Valley is kind of a metaphor for where innovation is happening. Just to give you an example, last week I was in Asia for a week and spent time in three cities in China and in Seoul, Korea. In every city I went to, 75 percent of my time was spent on GE or customer efforts, but I also made time to see what was happening in the marketplace. In Beijing, I spent time with the Xiaomi team. In Chengdu, I got to meet the Camera360 startup guys who have developed apps, and in Seoul, I participated in a roundtable innovation discussion with some incubators and founders. I do it with my venture cap, but more importantly I do it to keep the company tethered externally. It's partly my job but it's also a metaphoric way to describe that kind of sense of where innovation is happening.

Looking ahead either in terms of trends that you're seeing or just personal things that you would really like to get a handle on next year, what is on your priority list for 2015?

For the marketing mandate, I think just continuing to create stories that connect and scale. I think the journey is never done. I want to continue to find these different partners, media, and ways to tell stories that connect them in scale. We don't have a big budget so there's a lot of ongoing pressure for us as a team to raise the bar. That's always on our list.

I am a big believer in this idea of what we call the global brain. It's this idea of using digital connections to tap into people who don't work for us. It's called open innovation but you can also call it a digital workforce. There are a lot of ways you can get people who have insights and capabilities to do work with your company and I think it will continue to take off.

We have a culture of speed and simplicity and a kind of delight in things that can explain what we do at GE. I feel very committed to being a part of that in this coming year. The discovery agenda is still looming large. By the end of 2015, I hope to find three new trends of things that are just absolutely exciting.

KEY TAKEAWAYS

- *You don't have to come up with the ideas yourself to drive innovation—you just have to be open to them.*

- *Consistent innovation requires a process and a willingness to take risks. These risks can be mitigated via pilot projects.*

- *If you want to be perceived as an innovator, you must innovate at every turn which includes trying new media channels before your competitors.*

Further reading:

Brian Solis, *The End of Business as Usual: Rewire the Way You Work to Succeed in the Consumer Revolution*

Afterword

"The history of the periodic table is also a history of the discovery of the chemical elements. The first person in history to discover a new element was Hennig Brand, a bankrupt German merchant. Brand tried to discover the Philosopher's Stone—a mythical object that was supposed to turn inexpensive base metals into gold. In 1649, his experiments with distilled human urine resulted in the production of a glowing white substance, which he named phosphorus."

"History of the periodic table," Wikipedia, last modified July 23,2015, https://en.wikipedia.org/wiki/History_of_the_periodic_table

While the elements of marketing didn't have similar origins worthy of Mel Brooks or Monty Python, I want to wrap things up by calling attention to the first sentence of that excerpt, which does illustrate the most important similarity of all.

The ultimate evidence of Dmitri Mendeleev's genius is that he left spaces open on his initial version of the Periodic Table, knowing that there were still elements yet to be discovered and classified. He was not under the impression that his first version of the table would be the be-all and end-all of elemental organization.

Nor am I. Like its source of inspiration, *The CMO's Periodic Table* is very much a work in progress. As long as technology's breakneck pace continues and neural fireworks are still erupting inside the brains of great marketers, there will be new elements of marketing to master...and brilliant new CMOs to set the standard for how to do it right.

I'm still hopelessly afflicted with the interviewing bug, and even as this edition of the book goes to press I've got a long list of scheduled interviews, plus a shorter list of "dream" interview subjects I'm pursuing whose brilliance is certainly worth its weight in "Au"—that is, gold—to you, me, and every other marketer. Some of them will debut on thedrewblog.com, and all the best ones will have a place in the next edition of this book, which I fully intend to be a living, breathing document that evolves alongside marketing itself.

Like all world-changers, Mendeleev "stood on the shoulders of giants" to realize his amazing vision that was the Periodic Table. The prior work of Antoine Lavoisier, English chemist John Newlands, and others were essential building blocks of the then-contemporary scientific understanding that led the Russian to create the arrangement that chemists still use today.

I, too, stood on the shoulders of giants to create *The CMO's Periodic Table,* and I consider it a great privilege to have snatched a precious slot on the calendars of the sixty-four "giants" you've heard from in the preceding pages. These men and women embody the elements of quality marketing, and the greatest privilege of all is to share their wisdom with you.

My ultimate hope is that this book has embodied Renegade's core principle of Marketing as Service by helping you to do your job better, and will continue to do so in the future.

Please contact me any time at dneisser@renegade.com with questions, feedback, or just to say hi. Better yet, if you happen to be a CMO, look for me at one of The CMO Club Summits or at their dinners in New York City and let's talk about your "element."

Acknowledgments

The cliché "it takes a village" certainly rings true when it comes to pulling together a book like this. Without all sixty-four of my interviewees, this would simply be a Moleskine sans the nice soft cover. Without the relentless persistence and elevated writing standard of my editor and accomplice, James Houston, I suspect the general response may have been shrieks of "Why, Why?" Without the inspired design talents of Alan Irikura, no doubt the cover, the periodic table itself, and every other page of this book would be lacking his harmonious sensibilities. Without the continuous all-around help of Lindsey Gaon and Fiona Paladino, interns extraordinaire, I'd still be trying to get this done. And without the intrepid guidance, unwavering enthusiasm, and unprecedented promptitude from Pearson's Nikki McDonald, getting this tome published in 2015 would surely have been impossible. Then there is Dmitri Mendeleev, whose original and incomparable periodic table is not under copyright allowing me to join a long line of conceptual borrowers.

To my lovely and discerning wife Linda, god bless you for going through this from start to finish more times than marriage vows require and identifying opportunities for improvement each and every time!

To my friend Pete Krainik, founder of The CMO Club, thank you for bringing together so many exceptionally talented marketers and giving me the chance to meet many of them over the last eight years. I am forever in your debt.

And finally, I thank you, the reader. If you write a book, let me know. I promise to return the favor.

Index

About the Author

Drew Neisser is founder and CEO of Renegade, the NYC-based agency that helps CMOs transform marketing from mere messaging to programs of genuine value. Dubbing this approach "marketing as service," Drew and the Renegade team are on a quest to eliminate ad pollution. The author is also a recognized authority on guerrilla marketing having won numerous awards for creativity and campaign effectiveness.

Through a long-time partnership with The CMO Club, Drew has met and interviewed well over 100 CMOs in the last five years. Ranked among *Brand Quarterly*'s "50 Marketing Thought Leaders Over 50," he is an "expert blogger" for *Forbes, FastCompany,* CMO.com, and *MediaPost,* and pens the highly praised CMO of the Week column for *Social Media Today.* Drew is a trusted advisor to many CMOs and authors *TheCut,* a popular monthly newsletter. He regularly consults on digital and social media trends via the GLG network and currently sits on the boards of the Urban Green Council and Duke NY.

Diapered at Wells Rich Greene, trained at JWT, and retrained at Chiat/Day, Drew founded Renegade in 1996. He earned a BA in history from Duke University and lives in Manhattan with his wife Linda, their wondrous offspring Emma and Carl, and the agency's mascot, a French bulldog named Pinky. Somewhere along the way, Drew became obsessed with Benjamin Franklin. A native Californian, he dreams of becoming a surfer but is a long way from hanging ten.

Get the Elemental Companion Free!

This 65-page digital supplement provides further insights on all 64 elements covered in the book including more real-world examples, key questions to ask, and mistakes to avoid.

To access and download *The Elemental Companion to The CMO's Periodic Table*:

1. Visit peachpit.com/register.

2. Log in with your free Peachpit account, or if you don't have one, create an account.

3. Register using the book's ISBN: 9780134293783. This title will then appear in the **Registered Products** area of your account. Click the **Access Bonus Content** link to be taken to the page where *The Elemental Companion* is available for easy download.